Needlework Tools and Accessories
A Dutch Tradition

Woman busy with repair work. Brabant, South Holland, early 20th century.

Needlework Tools and Accessories
A Dutch Tradition

Kay Sullivan

Dedication

To my late father, who pointed me in the right direction, and to my mother, who has kept me company on many trips in search of thimbles and sewing tools. My appreciation goes to both of them for their unfailing encouragement always.

ISBN 1 85149 471 5

British Library Cataloguing-in-Publication Data
A catalogue record for this book is available from the British Library

Printed in Spain
by the Antique Collectors' Club Ltd., Woodbridge, Suffolk

THE ANTIQUE COLLECTORS' CLUB

Formed in 1966, the Antique Collectors' Club is now a world-renowned publisher of top quality books for the collector. It also publishes the only independently-run monthly antiques magazine, *Antique Collecting*, which rose quickly from humble beginnings to a network of worldwide subscribers.

The magazine, whose motto is *For Collectors-By Collectors-About Collecting*, is aimed at collectors interested in widening their knowledge of antiques both by increasing their awareness of quality and by discussion of the factors influencing prices.

Subscription to *Antique Collecting* is open to anyone interested in antiques and subscribers receive ten issues a year. Well-illustrated articles deal with practical aspects of collecting and provide numerous tips on prices, features of value, investment potential, fakes and forgeries. Offers of related books at special reduced prices are also available only to subscribers.

In response to the enormous demand for information on 'what to pay', ACC introduced in 1968 the famous price guide series. The first title, *The Price Guide to Antique Furniture* (since renamed *British Antique Furniture: Price Guide and Reasons for Values*), is still in constant demand. Since those pioneering days, ACC has gone from strength to strength, publishing many of today's standard works of reference on all things antique and collectable, from *Tiaras* to *20th Century Ceramic Designers in Britain*.

Not only has ACC continued to cater strongly for its original audience, it has also branched out to produce excellent titles on many subjects including art reference, architecture, garden design, gardens, and textiles. All ACC's publications are available through bookshops worldwide and a catalogue is available free of charge from the addresses below.

For further information please contact:

ANTIQUE COLLECTORS' CLUB

www.antique-acc.com

Sandy Lane, Old Martlesham
Woodbridge, Suffolk IP12 4SD, UK
Tel: 01394 389950 Fax: 01394 389999
Email: info@antique-acc.com
or
Antique Collectors' Club Ltd
Eastworks, 116 Pleasant Street, Suite #60B
Easthampton, MA 01027
Tel: (800) 252 5231
Email: info@antiquecc.com

Contents

Acknowledgements

Clementine Kuttschrütter, whose advice, patience, friendship and encouragement from the outset, and support throughout the period of compiling information for this book added greatly to its quality. She conscientiously read my texts, offered invaluable advice and was kind enough to write the Foreword.

Catherine Boon-Langedijk for her advice on the *Thimbles* chapter, and for kindly permitting me to use the excellent information contained in various published articles written by her.

Curators of museums mentioned in this book for their hospitality and willingness to spend time searching through archives and for supplying information and illustrations. I would like to say a special thank you to **Simon Honig** from the Nederlands Openluchtmuseum, who was prepared to carefully read and comment on some of the chapters, and for his kind assistance during my visits to the museum in Arnhem. I am also indebted to **Gieneke Arnolli** from the Fries Museum in Leeuwarden, and to **Ineke Tirion** and **Christel van Hees** from the Museum Boymans van Beuningen in Rotterdam for supplying and granting me permission to use images from these museums, and for their kindness during my visits. **Wiard Krook** from the Department Monumenten en Archeologie in Amsterdam for his kind assistance in providing original drawings of excavated items. To list the names of people who have helped me along the way would fill another volume. However, I gratefully thank all the museum curators for their indispensable help, as their contributions have enabled me to present a comprehensive view of needlework tools and accessories made in Holland throughout the past centuries.

Collectors, friends and dealers, too many to mention here, who have contributed by allowing me to borrow sewing tools to photograph, as well as supplying me with much helpful information. Their support is greatly appreciated.

Diana Steel, for her kind hospitality on my trips to Woodbridge and her many useful tips and advice. When deciding to write this book, I knew that the best publisher for the job would be the Antique Collectors' Club. I would like to thank Diana for making this wish come true through her confidence in me and her belief in my work. My appreciation also goes to my editor, Diana McMillan, for her suggestions and assistance whilst compiling the book, and to Craig and Richard, the production team, whose skill and precision produced a beautiful result.

My sister Pat, who painstakingly read my rough drafts and whose suggestions were gratefully accepted. I am confident that her contribution resulted in a better document and her constant encouragement helped me greatly in achieving my goal.

My neighbour Herman ten Brink, for his interest and stimulation, even when courage was lacking, and for teaching me the true meaning of an old Dutch saying:

> *Iedere dag een draadje is een hemdsmouw in 't jaar*
> (A thread every day is a shirtsleeve in a year)

Last but not least…

My husband Henny Holthuizen, whose rare talent for combining instinct with knowledge, and whose research during the past twenty years, have made this book possible. His contribution to the chapter *Marks on Gold and Silver Needlework Tools* has, in my opinion, added considerably to the usefulness of this book and I am confident that the marks and information will be of great assistance to the collector.

Foreword

In all literature published to date about sewing tools, Dutch items are almost completely under-exposed, or they are not recognized, or placed under the heading 'continental'. Therefore, when at the end of the last century, Kay came to me with the idea that she wanted to write a book on the subject, I supported it wholeheartedly, especially as I was also convinced that she could do it!

Many will ask themselves the question 'Can you write a book about sewing tools?' Scissors are only scissors and will always be scissors. That is true, but the variations throughout the centuries, even for such a small instrument, are so extensive that surprises are always possible. Sometimes after decades one can come across a decorating technique which is unfamiliar, or has never been previously encountered on a pair of scissors. This is what makes it so exciting for the collector to be out and about and to keep searching. During this exciting journey Kay led the way. In this book she has brought together an enormous collection of needlework tools; from simple needle cases to richly decorated silver spool knaves and thimbles, as well as exceptional wooden knitting sheaths and sewing boxes. In the Low Countries (Holland and Belgium) very many silver sewing items have been made and preserved. Many of the silver objects are provided with assay marks and can therefore be dated and given a place in time. Because of this, it is often also possible to ascribe a time margin to items made of other materials.

Kay provides a list of silversmiths who specialized in 'small work'. In Amsterdam this speciality was especially extensive. Mr. Wttewaall took the first step with the chapter in his book *Nederlands Klein Zilver* and Kay continues to amply embroider on the theme. Gold and silver needlework tools were not only made in the large cities such as Amsterdam, The Hague and Rotterdam. There were also silversmiths working and making sewing tools in smaller places like Heerenveen and Dokkum in the Province of Friesland. In the eighteenth century, the Dutch housewife often wore her sewing tools on a chatelaine and even in this small country there are distinct local differences. In Amsterdam the chains were mostly short, with small scissors, whereas in Friesland they were long, with large scissors.

With much pleasure I think back to our regular meetings, when the products of Kay's pen were discussed and our accumulated knowledge exchanged on this special area of collecting. Actually, it is an exceptional achievement that Kay, born and bred in England, has amassed such detailed knowledge about this specifically Dutch subject. This book, published in English, will reach large numbers of enthusiasts and collectors and will add to the knowledge and recognition of these unique Dutch implements.

I would like to thank Kay cordially and congratulate her on this fine success.

Clementine Kuttschrutter

Why This Book?

There are a number of books available for collectors of needlework tools and accessories. For many years one of the few books on this subject was Gertrude Whiting's *Old-Time Tools & Toys of Needlework* published in 1971 (originally published in 1928 under the title *Tools and Toys of Stitchery*). This book and *The History of Needlework Tools and Accessories* by Sylvia Groves, first published in 1966, were pretty much the only books to help us identify our hand-working tools, and we were very pleased to have such good reference material at our fingertips. In 1983 Gay Ann Rogers updated and complemented much of the information with the publication of *An Illustrated History of Needlework Tools*. This excellent book, with much historical background, has helped many collectors and dealers throughout the world. *Antique Needlework Tools and Embroideries* by Nerylla Taunton has added to our collecting libraries in more recent years.

However, all these books are sadly lacking in one area; that of the varied range of sewing tools made in Holland. Here must be mentioned that the addition of *Nederlands Klein Zilver* (Small Dutch Silver), written by B.W.G. Wttewaall and first published in 1987, has been of tremendous help in the identification of our treasures. This book covers the historical background of all types of small silver items made in Holland and contains a large section dealing with sewing items. Its addition to our libraries has greatly helped to increase our knowledge. Unfortunately, *Nederlands Klein Zilver* is only published in the Dutch language and for this reason it has not reached many overseas collectors who have therefore been unable to profit from the excellent information it contains.

For the reasons already mentioned, I chose to write this book in the English language. The Dutch people have always been great travellers, many having left their native country, taking household possessions and valuables with them. When browsing through this book it is most likely that, without having known it, you too may discover that some of your own treasures were in fact made in Holland.

Having lived in my adopted country of Holland for more than thirty years, a fascination has developed for the beautiful items made by the Dutch gold and silversmiths over the centuries. In the 1970s, my small antique business quickly became dominated by hand-working tools and in the early 1980s I published the first catalogue-cum-magazine in the Dutch language for collectors of thimbles and sewing accessories, which achieved great success. *De Vingerhoed* (The Thimble) was to achieve international recognition and within the first six months was also published in English and German.

In the 1970s there were important excavations during the building of a new underground railway in Amsterdam. Many household articles were found, including sewing items, dating back to the thirteenth century. From the Municipal Archaeological Department in Amsterdam we learnt, amongst other things, much about our thimble-making ancestors. This subject has kept my husband and I busy for many years.

Whilst giving lectures in England, America and Germany on the subject of sewing accessories, the interesting and beautiful sewing tools made in Holland are greeted with much surprise and admiration. Requests by collectors for this information to be recorded sowed the first seeds for this book.

Much of the information in *Needlework Tools and Accessories – A Dutch Tradition* has been accumulated over a number of years, and most of it has never been published before. I hope that I have now put it to good use, and that the information contained in my book will be a helpful addition to your library.

I wish you happy reading.

Kay Sullivan

Suzanna Cornelia Mogge and her daughter Johanna Ferdinanda, Hermanus Numan, 1776.

CHAPTER 1

Bags, Sewing Sets and Boxes

A little history

Silver and gold marks tell us that the majority of luxury sets of Dutch sewing tools were made in the cities, home to people from all walks of life. Amongst the affluent inhabitants were traders, bankers, magistrates, land-owners and noblemen, creating a ready-made market for the gold and silversmiths. It will be noticed that frequently recurring assay and makers' marks are those of the City of Amsterdam, whose lively history helps to explain this.

In 1275 Amsterdam received Toll Rights from the Court of Holland entitling the traders within the city to free trade their own goods and products throughout Holland. This new privilege meant that toll was levied on traders from outside the city, restricting trading possibilities, thereby creating a monopoly position for the Amsterdam traders.

Around 1300, Amsterdam would have been little more than a country town, mainly populated by traders, farmers, fishermen and sailors. The sea has always been a way of life for the inhabitants of Holland. This is inevitable, as the country is built for a large part on land reclaimed from the sea and is traversed by major rivers such as the Rhine, Meuse, Scheldt and Yssel, and the towns and cities are full of canals. Therefore, in 1400, when the *Hanze handel* (Hanseatic trading) was established permitting free trading with Scandinavian countries via the Baltic Sea, Amsterdam was quick to take advantage of the new horizons offered by this development. The new trading agreement presented possibilities to

Plate 1
'De Hofstede Trompenburg', an 18th century stately home on the River Amstel, just a short boat ride away from Amsterdam. The wealthy could afford luxury homes such as this, as well as houses near their work in Amsterdam. The lady of the house could spend her days making fine embroidery, often together with friends.
GEMEENTE ARCHIEF, AMSTERDAM

trade with neighbouring countries. Among others, free trading grew swiftly between Holland and Sweden, Denmark, Norway and north Germany.

The prosperity of Amsterdam attracted many immigrants and refugees, where rich and poor alike found the freedom to start a new life. The city became the cultural and financial centre of Europe and attracted artists and craftsmen like bees to a honeypot. It grew rapidly and all trades and services were soon required, allowing a variety of artisans to make a good living. Amsterdam was an ideal place for business folk to live and work, where the more affluent could afford a country house on the banks of the rivers Amstel, or Vecht, only a short boat ride away from Amsterdam. The picture of such a stately home in Plate 1 gives us an insight into the lives of this privileged group of people, and an impression of the style of clothing worn.

The influence of Jews from Portugal and of the French Huguenots was great. Driven from their native countries in the sixteenth and seventeenth centuries, they fled to a safe haven in the tolerant City of Amsterdam, bringing with them not only wealth, but also rich cultures still in evidence today. Amsterdam is a cosmopolitan city. The seventeenth century is referred to as 'The Golden Age'. The developments occurring in Amsterdam at this time were greater than in any other city in the world. Merchandise needed for the fast-growing metropolis was brought by boat from all over the world: fine fabrics, porcelain from China and Japan, spices, wine, precious stones and gold and silver. Therefore, as early as the seventeenth century, gold and silversmiths were making household items, including sewing tools. Tools were made for trade and for pleasure. Simple tools were needed for those who sewed to eke out a meagre existence, whilst ladies from the aristocracy and the wives of rich Amsterdam businessmen often engaged in fine embroidery, presenting an attractive market for the gold and silversmiths.

Chatelaine bags

Bags for carrying tools and other daily necessities have been used in Holland for hundreds of years. Mounts for chatelaine bags were excavated during the building of the underground railway in Amsterdam in the 1970s (Plate 2). These bag mounts date from the fifteenth century and were made of iron or brass.

During this period bags were worn by men to contain their keys, a knife or other small miscellaneous items. It is difficult to say exactly when women started wearing bags, but they were certainly a much-used, useful fashion accessory for women in the seventeenth century (see Plate 3). Although the contents varied over the centuries, money was not carried to any great extent. The contents tended to be everyday trivia such as keys, writing equipment, combs, mirrors, sewing implements and whatever the individual considered necessary for her daily use.

Whereas early bags for men would have been made of leather, bags for ladies were often more decorative. Expensive materials were used, embroidery talents were put to good use, and beads were used in abundance as decoration. Three eighteenth century examples, in exceptional condition, are featured in Plates 4, 5 and 6.

Plate 2
Iron bag mount excavated in Amsterdam. Mid-15th century.
<small>BUREAU MONUMENTEN & ARCHEOLOGIE, AMSTERDAM</small>

Plate 3
Painting by Dirck Hals (1591–1656) (younger brother of
Frans Hals). Lady holding a chatelaine bag, 1620.
MUSEUM BOYMANS VAN BEUNINGEN, ROTTERDAM

Plate 4
Velvet chatelaine bag with silver beads and silver bag mount
with classical vase pattern, made by Gabinus van der Lely,
Leeuwarden, c.1750. Hook with windmill made by his
nephew, Frederik Sylstra van der Lely, Leeuwarden, c.1760.
Pin pricked letters 'G.D.'
FRIES MUSEUM, LEEUWARDEN

Plate 5
Silk bag with gold braiding and tassels. Gold filigree mount
and hook made by Nicolaas Swalue, Leeuwarden. Marked
'I.V.L. 1779', probably a wedding gift.
FRIES MUSEUM, LEEUWARDEN

Plate 6
Blue silk bag with gold mount and hook with symbols of faith,
hope and love. Made by Lucas Oling, Leeuwarden, as a
wedding gift from Tiberius Bolman to his bride, Baukje
Rodenhuis, 1783.
FRIES MUSEUM, LEEUWARDEN

Plate 8a

Suzanna Cornelia Mogge and her daughter Johanna Ferdinanda, Hermuanus Numan, 1776.
RIJKSMUSEUM, AMSTERDAM

Plate 8b

Detail showing the sewing cushion box and casket in Hermanus Numan's painting.

Early sewing cushions

A number of Dutch Old Master paintings, a few of which are illustrated in this book, show a lady engaged in needlework with a large cushion on her lap. Some were indeed just a cushion, but others were covered boxes in the shape of a cushion, to be used as an aid whilst sewing as well as to store the tools. Those portrayed in paintings divulge little as to the interior of such a box. They are almost always shown as they were used, on the lap of a lady engaged in sewing. The silver miniature in Plate 7 gives an indication of how a luxury sewing cushion, with fitted compartments on the inside, must have looked. This toy, made around 1660, can be attributed to the Amsterdam toy maker, Wessel Jansen. Sewing cushions were still used in the eighteenth century.

The illustration on page 10 and Plate 8, of Suzanna Cornelia Mogge with her daughter, inside a well-to-do family home, shows the lady with a sewing cushion on her lap. She has some handwork tools on the cushion and in the corner on the floor is a basket containing fabrics. There is also a casket standing on the table into which she is placing an ivory or card thread winder.

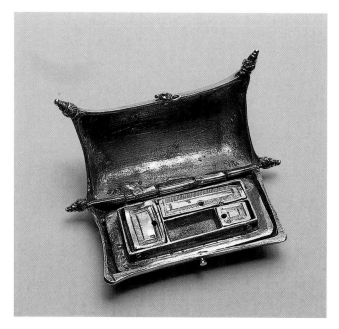

Plates 7a and 7b
Open and closed views of a miniature sewing box shaped as a cushion, made by a toy maker, Wessel Jansen (1642-1696), Amsterdam, c.1660. 6.3cm x 3.4cm x 2.1cm (2⅖in x 1⅜in x ¹³/₁₆in) high. PRIVATE COLLECTION

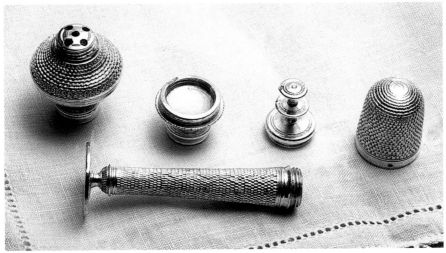

Plate 9a
Silver sewing compendium made in five sections. 10.5cm (4¼in) high. Probably manufactured in Germany, c.1775. Later marked with dolphin tax mark for old work used 1859-93. Base with seal of nobility.

KAY SULLIVAN ANTIQUES

Plate 9b
Five sections of the compendium shown in Plate 9a, needle case with seal, spools for thread, wax box, powder box and thimble.

18th century compendiums

In the second half of the eighteenth century it became fashionable to meet and sew with friends, creating a need for a combined set of easy to carry sewing tools. Thus a different type of sewing set began to appear. From this time, and well into the early twentieth century, small sewing sets in all shapes and sizes were produced in a broad range of materials.

One of the earliest combined sewing sets was the 'tower' type, otherwise known as a compendium. Silver compendiums were first made in the eighteenth century. These combined sewing sets would have been ideal to put into a chatelaine bag to take along when visiting friends. Although often believed to be of Dutch manufacture, it cannot conclusively be said that they were in fact made in Holland. We do know that similar compendiums were made in neighbouring Germany and it is therefore likely that some were imported into Holland, and then presented by the gold or silversmith to the Assay Office for a Dutch assay or tax mark. Most compendiums are unmarked, although occasionally they are found with a city mark. In the author's experience a maker's mark is, however, never present. The confusion experienced by today's collector is therefore

Plate 10
Silver sewing compendium shaped as a fish with moving scales and amethyst eyes. Marks: Amsterdam 1796–1807 and later tax mark 1853. Probably of German manufacture. 14cm x 2cm (5⅝in x ¹³⁄₁₆in).

PRIVATE COLLECTION

quite understandable. To hopefully shed some light on this matter, a number of compendiums are illustrated in Plates 9 to 15, all probably of German manufacture, but some with Dutch assay marks. There are three types of compendium. Plates 9, 11 and 12 show the type which unscrews, revealing compartments for needles, thread reels, perfume or talc, and wax. They are topped with a thimble, and the foot functions as a seal. The smaller type of compendium, shown in Plates 14 and 15, does not have the middle section and consists of a needle case, thread reels, thimble and seal.

A similar type of compendium shaped as a fish (Plate 10) would appear to have been made in Amsterdam, bearing the city mark used between 1796 and 1807. However, this too is more likely to have been made in Germany, where we know that such sets were made in Schwäbisch Gmünd. The fish's head, with amethyst eyes, can be removed revealing compartments for needles, spools for thread and a thimble.

Plate 11a
Silver sewing compendium made in five sections, with geometric pattern contained in spiral design. Marked with Rotterdam city mark and year letter for 1786. (Probably imported into Rotterdam.) Later mark 'O' for 1807. 11cm (4⅜in) high.   PRIVATE COLLECTION

Plate 11b
Five sections of the compendium shown in Plate 11a: needle case with seal, spools for thread, wax box, powder box and thimble.

Plate 12a
Silver sewing compendium made in five sections with leafy flower pattern contained in a spiral design. Marked: Amsterdam city mark (without year letter). Probably of German manufacture, c.1770-80 and imported into Amsterdam. 11cm (4⅜in) high.

KAY SULLIVAN ANTIQUES

Plate 12b
Five sections of the sewing compendium shown in Plate 12a: wax box, powder box, spools for thread, needle case with seal and thimble.

Plate 13a
Silver-gilt sewing compendium made in six sections, with fine wavy pattern and monogram 'MCG'. Probably of German manufacture, c.1780, and imported into Holland. Unmarked. 11cm (4⅜in) high.

Plate 13b
Six sections of the compendium shown in Plate 13a: Thimble, thread spools, wax box, powder box, needle case and seal.

Plate 14b
Four sections of the compendium shown in Plate 14a: Thimble, spools for thread, wax box, needle case with family seal.

Plate 14a
Silver sewing compendium in four sections with zig-zag wavy pattern. Probably of German manufacture, c.1770-90. 7cm (2¾in) high.

Plate 15a
Silver sewing compendium in four sections with flower, foliage and strap work decoration. Probably of German manufacture, c.1750-75. 8cm (3¼in) high.

Plate 15b
Four sections of the compendium shown in Plate 15a: Needle case with family seal, wax box, spools for thread and thimble.

19th century fitted sewing sets

In the nineteenth century, containers for sewing accessories were made in many varieties, including the use of textiles, precious and semi-precious materials. Much imagination went into the decorating of these cases and often wood or metal would be covered in leather, velvet, silk and other beautiful combinations, including mother-of-pearl, tortoiseshell, bone and ivory. It seems most likely that the jeweller presented a selection of tools to a box maker, who then provided a made-to-measure box or case to contain them. It is possible that a private individual could also make use of the services of the box maker. In this case perhaps she included tools handed down in the family, together with her own tools. This would certainly help to explain the many sewing sets found to contain tools of different dates, which appear to fit perfectly in the tray. A good example is the wooden sewing box shown in Plates 16a and 16b.

The unexpected combination of gold and ivory tools leads us to believe that this set of working tools was combined together in the wooden box at a later date. The gold tools, with the exception of a small knife type object (probably used for ripping seams), are all marked for 18ct. The needle case bears the maker's mark of C. Straater who operated in Amsterdam between 1816 and 1846. The other gold tools bear assay marks corresponding to this period.

An unusually comprehensive silver sewing set is that made by the Amsterdam silversmith, Uriot (Plate 17). With the exception of the thimble, all the items have a typical ribbed design, a decoration often found on items made in Holland in the first half of the nineteenth century. It is possible that the thimble is also original, as apart from sewing rings from this period, thimbles with this ribbed design are unknown to the author. As with the previous set, an unfamiliar frivolity for a Dutch sewing set is the cut glass perfume bottle.

French influence on style and decoration of silver and gold, and also on sewing tools, started to seep in during the fourth quarter of the eighteenth century. The similarity between French and Dutch sewing tools increased when Holland became a Kingdom in 1807 under the reign of Louis Napoleon, brother of Napoleon Bonaparte, and later a department of France. There were few countries where complete boxed sets of sewing tools were made. The so-called French Palais Royal boxes found their follower around 1840 in the Dutch tortoiseshell boxes with gold sewing implements.

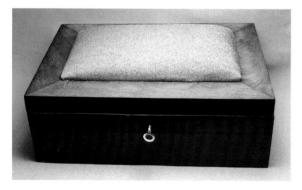
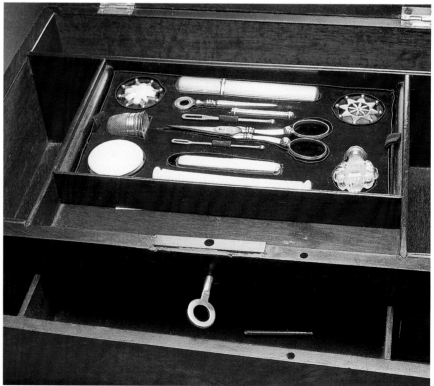

Plates 16a and 16b
Wooden sewing box with pincushion on lid and a drawer for sundry items, fitted with gold and ivory tools c.1825-40. Needle case: Maker: C. Straater, Amsterdam 1816-46. 18ct. lion mark 1814-1905 (style 1825-40). Thimble: 18ct. lion mark 1814-1905 (style 1825-40). Thread winders: 18ct. lion mark 1814-1905 (probably 1825-40). Scissors: 18ct. lion mark 1814-1905 (style 1825-40). Stiletto: 18ct. 1814-65. Maker's mark indistinct. Two bodkins: unmarked. Perfume bottle: cap unmarked. Small gold knife: English, marked with Dutch import mark 1817-31. Ivory items: needle case, knife and pin box. 28.5cm x 18.5cm x 10cm (11⅛in x 7⅜in x 4in) high. Courtesy of Inez Eikelenboom/Mrs. Oaktree

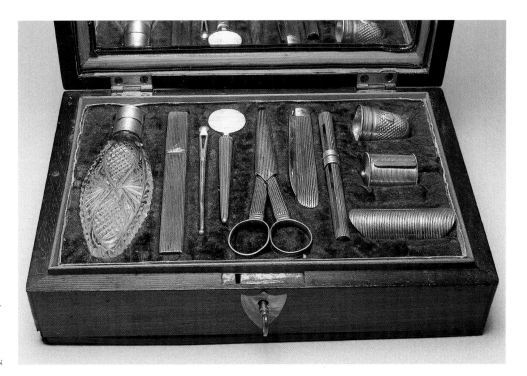

Plate 17

Wooden sewing box containing silver tools, 1820-35. Needle case, stiletto, tape measure, finger shield, all bearing maker's mark: Pierre Louis Uriot, Amsterdam (1812-62). Bodkin: maker's mark: Jacob Kooiman, Schoonhoven 1812-53. Thimble and all other parts are marked with Dutch assay for 925/1000 silver 1814-1905. Perfume bottle with silver mount: maker's mark indistinct. Assay 1814-1905. 18cm x 11.7cm x 5cm (7¼in x 4¹¹⁄₁₆in x 2in) high.

PRIVATE COLLECTION

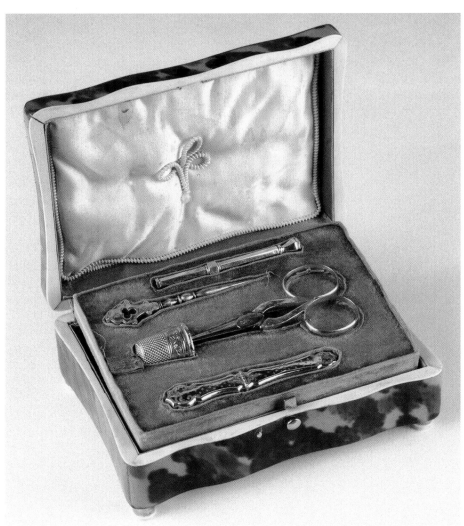

Plate 18

Luxury gold sewing set in a tortoiseshell box on ivory ball feet and with ivory trimmings. Amsterdam c.1830-50. The implements are in a tray lined with blue velvet, which is removable, revealing a section to store embroidery threads and other small items. Lid fitted with a white silk cushion. 11cm x 7.5cm (4⅜in x 3in).

KAY SULLIVAN ANTIQUES

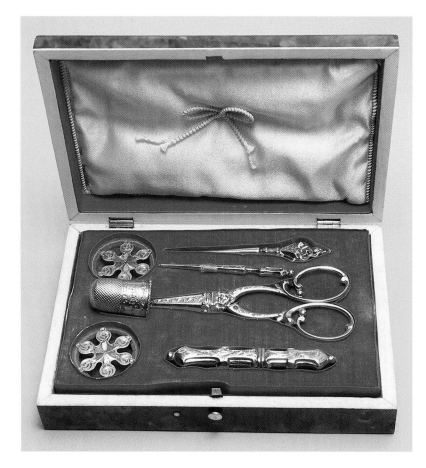

Plate 19
Tortoiseshell and ivory box containing seven gold implements.
Amsterdam c.1852-53. Thread winders: Maker's mark
Nicolaas Hermanus van Veen, Amsterdam (1844-82) and oak leaf
assay mark 1853-1906. All other pieces with wild boar's head tax
mark, used 1831-53 for work of national origin below legal alloy.
14.5cm x 9.6cm (5¾in x 3¹³⁄₁₆in).

PRIVATE COLLECTION

Plate 20
Tortoiseshell and ivory box containing 18ct. gold sewing tools.
Amsterdam c.1850-60. Needle case: maker's mark J. Nieuwmeyer
& J.W. Schwab (1834–75). Scissors and thread winders: maker's
mark Pieter Keizer, Amsterdam (1850-66). Thimble: H.W. van
Riel, Amsterdam (1837-80). All parts assay for 18ct. gold 1814–
1905. 14.4cm x 9.5cm (5¾in x 3¾in).

KAY SULLIVAN ANTIQUES

Plate 21
Tortoiseshell box with ivory trimmings containing six gold
implements c.1870–80. Needle case: maker's mark P.F. van
Maarseveen, Amsterdam (1868–80). All other parts marked with
assay mark for 14ct. gold. 15.5cm x 10.5cm (6¼in x 4¼in).

KAY SULLIVAN ANTIQUES

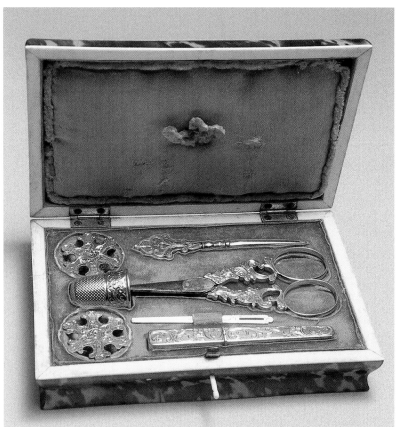

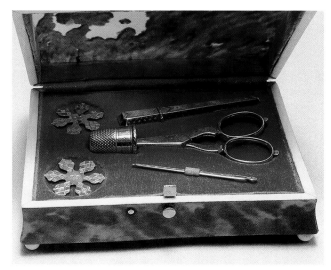

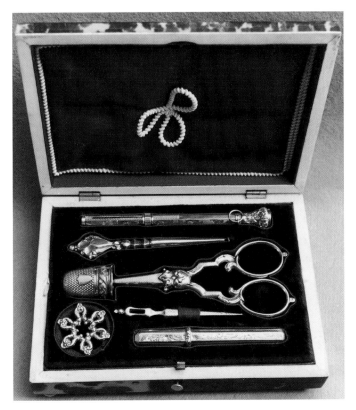

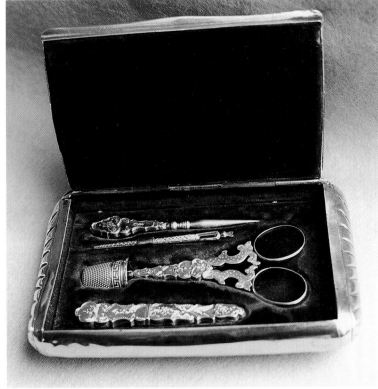

Plate 22
Tortoiseshell box with ivory trimmings containing seven 18ct. gold tools c.1830-50. Thimble: maker's mark: Widow B. Gilles, 's–Hertogenbosch (1833-59). Pencil with agate top, bodkin, stiletto, scissors in sheath, thread winder and needle case all bear boar's head mark, used 1831-53. 15.1cm x 10.2cm (6in x 4in). PRIVATE COLLECTION

Plate 23a (above right) and 23b (detail)
Silver gilt box (possibly previously tobacco box) containing five gold sewing tools. Maker: Widow Teuntje van Halteren, Schoonhoven (1863-95). All tools bear Dutch mark for 14ct. gold. PRIVATE COLLECTION

These luxury tortoiseshell boxes often have small ivory ball feet and trimmings, and are completed with a silk cushion. The tray of tools can be removed to reveal a section in which to store embroidery threads and other small items.

The gold sewing set in Plate 19 can be accurately dated to 1852-53 for the following reason. The thimble is made of 14ct. gold, which was not introduced as legal standard until 1853. The remaining tools are marked with the boar's head, which ceased to be used after 1852 for objects of national origin below legal alloy.

The exquisite set of gold tools in a tortoiseshell box (Plate 22) can be attributed to a lady jeweller. From records we know that the 'Widow B. Gilles' continued her husband's business after his death and between 1833 and 1859 she is recorded as having used her own maker's mark. As all seven tools bear marks consistent with this period, we can conclude that the set was made at this time.

An inventive sewing set, contained in what could have once been a tobacco box (Plate 23), bears the marks of another lady jeweller. The beautifully engraved box is made of silver gilt. It is marked with the year letter for 1874 and the maker's mark of Widow Teuntje van Halteren who lived in the Lopikerstraat in Schoonhoven. She took over the business of her deceased husband on 15th August 1863. When she died on 1st January 1895, her son Johannes continued the business until 1908. All implements bear matching marks. Schoonhoven is famous for its silver and a similar silver tobacco box can be found in the Silver Museum of this city.

Plate 24a
Mother-of-pearl sewing box
containing seven gold
implements. Amsterdam. c.1860.
Text inside box: 'Benten &
Zonen' (1853-83). All tools bear
an indistinct maker's mark and
assay mark 1814-1906.
14.5cm x 9.5cm (5⅞in x 3⅞in).
Private collection

In accordance with the Dutch tendency towards the style of Calvinistic teachings, their sewing tools are generally functional rather than pretty. That the people sometimes felt a need to stray from this path is illustrated by two elaborate sewing boxes decorated with mother-of-pearl (Plates 24 and 25).

As the maker's marks on the various gold tools are indistinct, the text, printed in gold within the box, helps to date the sewing set shown in Plate 24. The message tells us that the jewellers Benten & Sons compiled this set and enclosed it in this exquisite and intricately crafted mother-of-pearl box.

Plate 25 illustrates an exceptional combination of gold tools. Each piece is engraved with leaves and bunches of grapes and is the work of a skilful goldsmith. The tools in the box are of high quality and all marked 18ct. The only maker's mark is to be found on the thimble, which tells us that it is the work of Canté in Amsterdam between 1852 and 1870. The perfume bottle is decorated with a small round mosaic of roses and bunches of grapes. The box lid is fitted with oval mosaics of butterflies, birds and fruit, with a larger mosaic of a basket of flowers in the centre.

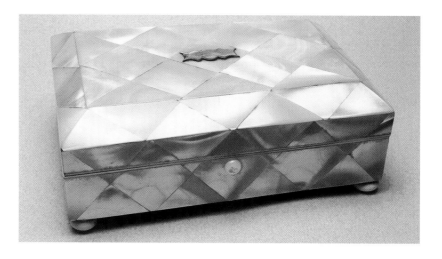

Plate 24b
The faceted mother-of-pearl box.

Plate 25a
Mother-of-pearl box with ivory trimmings containing 18ct. gold tools c.1850-70, possibly Amsterdam. Thimble: maker's mark Cornelis Canté, Amsterdam (1852-70). Thread winders: Dutch 18ct. mark 1814-65 Needle case with mosaic decoration. Other tools unmarked.
14cm x 9.5cm (5⅝in x 3¾in).

Plate 25b
The box, decorated with six small Italian mosaics from the period 1850-80, with butterflies, birds and fruits and a larger centre mosaic of a basket of flowers.

23

An Amsterdam mark regularly recurring on sewing items is that of H.W. van Riel who was an assay master. Van Riel was allowed to place his mark on goods presented by independent gold and silversmiths and he operated from 1854 to 1880. The sewing set shown in Plate 26 is made of 14ct. gold in Biedermeier style and bears van Riel's assay mark. An Amsterdam maker's mark often found on gold sewing tools is that of Cornelis Canté, whose mark was registered with the Assay Office in the period 1852-70 (Plate 27).

Early in the nineteenth century, sewing sets housed in an ivory box became fashionable, a fashion

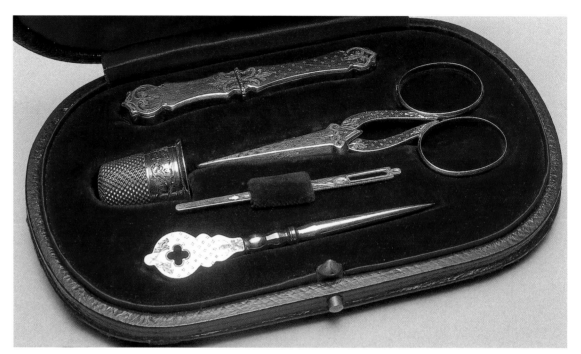

Plate 26
Red leather-covered box lined with red velvet and satin, containing five 14ct. gold sewing tools in Beidermeier style. Amsterdam c.1860-70. Marked: H.W. van Riel (1854-80) and oak leaf – assay mark for 14ct. gold 1854-1905. 10.5cm x 5.3cm (4¼in x 2⅛in).
KAY SULLIVAN ANTIQUES

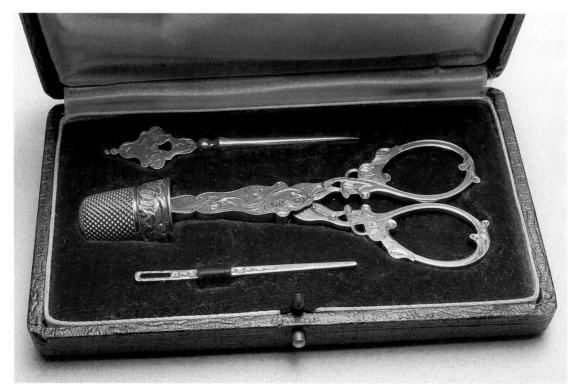

Plate 27
Leather-covered box containing three-piece 18ct. gold sewing set with asymmetrical engraving and foliage in Biedermeier style. Amsterdam c.1860. Thimble: Maker's mark Cornelis B.H. Canté (1852-70). Scissors, bodkin, stiletto: assay mark 18ct. 1814-65. 9.5cm x 6.2cm (3¾in x 2½in). KAY SULLIVAN ANTIQUES

which was to continue until well into the twentieth century. These sets are generally quite small in size and will fit into the palm of your hand. The appropriate name given to these little sets by the Dutch people, is *zeepje* meaning little soap. Appropriate, because that's just how they feel in your hand, nice and smooth, just like a tablet of soap. An early example of a gold sewing set contained in an ivory box bears the marks of Martinus Wouters, 's-Hertogenbosch (Plate 28). It contains 14ct. gold tools and can be accurately dated to 1852-53. Although it is quite common to find these ivory cased sets, an unusual aspect of this one is the intricately carved box, to take two thread winders.

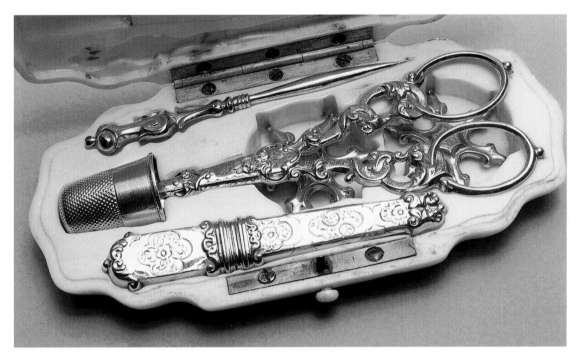

Plate 28a
Ivory sewing companion containing six 14ct. gold tools. 's-Hertogenbosch, 1852-53. All pieces original and marked with maker's mark: Martinus Wouters (1841-52) and oak leaf for 14ct. gold 1853-1906.
Note the unusual addition of the thread winders and their position in the box, in carved-out sections under the scissors. 10.9cm x 5.5cm (4⅜in x 2⅛in).

Plate 28b
The tools contained in the ivory *zeepje*, Plate 28a.

20th Century sewing sets

Eersten & Hofmeijer is a reputable firm of jewellers in Amsterdam. A number of ivory sewing sets *(zeepjes)* from the early twentieth century can be attributed to this company. The tiny 14ct. gold set in Plate 29 contains only a thimble and scissors with a cable-ribbed design. It was made in Amsterdam, between 1906 and 1920. Another gold set bearing this jeweller's mark can be seen in Plate 30.

The gold lettering on the blue silk inside the lid of the box in Plate 31 reads 'S.W. Osenbruggen & Zn. Kalverstraat 147, Amsterdam'. This label leads us to believe that the set was made in

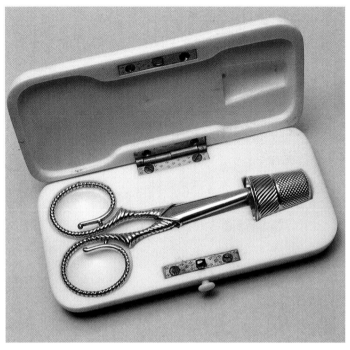

Plate 29
Two-piece 14ct. gold sewing set contained in an ivory case with thimble and scissors, c.1910. Maker's mark used between 1906-20. Eersten & Hofmeijer, Amsterdam. 8.5cm x 4.3cm (3⅜in x 1⅝in).

KAY SULLIVAN ANTIQUES

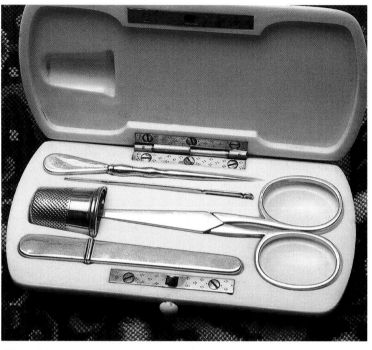

Plate 30
Five-piece 14ct. gold sewing set contained in an ivory case. Maker's mark used between 1906-20. Eersten & Hofmeijer, Amsterdam. 10.7cm x 5.3cm 4⅛in x 2⅛in).

KAY SULLIVAN ANTIQUES

Plate 31
Five-piece 14ct. gold sewing set c.1906-26. Maker's mark: Samuel Machoel Wolf, Breda (1901-26). Assay mark: oakleaf 14ct. gold, 1906-53. Scissors, needle case, bodkin, stiletto and thimble. 10.8cm x 5.3cm (4⅜in x 2⅛in).

KAY SULLIVAN ANTIQUES

Amsterdam, whereas the gold tools bear the mark of Samuel Machoel Wolf, who worked in Breda, in the south of Holland, between 1901-26. The Amsterdam jeweller, S.W. Osenbruggen, probably contained the tools in his own box at a later date. It is noticeable that the style of twentieth century sewing sets becomes plainer around the time that Art Deco design came into fashion. This trend can be seen in the sets in Plates 32 and 33, both contained in simple, fitted cardboard covered boxes. Although the gold set in Plate 32 has all the original tools, the thimble is of German manufacture. It was not uncommon in this period, when thimbles were not made in any great quantities in Holland, to import them from the still very active German factories for inclusion in a Dutch sewing set.

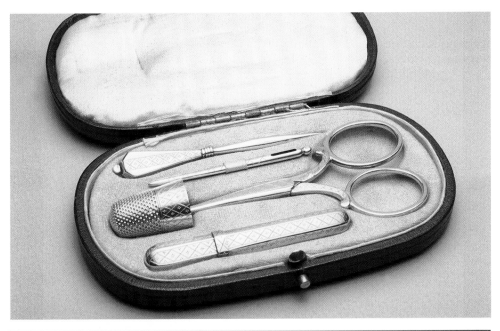

Plate 32
Sewing set, c.1905-10 with five-piece 14ct. gold implements: Needle case, scissors in sheath, stiletto, bodkin and thimble. Needle case and scissors: Assay mark for 14ct. gold (1853-1905). Thimble and bodkin: Assay mark for 14ct. gold (1906-53) Stiletto: unmarked. Maker's mark indistinct.
11.2cm x 5.6cm (4½in x 2¼in).
KAY SULLIVAN ANTIQUES

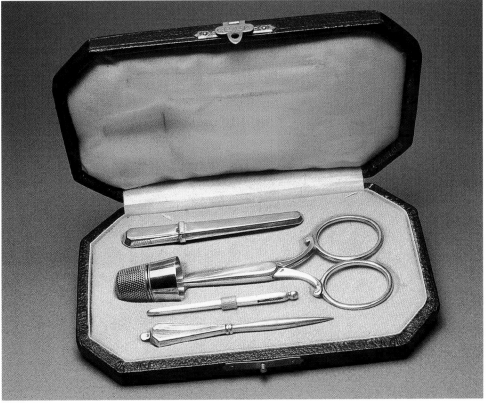

Plate 33
Five-piece silver sewing set containing tools of Art Deco design, c.1935. All implements: Assay mark 1906-53.
Thimble: tax mark 1906-53.
Maker's mark: Zilverfabriek 'Voorschoten' N.V. (1925-61).
11.2cm x 5.8cm (4½in x 2⁵⁄₁₆in).
KAY SULLIVAN ANTIQUES

Wooden sewing aids and boxes

The folk-art *Kerfsneewerk* (chip-carving) was extensively carried out in Holland from the seventeenth century until well into the twentieth century. Every imaginable household item was made – boxes of all shapes and sizes, barometers, wooden shoes, cases for clocks, mirrors, photo frames, closet roll holders, spoon racks, pipes and pipe racks, and anything else which was useful in daily life, both inside and outside the home (Plate 34). Especially in slack times, and during times of unemployment, folk living in the country could fill their days making these useful objects for their own use or as gifts. The high quality and intricate decorations are composed of incised triangles formed in circles and/or straight lines. This particular type of wood-carving is often referred to as *Fries houtsnijwerk* (Friesian wood-carving) as it was especially active in the north of the country, in Friesland. However, it was carried out all over the country (see Chapter 10, The Wiegersma Collection (page 156)

The unusual triangular-shaped wooden box shown in Plate 35 was used to store sewing tools. It is decorated with Friesian wood-carving. The little wooden wall-hanging plaque (Plate 36) was made around 1875. This convenient sewing aid ensured that all the necessary tools were easily within reach. Two boxes with intricate Friesian wood-carving decoration can be seen in Plates 37 and 38. The high box was used as a darning cabinet.

Plate 34
Collection of wooden household articles decorated with the Friesian wood-carving method, 19th-early 20th century.

PRIVATE COLLECTION

Plate 35
Wooden triangular-shaped box decorated with Friesian wood-carving. Dated 'Anno 1786'.

NEDERLANDS OPENLUCHTMUSEUM,
ARNHEM

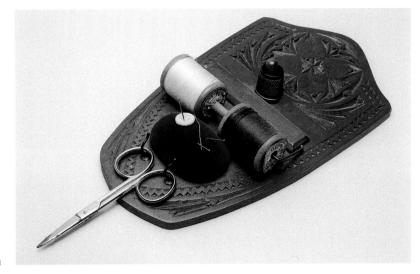

Plate 36
Wall plaque sewing aid decorated with Friesian wood-carving,
c.1875, providing easy access to thimble, threads, pins and scissors.
22.5cm x 12.5cm (9in x 5in).

Plate 37
Wooden box to contain sewing tools, materials and
threads. Decorated with Friesian wood-carving.
Late 19th-early 20th century.

Plate 38
Wooden cabinet for darning and appropriate tools,
decorated with Friesian wood-carving. Late 19th-
early 20th century.

29

No. 145. Naaidoos 25 × 18 × 10 c.M.
Prijs f

No. 96. Naaidoos 28 × 18 × 10½ c.M. Prijs f
No. 96a. Kapdoos 28 × 18 × 10½ c.M. Prijs f

No. 225. Naaidoos 30 × 21 × 11 c.M.
Prijs f

No. 186. Naaidoos 27 × 19 × 10 c.M.
Prijs f

No. 207. Naaidoos 30 × 21 × 11 c.M.
Prijs f

No. 198. Naaidoos 37 × 25 × 12 c.M. Prijs f

No. 209. Doos met slot 15 × 10 × 6½ c.M.
Prijs f

No. 54. Naaidoos 33 × 23 × 11 c.M. Prijs f

Plate 39
Front cover of W.H. Steelink & Zonen's catalogue, c.1920.

Plate 40
A page from Steelink's catalogue advertising paper patterns for sewing boxes, c.1920.

The company W.H. Steelink & Zonen in Amsterdam issued a catalogue offering for sale paper patterns for wood workers (Plates 39 and 40). On page 20, patterns for *naaidozen* (sewing boxes) are displayed. These came in many varieties and in all different sizes. Although not dated, the Art Deco decoration on the cover tells us that the catalogue was issued in the 1920s.

This factory sold all articles needed for all sorts of wood chipping and carving, including the tools and if necessary, the wood. That the practice of Friesian wood-carving, shown on some of these sewing boxes, was still very active at the beginning of the twentieth century is evident from the following excerpt from their sales catalogue:

> *Working with wood for making objects of art, is certainly one of the oldest existing arts. People are surprised to see with which primitive working tools these magnificent figures have been carved in wood. If we take our own part of the world, then it was especially the inhabitants of the North who were the real wood carvers. Norwegians, Swedes and Friesians are famous for this. Supposedly there were two reasons that especially in the North of Europe much wood-carving was carried out. First, the abundance of wood and second the long winter. The practice of Friesian wood-carving has, here as well as in Germany, gained much territory.*

Plate 41a
Wooden sewing box with gold and silver inlay and wooden 'pearl' beaded border, c.1840-60. 27cm x 17.5cm x 11.2cm (10¾in x 7in x 4½in) high.

PRIVATE COLLECTION

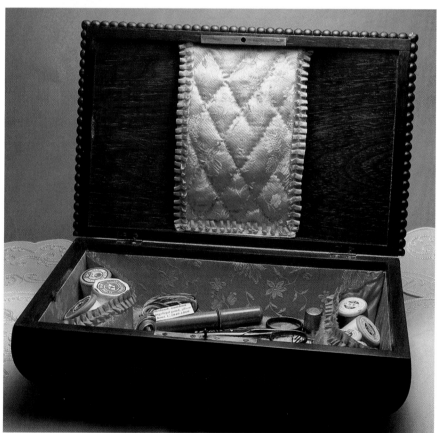

Plate 41b
Inside of sewing box, showing red flowered silk lining with pocket for work in progress. Tools mostly contemporary.

Throughout the centuries, wood has been a popular material with which to make sewing boxes. Not only Friesian wood-carving, but other wood-carving and wood-chipping methods were used to decorate boxes. A fine example is illustrated in Plates 41a and 41b. This nineteenth century wooden box is elaborately decorated with three colour gold and silver inlay. The lid is arched in the middle and bordered with wooden 'pearl' stringing. The inside is lined with red flowered silk with a pocket in the arched lid for work-in-progress.

Plate 42
Carved wooden box showing a lady sitting at a spinning wheel. Text: *Wie Spint Gewint* (She who spins gains).
First half 20th century.   NEDERLANDS OPENLUCHTMUSEUM, ARNHEM

The sewing box made by Pieter Buys from Middelburg in Zeeland carries a special message (Plate 42). A lady is shown sitting at a spinning wheel and the wise text reads *Wie Spint Gewint* (She who spins, gains). The beautiful carved decoration on this box, although undoubtedly wood-carving, cannot be attributed to the Friesian method as the typical circle and triangle patterns are lacking.

A delightful early twentieth century sewing standard decorated with a typical Dutch design is shown in Plate 43. The hand painted wooden dish-shaped base houses all the necessary sewing attributes bringing them easily to hand.

Not many sewing sets were made after the first quarter of the twentieth century. During the turbulent wartime years of the 1940s, materials needed for such luxury items were put to other uses. In the 1950s, sewing sets were often combined with manicure implements as the need and time for handwork declined. Some attractive travel sets were made, amongst others the 'hussif' type set containing needles and threads. These were mostly made as souvenirs or for advertising purposes, and can sometimes be found with a Dutch text, but few, if any, were actually made in Holland. Plate 44 shows a number of examples.

Plate 43
Wooden dish-shaped base with reels of thread, pincushion with blue and white cotton print and a thimble standard with brass thimble. Hand painted decoration of flowers and a windmill, c.1925.

PRIVATE COLLECTION

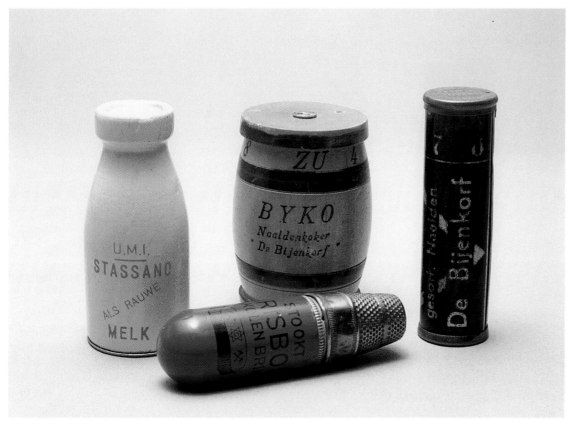

Plate 44
Left to right: White wooden bottle containing threads and thimble, 'U.M.I. STASSANO als rauwe MELK' (milk advertisement). A wooden barrel needle case 'BYKO Naaldenkoker De Bijenkorf' (a large department store in Holland). Metal tube needle case 'De Bijenkorf – Naaldenkoker bevattende 50 gesort.Naalden' (same department store, a needle case with 50 assorted needles), text on end of case 'Best quality steel needles. Made in Germany – Importe D'Allemagne'. Red painted wood with steel thimble, 'Stookt CARISBORG BRUINKOLEN BRIKETTEN' (Stoke Carisborg lignite nuggets). All early 20th century.

PRIVATE COLLECTION

The oldest daughter of the family Thoe Schwartzenberg en Hohenlansberg, Rienk Keijert, 1743.

CHAPTER 2
Chatelaines

The chatelaine

Our journey through the centuries in the quest for information about needlework tools and accessories made in Holland leads us inevitably to the chatelaine. The word is derived from the French *châtelaine,* meaning the lady of the castle or stately home. This lady was in charge of the household and carried the keys and other necessary tools on chains fastened to her belt, so that they were to hand when needed. In the nineteenth century the name *chatelaine* passed on to the object itself. In the Dutch language various words have been used to describe a chatelaine: *Tuigje, Raexc, prak* and also the internationally used word, *chatelaine.*

The chatelaine in the Middle Ages

Chatelaines were worn in medieval Holland. The Amsterdams Historisch Museum houses a simple brass chatelaine with hooks (Plate 1), bearing the following text:

Chatelaine c.1450.
The long chain was called in Medieval Dutch a 'RAEXC' and fastened to the belt. Objects such as keys, scissors, sewing needles or a purse could be hung from the hooks on the chain. The key 'raexc' formed part of the women's clothing.

Seventeenth century costume

It is not evident that there were pockets in men's clothing before 1680. Therefore the chatelaine was an essential accessory to a man's costume, being something upon which to hang tools for his daily use. His chatelaine would contain items such as keys, a container for tobacco and a knife in a sheath.

In the seventeenth century men and women wore belts on which to hang a hook with chains to suspend tools. Some belts were made of silver and were elaborately decorated, others were made of leather or fabric, with silver decoration, and some were simply a piece of rope (Plate 2).

The objects on a lady's chatelaine could consist of sewing tools, most commonly a needle case, thimble holder, scissors and a pincushion. However, anything could be included such as a bodkin, knitting needle sheath, perfume bottle, bag or purse, keys, mirror, knife, tweezers or any other small items considered useful. Unfortunately, as the belt, or girdle, was traditionally worn under the top layer of the lady's skirt, it was not readily seen and was therefore rarely portrayed in paintings before 1700. Only when the need arose to use one of the attachments would the top layer of the skirt be pulled up, and a glimpse caught of the chatelaine.

The Fries Museum, Leeuwarden, has a rare

Plate 1
Medieval brass chatelaine with hooks for tools, c.1450.
BUREAU MONUMENTEN & ARCHEOLOGIE, AMSTERDAM

Plate 2
Two etchings by Rembrandt, dated 1634.
Peasants with knives, other tools and bags hanging on belts around their waists.

seventeenth century silver girdle (Plate 3) with two hooks and chains, complete with various personal items. This unique item was handed down within the same family since its acquisition late in the seventeenth century. The history of this girdle with chatelaines shows that such an item was a gift to a woman and, even after her marriage, remained her own personal property. The provenance also proves, without a doubt, that such luxury accessories were inherited via the female line of the family. It was presented to the museum by the last heir and benefactor, accompanied by all relevant information appertaining to dates, origin, maker and family history. Both girdle and chatelaines are in remarkably good condition. Plate 3a demonstrates how the belt was worn, although in normal practice an apron would have been worn over the top, hiding the chatelaine from view.

A rare gold chatelaine in the possession of the Nederlands Openluchtmuseum, Arnhem shown in Plate 4, dates from 1680. It is believed that this noteworthy chatelaine was made either in Friesland or Amsterdam. The five attachments are hung from five finely-woven gold cords. The tools consist of a thimble house containing a gold thimble and a bodkin with earspoon, a scent bottle, a case for scissors, a sealing wax holder and a carved crystal seal, mounted in a filigree surround.

The Fries Museum also houses a gold chatelaine, fashionable in the first half of the eighteenth century (Plate 5). The hook is decorated with love symbols and the tools consist of two thimble holders, a needle and bodkin case and a case for scissors.

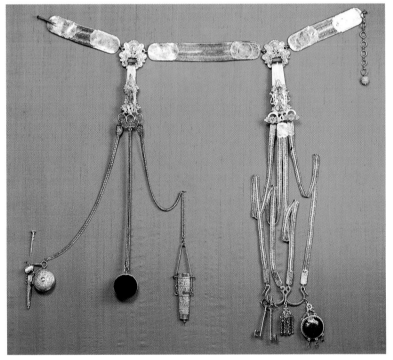

Plate 3b

Detail of girdle and chatelaines. The oldest chatelaine dates from 1669 with three chains and four tools: stiletto in sheath, sheath for knife and fork or for sewing items, black velvet pincushion and a pin box.

The second chatelaine has four chains, held together at the bottom with a W-shaped hook, on which are two silver keys and a lacquered leather scent bottle. The gold bell or pomander is exceptional.

Plate 3a

Silver girdle with two chatelaines of silver, gold, leather and velvet, made at the end of the 17th century by Thomas Sibrand Hicht in Dokkum, Friesland.　　　　　FRIES MUSEUM, LEEUWARDEN

Plate 4b
Detail of gold chatelaine, showing close-up of an extraordinary crystal seal.

Plate 4a
Gold chatelaine, dated 1680. Probably made in Friesland or Amsterdam. 16.5cm (6⅜in) long.

NEDERLANDS OPENLUCHTMUSEUM, ARNHEM

Plate 5
Gold chatelaine c.1725-50 with two thimble holders, two needle cases and a scissors case. The hook is decorated with a figure of Cupid. 17.5cm (7in) high.

FRIES MUSEUM, LEEUWARDEN

Plate 6
'Whitsun Bride' on the Isle of
Texel, wearing chatelaines and
chatelaine bags.
NEDERLANDS OPENLUCHTMUSEUM,
ARNHEM

The 'Whitsun Bride' and the chatelaine

To explore the chatelaine in more detail, we have to know something about Dutch folklore, in
which the chatelaine plays an important role. From medieval times a festival was held in the north
of Holland to celebrate Whitsun. This occasion finds its roots in the Middle Ages when it was called
'Maria Month'. In the sixteenth century the celebrations had already expanded into a true folk
festival lasting for four days, starting on the Friday before Whitsun. Whit Monday was the day of the
'Whitsun Bride', as she was commonly called.

Plate 7
Whitsun tradition of the 'bride'
decorated with accessories,
being paraded through the
streets. Bernard Picart,
Schermerhorn, 1732.
NEDERLANDS OPENLUCHTMUSEUM,
ARNHEM

Following the tradition at that time, family and neighbours would dress a young girl in the finest clothes they could muster and gather together as many accessories as possible to complement her gown. On this special occasion, the chatelaine was an important addition to her dress. She was then paraded through the streets, surrounded by a crowd of white-clad virgins. Plate 7 portrays a 'Whitsun Bride' early in the eighteenth century. This ceremony was a rare phenomenon in Schermerhorn and people flocked from far and wide to see the 'bride'. Plate 6 shows a 'bride' on the Isle of Texel, in the extreme north of Holland, where the Whitsun ceremony is known to have continued until early in the twentieth century.

In the Openlucht Museum in Arnhem, a number of exhibitions have been held over the years on the subject of Dutch folk costume. During an exhibition in 1963, *Feest en Vermaak* (Festivities and Pleasure), a Whitsun Bride was authentically reconstructed (Plate 8). In this picture we see a 'bride' in north Holland circa 1750, wearing a dress with tambour embroidery, a silk damask jacket and the cap of the local costume. Apart from the normal jewels appropriate to this costume, the 'bride' is shown to be wearing three necklaces, two chatelaine bags, two chatelaines and four spoons.

At the exhibition *Sieraden uit de tijd* (Jewels from the Past) held in Arnhem in 1990, a 'Whitsun Bride' was shown (Plate 9) wearing many appendages, including a chatelaine, a spool knave, corset pins, a chatelaine bag, many silver spoons and two silver wine flasks.

Plate 8
'Whitsun Bride' dressed in traditional costume and wearing chatelaines. Exhibited in 1963. *Feest en Vermaak* (Festivities and Pleasure). NEDERLANDS OPENLUCHT MUSEUM, ARNHEM

Plates 9a and 9b
'Whitsun Bride' dressed in traditional costume and decorated with valuable silver and gold chattels, including a gold chatelaine. Exhibited in 1990. *Sieraden uit de tijd* (Jewels from the Past). NEDERLANDS OPENLUCHT MUSEUM, ARNHEM

Eighteenth century chatelaines

At an important antique fair in Amsterdam, the author saw a gold chatelaine consisting of a needle case, two thimble holders and a pair of scissors, on a figural decorated hook (Plate 10). According to the information card with the chatelaine, the Amsterdam maker was Nicolaas Siedenburg and the chatelaine could be dated to 1776.

Dutch chatelaines are difficult to find today and with matching pieces, a rarity. The silver filigree chatelaine illustrated in Plate 11 was found in an American collection. The chatelaine, in perfect

Plate 10b
Detail of hook decoration of chatelaine, symbolizing the Creator with compasses and globe.

Plate 10a
Gold chatelaine with two thimble holders, needle case, bodkin case and scissors case. Amsterdam, 1776. Maker: Nicolaas Siedenburg I (1757-1802).
COLLECTION EX-DREESMANN
COURTESY OF JOHN ENDLICH, HAARLEM

Plate 11b
Detail of chatelaine chains.

Plate 11a
Silver filigree chatelaine with six decorative chains and original tools, c.1730. Thimble holder, scissors, tape measure and a thimble house (thimble-cum-needlecase). Maker's mark, hook: Jan van Beuningen, Amsterdam (1701-post-1754), scissors: Jan van Stavoren, Amsterdam (1727-50). Amsterdam city mark: 1717-33. Other pieces unmarked. Length approximately 35cm (14in).
PRIVATE COLLECTION

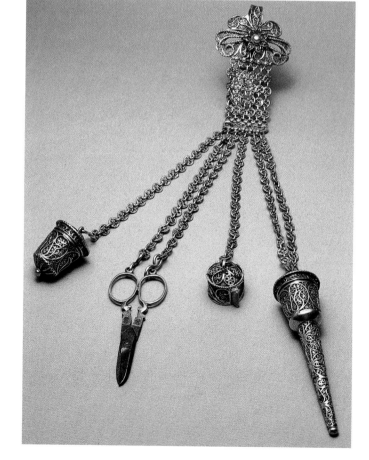

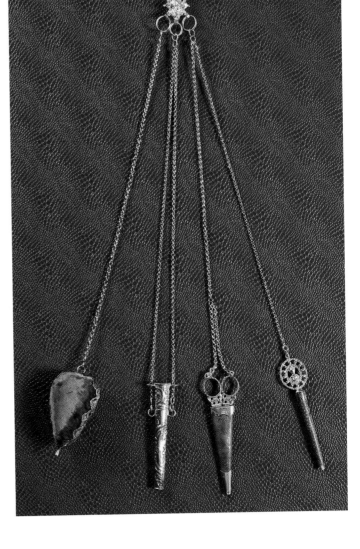

Plate 12
Chatelaine with three tools: needle case, scissors and hand-embroidered pincushion with silver mount. Friesland, c.1780. 50cm (20in) long.

Plate 13
Chatelaine with hook and four implements: pincushion, needle case, silver scissors and stiletto, both covered in shagreen. Chains extended from hook with mother and child deocration (love symbol). Maker's mark, needle case: Anthony de Hoop, Amsterdam (1767-85). Amsterdam city mark. Scissors: city mark, Amsterdam. Pincushion and stiletto: marks not clear. Length approximately 50cm (20in).

condition, has weathered the centuries remarkably well. The appendages are a thimble case, needle-cum-thimble case, scissors and a tape measure. The silver marks tell us that it was made in Amsterdam circa 1730. Whether the intention of the silversmith or not, the decoration of the chains appears to resemble a button (Plate 11b). The silver chatelaine in Plate 12 was made in Friesland about 1780 and, consistent with Friesian chatelaines of this period, has three chains for an embroidered pincushion, needle case and scissors.

The Zuiderzeemuseum in Enkhuizen is in possession of a chatelaine with unusual ray skin (shagreen) covering on two of the implements (Plate 13). It is rare to find such a combination on Dutch sewing tools. The hook has a decoration of mother and child, symbolizing love. The needle case bears the mark of Anthony de Hoop, who worked in Amsterdam between 1767 and 1785.

Chatelaines were also made for children, as was probably the case with the one shown in Plate 14. Made in Amsterdam circa 1757, this chatelaine is only 22cm long, compared to some of more than double the length. It consists of a thimble house, separate thimble holder, scissors and a scent box. The decoration on the lid of the scent box depicts Christ and the woman of Samaria at the water well (John 4:1-42). Both the thimble house and thimble holder have a portrait of a lady on the lid. The hook bears the Amsterdam city mark for the period 1752-71 but the actual year mark is not definable, as is the case with the maker's mark.

The scent box is marked with the year letter 1757 and maker's mark for Johannes van Somerwil I. The scissors were made by Frans Morellon La Cave, a coin maker and an engraver, as well as a specialist in cast forks and spoons. La Cave made not only the scissors, which bear his mark, but also, as he was experienced in coin making, the lids for the thimble holders. The silversmiths lived close together in the city of Amsterdam, and often pooled their resources. The intricate chains are beautifully detailed and very decorative. Johannes van Somerwil's father, Pieter van Somerwil I (active 1706-53) was a silversmith who specialised in toys and other small items. A number of tiny chatelaines have been known to bear his mark (see *Chatelaines for Dolls,* page 50).

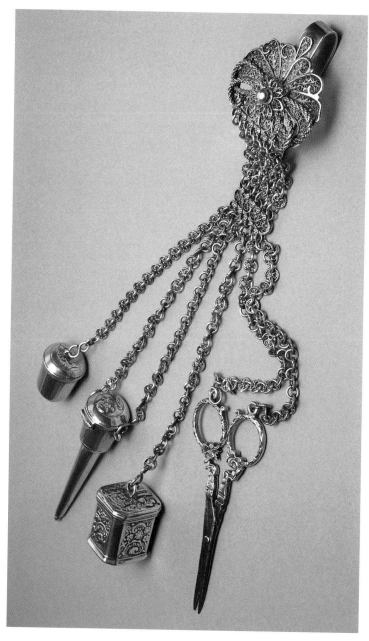

Plate 14a
Child's chatelaine containing thimble holder, thimble house for needles and thimble, scent box and scissors, c.1757. Waist plaque marked Amsterdam 1752-71. Scent box, year letter 1757. Original tools by two makers: total ensemble, hook, scent box, thimble holder and needle case: Johannes van Somerwil I (1737-64). Scissors, lids of thimble holder and needle case: Frans Morellon La Cave (1753-86). 22cm (8¾in) long.
Private collection

Plate 14b
Details of lids: Needle case with portrait of a lady. Scent box showing Christ and the woman of Samaria at the well.

Traditional costume up to the twentieth century

Until the end of the nineteenth century the chatelaine was still in use, especially in Friesland where folk costume was still customarily worn. Early twentieth century picture postcards (Plates 15-18) show ladies wearing chatelaines and chatelaine bags.

Plate 15
Postcard showing group photo of folk in Friesian costume, the ladies wearing chatelaines. Stamped 30-VII-23 (30th July 1923). PRIVATE COLLECTION

Plate 16
Postcard of a lady in Friesian costume, wearing a chatelaine. Early 20th century.
PRIVATE COLLECTION

Plate 17
Postcard of a lady in Friesian costume, wearing a chatelaine. Early 20th century.
PRIVATE COLLECTION

Plate 18
Postcard of a lady in Friesian costume, wearing a chatelaine. Early 20th century.
PRIVATE COLLECTION

Queen Wilhelmina's chatelaine

The young Queen Wilhelmina was featured on the front page of a French newspaper at the end of the nineteenth century wearing a chatelaine (Plate 19). The article in *Le Petit Journal*, dated 29th November 1896, shows Queen Wilhelmina with the chatelaine, and a chatelaine bag hanging from her apron band. The attachments on her chatelaine consist of a pincushion, a needle case and a needle case with a section for a thimble. A short summary of this article goes as follows:-

THE GUESTS OF FRANCE
The Queen of Holland
The young Queen of Holland came to France for a short stay accompanied by her mother, the Regent Queen. Everybody to whom she was introduced was charmed by her friendly disposition.

The article goes on to tell us that, with the Pope's permission, she was admitted to The Big Monastery ('*La Grande Chartreuse*'), which was forbidden for women. The reporter commented that the 'Queen of Holland, at only 16 years of age is in the bloom of her youth'.

When Wilhelmina was inaugurated as Queen of The Netherlands in 1898, an exhibition was organised in the Stedelijk Museum, Amsterdam, entitled 'National Folk Costume'. This exhibition was a great success and when finished, every effort was made to keep the collection together. The entire collection was therefore presented to the Rijksmuseum in Amsterdam. In 1916 it was moved to the Nederlands Openluchtmuseum in Arnhem, where it attracted many visitors. Unfortunately, during the war years the collection was lost.

Plate 19
Detail of Queen Wilhelmina's chatelaine and bag as featured in *Le Petit Journal*, 29th November 1896.

Matching tools

For centuries, the chatelaine was a love token. In the Northern Provinces of Holland, a chatelaine was considered an appropriate gift for the bridegroom to present to his wife-to-be, thereby symbolising his love for her. The chatelaine was more than just a useful set of tools, it was also a status symbol.

A bride may have started her married life with a new chatelaine, but chatelaines found today rarely have matching tools. There are a few simple explanations. A chatelaine was passed down from generation to generation and it would frequently be specified in a Will that it be divided between the heirs. The chatelaine was split up after the reading of the Will and each child received a 'portion', in this case a tool. The recipient then replaced the missing items. This tradition has been carried on throughout the centuries, which has had sad consequences for our chatelaines.

On the other hand, chatelaine hooks with chains were offered for sale as separate items. The user could then make up her own chatelaine, using pieces already in her possession or add new attachments. When these wore out, or were lost, they could be replaced. A case in point is the example in Plate 20. The hook, made by Christiaan Faust in Kollum, Friesland, between 1792 and 1811 is about the same age as the pincushion. However, Pieter van Gelderen from Schoonhoven made the scissors between 1819 and 1842. It is possible that the chatelaine dates from around 1800 and that the tools are original, but it is more likely that the scissors were, for whatever reason, added at a later date. Originally, this chatelaine would have had three chains, including one in the middle, on which perhaps a thimble house, or needle case was suspended. The third chain and accessory are long gone, and an old repair to the hook where the chain was removed is visible. On the hook is a design featuring a peacock, symbolising vanity. Similar designs are regularly found on silver objects from Friesland.

Plate 20a
Silver chatelaine with two chains suspending scissors and pincushion, c.1800. Maker's marks: Hook, Christiaan Faust, Kollum, Friesland. Dolphin tax mark used between 1.8.1859 and 1.11.1893 for old, Dutch work. Maker's mark on pincushion indistinct. Scissors: Pieter van Gelderen, Schoonhoven (1819-42).

PRIVATE COLLECTION

Plate 20b
Detail of hook depicting a peacock.

Plate 21a
Friesian silver chatelaine c.1781. Silver hook with peacock design and five chains. Year letter: crowned D for 1781, no maker's mark. Maker's marks, vinaigrette: Jacob Boltjes, Leeuwarden (1760-83), thimble holder: Dirk Goedhart (1782-1816), marked Amsterdam 1786. Pen/pencil unmarked, but decoration and portraits indicate period 1775-90. Folding knife: Likely Sacco Visscher, Dokkum, Friesland c.1764-86. Scissors: indistinct. Dolphin mark used between 1859-93 for old Dutch silver. Bible/book closure bears year letter 1845.   PRIVATE COLLECTION

Plate 21b (above)
Detail of hook to chatelaine, depicting a peacock.

When the wearing of national costume declined early in the twentieth century, and people became interested in maintaining the folklore, chatelaines were reconstructed from old tools and hooks which were still available. This practice is still carried out today, sometimes resulting in curious combinations.

The Friesian chatelaine in Plate 21 also has a hook with a peacock, marked with the year letter for 1781. This extensive chatelaine has five tools, some of which are suspended on double chains. The scissors have an extra chain to keep the sheath attached. The crowned doves decoration on the handles of the scissors is a typical feature for this period. The oblong silver vinaigrette has a snugly fitting lid which, when pressed on the sides, springs open. A folding knife is decorated with a figurehead and is similar to a type used in Friesland at this time. One object, probably a pen or pencil holder, has no marks. However, the decoration indicates the Louis XVI period (1775-90). The thimble holder has an Amsterdam mark for 1786. To sum up, although the tools on this chatelaine were made in different places throughout the country, with the exception of the pencil and thimble holder, the various makers all operated at the time that the hook was made in 1781. Therefore, it seems likely that the tools for this chatelaine hook were assembled around 1781, including the older pencil holder, and that the thimble holder was added at a later date. A medallion suspended from chains in the middle is a book clasp with the year letter 1845. This was probably added much later as a remembrance of an old family book, such as a Bible.

The Nederlands Openluchtmuseum in Arnhem has an interesting collection of chatelaines dating from the early nineteenth century (Plates 22-26). The pincushion belonging to the chatelaine pictured in Plate 22 is covered in cotton with a chintz flower design in red, blue and white on a red background. The silver pincushion mount bears the year letter for 1827. A hook from a chatelaine bag has been used for the waistband clip, and chains have been added to suspend the tools. The screw thread under the decorative top of the bodkin indicates that a sheath to protect the point is missing. It is probable that this chatelaine was composed later, perhaps even as late as the twentieth century. The pincushion of the chatelaine in Plate 23 bears the monogram 'FA' mapped out in pins. The hook, scissors and etui for sewing tools are decorated with figures and pastoral scenes of farming life.

Plate 22
Silver chatelaine used in the Friesian city of Hindelopen. Hook showing design of an urn with three double chains on which scissors, stiletto and pincushion are suspended. Silver mount of pincushion bears a year letter, 1827.

NEDERLANDS OPENLUCHTMUSEUM, ARNHEM

Plate 23
Silver chatelaine worn in Friesland, 19th century. Hook with three double chains. Hook, scissors and etui are decorated with figures and pastoral scenes of farming life.

NEDERLANDS OPENLUCHTMUSEUM, ARNHEM

The hook of the chatelaine shown in Plate 25 is made from a coin or medallion. There is only one eye on which to hang the chains. The tools bear designs used on Friesian silver from this period and the scissors in sheath bear a maker's mark.

Plate 27 features a chatelaine which has, as well as the 'standard' attachments expected of a Friesian chatelaine, an additional chain connected to the middle eye of the hook, on which hangs a sailing ship with three masts. This can again be an indication as to the trade of the family or owner of the chatelaine.

Plate 28 demonstrates how a chatelaine would undergo changes during its lifetime. The early part dates from 1730, and the most recent addition is from 1854. The chains are original but the original tools have been replaced, either due to wear and tear or they have been subjected to inheritance as explained earlier.

Plate 24
Silver chatelaine, Friesland c.1820-50. Waist plaque with peacock, typical for Friesland. Heart-shaped brown velvet pincushion mounted in silver. Scissor handles as flower baskets. Needle case, engraved pin-head and line design with shield for initials.

NEDERLANDS OPENLUCHMUSEUM, ARNHEM

Plate 25
Silver chatelaine, Friesland, c.1820. Hook made from coin with text 'Ferdinand VII Dei Gratia', 1818. Velvet pincushion in silver mount with bird and figures. Scissors in sheath, handles with figures, probably Hendrik Joekens, Leeuwarden (1810-20).

NEDERLANDS OPENLUCHTMUSEUM, ARNHEM

Plate 26
Silver waist plaque c.1820. Scissors, Schoonhoven 1820-40. Pincushion with embroidered design in heart-shaped silver mount, Friesland c.1820-40. Needle case, Friesland c.1820, possibly S.T. Reitsma, Lemmer.

NEDERLANDS OPENLUCHTMUSEUM, ARNHEM

Plate 27
Silver chatelaine with hook decoration of 'Steadfastness', c.1824. Chains with needle case, pincushion, scissors and a ship with three masts. Maker: Albert H. Kuipers, Workum (before 1807-31).

FRIES MUSEUM, LEEUWARDEN

Plate 28
Silver chatelaine with Rococo hook decoration and chains with etui for sewing tools, pincushion and scissors in sheath. Hook and etui, Sneek, c.1730. Pincushion, c.1810. Scissors in sheath marked 'D.R.S.', 1854.

FRIES MUSEUM, LEEUWARDEN

Chatelaines for dolls

In the eighteenth century, large costume dolls became popular. These dolls wore replicas of authentic costume, complete with all accessories. Only the fortunate few could indulge in this luxury and tiny doll's chatelaines were made at this time to complete the costume. Pieter van Somerwil I, an Amsterdam silversmith, advertised in *De Amsterdamse Courant* on the 9th May 1737, that he made silver jewellery for dolls.

In plate 29, the size of a doll's chatelaine can be compared to the pincushion from a full size chatelaine. Both the thimble house and scent box bear the maker's mark of Pieter van Somerwil I, as well as the Amsterdam city mark and year letter for 1738.

The doll's chatelaine in Plate 30 was made by two toy makers. Pieter van Somerwil I made the hook and Jan de Hoop made the tools. The hook carries the Amsterdam city mark used in the period 1716-34. The thimble holder and thimble house-cum-needle case are both marked with the year letter for 1735

Plate 29
Doll's silver chatelaine, c.1738. Waist plaque, Amsterdam mark and Provincial mark 1734-51. Thimble house, Amsterdam mark and year letter D for 1738. Maker: Pieter van Somerwil I (1706-53). Scent box, same marks as thimble house. Scissors unmarked. (Full size pincushion to show scale.) 14cm (5⅝in) long
COURTESY OF MARIAN STERK ANTIEK, AMSTERDAM

Plate 30
Doll's silver chatelaine, c.1735. Thimble holder, Amsterdam mark and year letter 1735. Maker, Jan de Hoop (1731-69). Hook, Amsterdam city mark used in the period 1718-34. Maker, Pieter van Somerwil I (1706-53). Scissors unmarked. (Full size thimble for scale). 14cm (5⅝in) long.
PRIVATE COLLECTION

Plate 31
Doll's silver chatelaine, c.1760-70. Filigree 'butterfly' hook with six chains attached to which are a thimble holder, thimble house with needle case, scissors, filigree seal and a boat charm. 11cm (4⅜in) long.
Marks: Amsterdam 1752-71.
Maker: Magdalena Rembrants (1753-1787).
PRIVATE COLLECTION

Plate 31b
The boat charm from the doll's chatelaine.

Plate 31a
The seal from the doll's chatelaine.

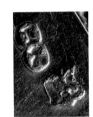

Plate 32a
Doll's silver chatelaine, including needle case, scissors and case containing a knife and fork. Marks, see Plate 32b. Length approximately 16cm (6⅜in).
COURTESY OF DEKKER ANTIEK, AMSTERDAM

Plate 32b
Detail of marks on chatelaine hook. Maker: Pieter Stuurman, Alkmaar. Alkmaar city mark and year letter for 1793.

Plate 33
Doll's silver chatelaine with red silk purse and tools, including two pairs of scissors, thimble house and a scent box. 19th century. Bag 4.2cm (1¹¹⁄₁₆in) high. Chains 25.5cm (10¼in) long.
FRIES MUSEUM, LEEUWARDEN

Plate 34
Doll's 14ct. gold chatelaine c.1860-75. Hook, clips and pincushion, assay mark 14ct. 1853-1905. Chains, assay mark 1831-92. 9cm (3⅝in) long.
PRIVATE COLLECTION

and the maker's mark of silversmith Jan de Hoop, who also had his business in Amsterdam and was known as a maker of small objects, including toys and rattles.

Other silversmiths were also employed in the making of chatelaines for dolls. The example in Plate 31 has an unusually large number of tools, one of which is a rare miniature filigree seal. The other pieces are a thimble holder, thimble house with needle case, scissors and a little boat charm. The boat could symbolise that the doll wearing the chatelaine belonged to a wife or daughter whose family had connections with the water.

The silversmiths in Amsterdam appear to have had the monopoly for most of the doll's chatelaines found today. The city of Alkmaar, just north of Amsterdam, usually associated with its famous cheese market, is where the silversmith Pieter Stuurman had his business. The doll's chatelaine in Plate 32 bears his maker's mark, as well as the city mark of Alkmaar and the year letter for 1793. It consists of a decorated hook with six chains, holding a pair of scissors, a needle case and a container holding a tiny knife and fork.

A miniature chatelaine made for a costume doll, including a charming red silk purse, was part of an exhibition at the Fries Museum, Leeuwarden (Plate 33). Also on this chatelaine are two pairs of scissors, a thimble house and a scent box. The miniature tools conform to those used at the time for a doll's chatelaine, but the hooks and purse are probably a 'marriage'.

A luxury doll must have worn the 14ct. gold chatelaine in Plate 34. The fine filigree hook is shaped as a butterfly. The hook, pincushion and chain with scissors bear Dutch assay marks used between 1853-1905. The thimble is unmarked and probably a charm from the late nineteenth or early twentieth century. This chatelaine, made by an unknown goldsmith around 1860-75, is the smallest of them all, with a total length of only 9cm.

Surgeon Jacob Fransz Hercules with his family in his practice at home, Egbert Heemskerck the Younger, 1669.

CHAPTER 3
Thimbles

A little background

Interest in thimbles has increased considerably since the 1970s and from this time, more and more information has become available. Excavations in Amsterdam during the building of an underground railway, shipwrecks, archive research and collectors' books published on the subject have greatly added to our knowledge of Dutch thimble makers.

Copper alloys were the most common materials for making thimbles before the seventeenth century. It was not until the Spaniards supplied Europe, via the New World, with large amounts of silver in the sixteenth century that silver was used in any quantity for making thimbles. Only a few thimbles have survived from this period.

The earliest recorded thimbles to have been produced in Holland were made of silver and date from the sixteenth century. The puzzle of dates, makers and origins has been fitted together with the help of ancient documents from archives, occasionally revealing the name of a silversmith who had thimbles on his list of inventory, marriage documents from County registers and articles on the subject. Some of these rare thimbles have been preserved as family possessions or have been found at excavation sites, but today nearly all are in private collections or museums.

From a publication by G. van Klaveren in 1917, it would appear that even at that time the study of thimbles was a captivating subject. This study, entitled *Bescheiden betreffende een verdwenen Nederlandsche Nijverheid: De Vingerhoed-Industrie* (Documents Relating to a Vanished Dutch Industry: Thimble Making), covers thimble makers operating in Holland on an industrial basis in the seventeenth and eighteenth centuries. It tells us not only about thimble making, but also contains details about the lives of the families involved, giving an insight into how they lived and worked.

Early silver thimbles – sixteenth to eighteenth century

The most talked about Dutch silver thimble must be that found in the Zeeuws Museum in Middelburg (Plates 1a and 1b). It was made in two parts, the outside thimble with entwined hands on the top, indicating that it was made as a wedding gift. The text on the thimble reads *Sara Reigersberg 1594* and records from the Reformed Church of Veere show that Sara Reigersberg did indeed marry Ingel Leunisz from Vlissingen there on 20th November, 1594. The inner thimble shows four allegorical scenes depicting fidelity, hope, love and justice. On the top is an engraved angel. This silver thimble has gilded highlights.

Silver thimbles were given as gifts and are sometimes engraved with a man's name, presumably

Plate 1a
Silver wedding thimble with gilded detail made in two parts. 'SARA REIGERSBERG 1594' with entwined hands on the top.

ZEEUWS MUSEUM, MIDDELBURG

Plate 1b
Both parts of the double thimble in Plate 1a. Inside thimble with allegorical scenes: fidelity, hope, love and justice. On the top is an engraved angel.

Plate 2
Silver thimble with strapwork design, c.1574. Text on band: 'Bauck Hettes 1574'.
FRIES MUSEUM, LEEUWARDEN

Plate 3
Silver thimble, c.1594. Strapwork design with text 'X SVAENTIEN X GEERS X 94' with flower in top. Probably made in Friesland. 2.5cm (1in) high. PRIVATE COLLECTION

Plate 5
Silver thimble c.1600-25 with circular indentations and top decoration, probably of a duck. Initials in band 'F★D'. 2.4cm (¹⁵⁄₁₆in) high. PRIVATE COLLECTION

2
3
4

5
6
7

Plate 4
Silver thimble. Friesland, c.1598. Text: 'EBEL HAISMA D 1598'.
FRIES MUSEUM, LEEUWARDEN

Plate 6
Silver thimble with top to be used as seal. Year letter H for Nijmegen, 1661-62. 2.4cm (¹⁵⁄₁₆in) high. PRIVATE COLLECTION

Plate 7
Child's silver thimble with waffle top. Amsterdam city mark 1663-98. Year letter likely 1668. Maker's mark indistinct.
PRIVATE COLLECTION

the giver. The earliest known silver thimble bears the name 'Bauck Hettes' and is dated 1574 (Plate 2). This thimble, and that shown in Plate 3 bear designs resembling English strapwork. The thimble with the name 'EBEL HAISMA D' is dated 1598.

An early seventeenth century thimble bearing the initials 'F★D' between two bands with raised edges can be seen in Plate 5. On its top is a decoration, portraying a duck. Silver thimbles from the late sixteenth and early seventeenth centuries often have a protruding ring added between the rim and the indentations. In the later part of the seventeenth century, a similar ring tends to be flatter and less prominent.

The thimble illustrated in Plate 6 bears a year letter from the city of Nijmegen, dating it to 1661-62. Its top has been made to use as a seal. Plate 7 shows a child's silver thimble, bearing marks of Amsterdam. Although not entirely clear, the year letter is likely to be from 1668. Early children's silver thimbles are rare. The child's thimble illustrated in Plate 8 would possibly have been contained in a thimble holder belonging to a child's chatelaine. A Friesian thimble engraved with simply a name and the date 1763 can be seen in Plate 9.

An important notarial act was passed in 1608, when Baptista van Regemorter bought an invention from Gerart van Slangenborg for making silver, brass and iron thimbles. Van Slangenborg promised to hand over the 'know-how and everything belonging to it'. This was a multiple knurling wheel which considerably increased the speed and accuracy of making the indentations. Van Slangenborg kept the 'instruments' himself, possibly to continue making thimbles. Six months later, van Slangenborg had still not handed over the 'know-how' and was even negotiating with someone else. In 1613, the same van Regemorter bought a new invention from Jacob Seyne, presumably to do with the making of the top of the thimble. In the meantime, having become more careful in his negotiations, he made sure that the act stated that he had sole use of the invention. Around this time, he had moved from Haarlem to Schoonhoven, a village known for its silver industry. Although there is little information on van Regemorter after this time, we do know that in the first half of the seventeenth century silversmiths from Schoonhoven specialised in thimble making and that Henrick Jacobsz was registered in the records as a thimble maker when his son was born in 1625, and Aryen Heyndricks Groenevelt was noted in 1636 in the Citizen's Registration Book as being a thimble maker. This last gentleman made thimbles for Jan Willemsz van Schalckwijck. When this silversmith died in 1653, during a business trip to Antwerp, he was found to have forty dozen silver thimbles in his possession. Another notarial act from 18th April 1749 states that Paulus Theodatus Benthem had received a lathe and all necessary equipment from his aunt for the purpose of making silver thimbles. Benthem was later master silversmith in Utrecht and a year later had his place of business in Vianen, another town closely associated with thimble making.

Thimbles were also made in Friesland. The inventory of Johannes Langueer, a gold and silversmith in Leeuwarden who died in 1662, lists '25 silver thimbles'.

Decorative bands – seventeenth and eighteenth centuries

Silver thimbles with decorative bands of various designs were made in the seventeenth and eighteenth centuries. An early example can be seen in Plate 10 (outside right), showing a decorated band of flowers and leaves. The indentations are handmade. The thimble bears an Amsterdam city mark, but unfortunately the maker's mark is indistinct. Also shown on Plate 10 (outside left) is a thimble with a decorative band featuring a hunting scene with a hunter on horseback, a deer, a dog and a hare. The two remaining thimbles in this picture were made early in the eighteenth century, one with a clear impression of the Amsterdam city mark. The other is a classic child's thimble.

The exceptional band design on the thimble in Plate 11 depicts the Bible story of the Flight to Egypt (Matthew 2:13-18). The flower decoration on top of the thimble indicates an origin from Zeeland in the period 1775-1800. A thimble with a clear impression of a hunting scene is shown in Plates 12a and 12b.

Plate 8
Silver thimble, possibly from a child's chatelaine, c.1700. Hand indentations. Unmarked. 1.5cm (⅝in) high.
PRIVATE COLLECTION

Plate 9
Silver Friesian thimble engraved with the text 'Meye Foppes 1763'. 2.4cm (¹⁵⁄₁₆in) high.
PRIVATE COLLECTION

Plate 11
Silver thimble c.1775-1800 depicting scene of 'The Flight to Egypt'. Unmarked, probably Zeeland.
PRIVATE COLLECTION

Plate 10
Silver thimbles, left to right:
1. Hunting scene with horse and rider, deer, dog and hare. c.1700. Unmarked.
2. Plain indentations c.1725, Amsterdam mark.
3. Child's thimble with waffle top, c.1700-50.
4. Flower and leaf patterned band with handmade indentations. Amsterdam maker's mark indistinct, c.1625.
ALL PRIVATE COLLECTION

Hares and hounds

Silver thimbles with the familiar band of running hounds, with or without hares, were made for an extended period. The earliest the author has come across dates from the mid-seventeenth century and they continued to be made until late in the eighteenth century.

Sewing rings were made for use by tailors, shoemakers and other tradesmen. These are less difficult to find today than regular thimbles. Two of the sewing rings in Plate 13 are decorated with hares and hounds. Plates 14-16 illustrate thimbles and sewing rings with bands of hares and hounds which were made in the seventeenth and eighteenth centuries.

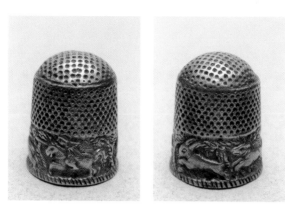

Plates 12a and 12b
Silver thimble with hunting scene, c.1700. Left: Horse and rider. Right: dog and hare.   PRIVATE COLLECTION

Plate 13
Silver sewing rings, from left to right:
1. Band of running hares and hounds, c.1725.
2. Plain sewing ring, c.1700. Maker: Jan Breda, Amsterdam. (1688-1725).
3. Running hares and hounds. Unmarked c.1650-1700.
4. Plain sewing ring with raised band above rim c.1625-50.
          KAY SULLIVAN ANTIQUES

Plate 14
Silver sewing ring with band of hares and hounds, c.1650-75. Unmarked.
          KAY SULLIVAN ANTIQUES

Plate 15
Left: Silver thimble with band of hares and hounds, c.1756. Maker: Frans Morellon La Cave (1753-86). Amsterdam year letter 1756. Right: Silver thimble with band of hares and hounds, c.1700.
          PRIVATE COLLECTION

14

15

Plate 16
Left: Traditional pattern of springing hounds c.1750-90.
Right: Band of hares and hounds. Amsterdam mark, year letter 1766. Unusual twisted rope rim and middle band design.
          PRIVATE COLLECTION

Thimble houses

Plates 17a and 17b show an important thimble, probably made in Friesland in the last quarter of the eighteenth century. All around the thimble are panels containing elaborately carved cupids and other figures. Half of the maker's mark is present, but we shall probably never know who it was. It was found contained in a holder, referred to in Dutch as a *vingerhoedhuisje* (thimble house), designed in this case to contain needles as well as a thimble (Plate 18). This thimble is a discussion point in an article written by Edwin Holmes in his *Notes and Queries* no. 2, Spring 1989, when its origin and date are considered. Since the thimble came in its original pedestal thimble house which is marked with a Dutch-type maker's mark, unfortunately somewhat rubbed and therefore not identified, the conclusion is that it was made in Holland, late in the eighteenth century.

Another example of a thimble house incorporating a needle case is shown in Plate 19. The maker, Hendrik Grauhart, whose father was a tailor, worked in Amsterdam from 1683 until his death in 1732. Plate 20 shows a thimble house intended for a thimble only. Both containers are decorated with a basket-weave pattern. Isaac Lingenaar, a silversmith working in Amsterdam in the eighteenth century, is known to have made items for sewing. The thimble house with needle case shown in Plate 21 is a fine example of his work. The needle case and adjoining thimble case are decorated with a pastoral scene of shepherd and sheep.

17a   17b

Plates 17a and 17b
All-round view of silver thimble with decoration of cupids and figures. Friesland, c.1775–1800.

Plate 18
Silver thimble house with needle case and original thimble (see also Plates 17a and 17b). Thimble house: study of sheep with scrolls and laurel swags, c.1775–1800. 10.1cm (4in) long. Thimble: cupids and other figures. 2.1cm (¹³⁄₁₆in) high.   PRIVATE COLLECTION

Plate 19
Silver thimble house with needle case from a chatelaine, Amsterdam, c.1710. Beautiful basket-weave stampwork. Amsterdam city mark 1699–1716. Maker's mark: Hendrik Grauhart, Amsterdam (1683–1732).   PRIVATE COLLECTION

18

19

20   21

Plate 20
Silver thimble house with basket-weave pattern. Amsterdam, c.1750. Maker's mark: Johannes Gastmans, Amsterdam (1696–1774). 3.8cm (1½in) high.   PRIVATE COLLECTION

Plate 21
Silver thimble house with needle case. Amsterdam, c.1765. Maker's mark: Isaac Lingenaar, Amsterdam (1751–1802). 9.7cm (3⅞in) long.   PRIVATE COLLECTION

Brass thimbles in the seventeenth century

Prior to the seventeenth century, and before the blossoming of the Dutch thimble making industry, the majority of brass thimbles used in Holland were imported, most likely from Belgium and Nurnberg in Germany. By the beginning of the seventeenth century, thimble making in Holland on an industrial scale was well under way. From records we know that Marichgen Peters Dochter (Marichgen Peters' daughter – who we will now refer to as Mariken), was granted permission from the City of Utrecht in 1628 to build a watermill on the Zwarte Water (Black Water) outside de Weerd, near Utrecht, for the purpose of making thimbles. Mariken originally came from Dordrecht, and married Claes Jacobs Schodt from Brussels in 1597. Their first son, Jacob, was born in Dordrecht in 1600, and they moved to Schoonhoven in 1601, where Claes's occupation was registered as an armourer. Claes must have learned to make thimbles in Schoonhoven – he is recorded as being a thimble maker when he moved to Vianen in 1621. Mariken had learned her thimble making skills in Schoonhoven.

Claes and Mariken really started something. There were four thimble mills, one of which remained in the family for 170 years. Three of Mariken's sons, Samuel, Jacob and Jan, inherited her skill, and most probably also the funds, to start their own thimble mill. Two other sons, Claes and Isaack are known to have been trumpet makers, but were sometimes referred to as thimble makers. Exactly when Mariken's first husband Claes died is not known, but she was registered as a widow in 1625. She married Antonis Hendricks van Gesteren and in 1629, according to records, they were still living on the Zwarte Water. Although Antonis is not known to have originally been a thimble-maker, it seems likely that he learned the trade from his wife, as directly after her death in 1632 he is known to have had the occupation of thimble-maker, and did indeed continue with the business. In her will, made in 1632, Mariken left the thimble mill to her son Jacob who was a thimble maker in Vianen. Samuel had his thimble mill in Aachen, just over the German border, and in 1638, Jan was making thimbles in de Weerd. In 1632 a patent was granted for nine years to Jacob Schodt when he was in Vianen. It covered the casting of thimbles. In the early days of brass thimble making, the shapes were similar to the early silver thimbles. The tall, elegant example illustrated in Plate 22 could well have been made in Mariken Peters' thimble mill.

It has been said that iron thimbles were also made, although very few have survived. Therefore, the iron sewing ring with pewter lining illustrated in Plate 23, excavated in Amsterdam, is indeed a rarity.

A thimble made of brass, with a pewter lining, bears a name, or monogram, on the band (Plate 24). Personal messages, although often portrayed in the sixteenth century on silver thimbles, are rarely found on seventeenth century brass thimbles, when the accent lay on utility rather than decoration. This thimble is an exception. Although the top layer of brass is damaged, the letters E...V (or W) can be deciphered.

The elegant shapes of early seventeenth century brass thimbles are illustrated in Plate 25. These thimbles were cast in one piece. This was not always the case, as can be ascertained from the thimbles in Plate 26, showing one where the separate top has fallen out.

Early Dutch brass thimbles with a maker's mark are rare. The three thimbles in Plate 27 were excavated in Amsterdam and date from the period 1590-1630, the middle one probably being the oldest. A maker's mark required an additional tool and the early thimble maker would not have stamped his products for advertising purposes. The marking was most probably a requirement of the Guild, as this was also the case in Nurnberg. It seems that marking of thimbles was abandoned around 1630. The makers of these thimbles are as yet unidentified. The different indentations illustrated, comprising stars, diamonds and circles, are probably individual to the master and for his use only. These thimbles do not yet have the characteristic waffle top of late seventeenth and eighteenth century thimbles.

22   23   24

Plate 22
Early 17th century brass thimble of high quality, possibly made in Mariken Peters' thimble factory. 2.3cm (¹⁵⁄₁₆in) high.   KAY SULLIVAN ANTIQUES

Plate 23
Iron sewing ring lined with pewter, c.1650. 1.6cm (⅝in) high.   KAY SULLIVAN ANTIQUES

Plate 24
Brass thimble with pewter lining, c.1675. Initials on band E....V (or W). 2.5cm (1in) high.
   KAY SULLIVAN ANTIQUES

Plate 25
Brass thimbles, made in one piece, c.1600-50.   KAY SULLIVAN ANTIQUES

Plate 26
Brass thimbles, made in two pieces, c.1625-1700.   KAY SULLIVAN ANTIQUES.

28a   28b   28c

27

Plate 27
Brass thimbles excavated in Amsterdam. All have makers' marks c.1590-1630. 2.5cm, 2.8cm and 2cm (1in, 1⅛in and ¹³⁄₁₆in) high.   KAY SULLIVAN ANTIQUES

Plate 28a
Brass thimble from Plate 27 (left) showing maker's mark and round indentations.

Plate 28b
Brass thimble from Plate 27 (centre) showing maker's mark and square star indentations.

Plate 28c
Brass thimble from Plate 27 (right) showing maker's mark and diamond indentations.

Plate 29
Tops of thimbles shown in Plate 27, showing a variety of indentations.

29

The Dutch Monopoly – seventeenth and eighteenth centuries

Signatures of Dutch thimble makers can be found at the bottom of a deed dated 1689 (Plate 30). This deed extended the 'monopoly' formed in 1687 by the thimble mills in existence at that time. The rules laid down by the monopoly were strict and excluded any competition for producing thimbles in Holland as well as dictating prices, methods of packaging, quantities and many other things. One consequence of the monopoly was that the thimbles produced after 1687 were never marked.

The first signature on this historical document is that of Willem van Rijssel, an important member of another large thimble-making family. It is said that his father, Aelbert van Rijssel, came in 1656 to Holland as a Protestant refugee from the city of Lille in the north of France. This is quite possible, since the Flemish name for Lille is 'Rijssel'. The most important representative of this family was undoubtedly Aelbert's son, Willem. He was the owner of thimble mills in Vianen and Amsterdam and around 1710 he also bought the old mill from his father. The family produced thimbles for eighty years.

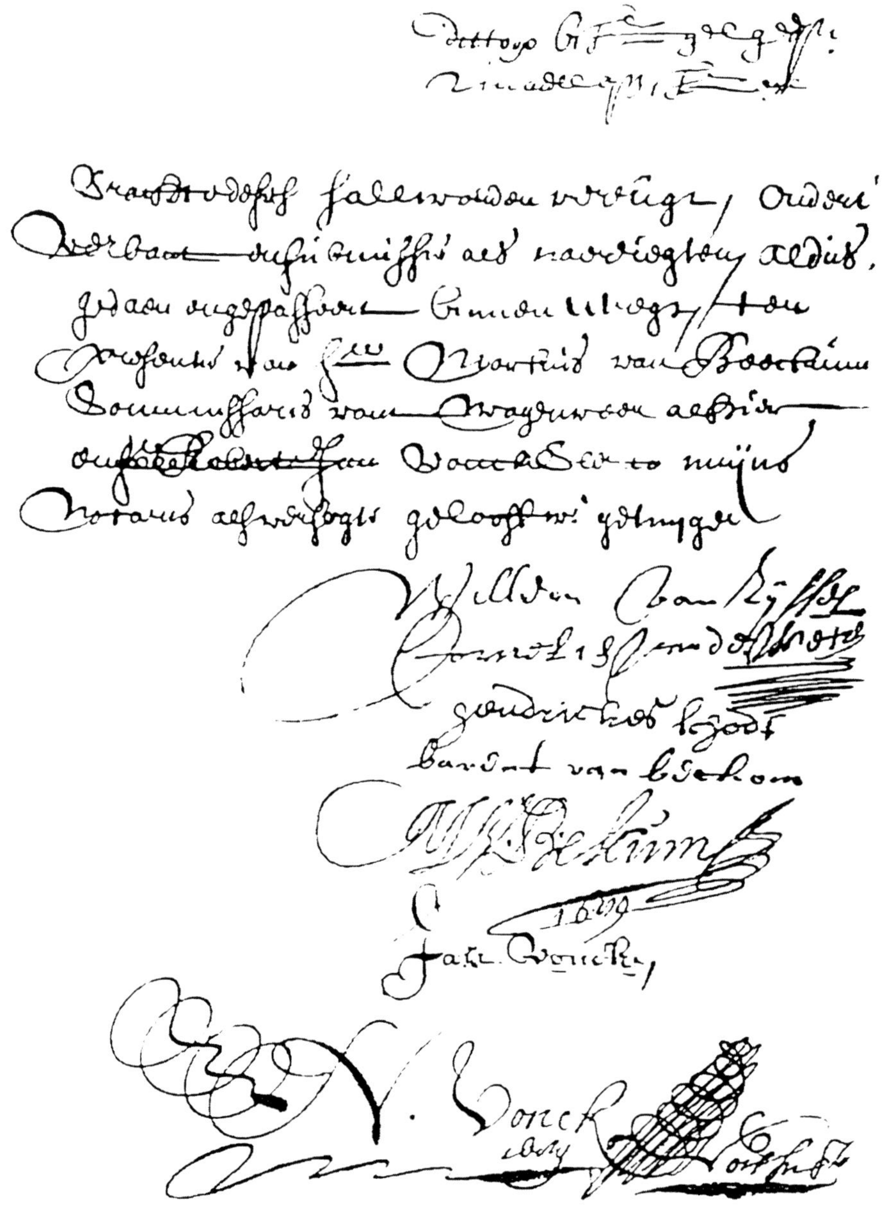

Plate 30
Document dated 1689 signed by thimble makers of 'the Monopoly' formed in 1687: Willem van Rijssel, Cornelis van de Wetering, Hendrik Schodt, Barend van Beckom.
Gemeente Archief, Utrecht

A story about the van Rijssel family takes place in April 1698. It was handed down through the generations, until it was recorded in 1952, and gives us not only an insight into the life of a thimble maker at this period, but also provides a number of otherwise unknown details. As the author, Piet Horden, is rather elaborate in his style, his writing has been condensed to relate the essential details, and it is assumed that these events did actually occur.

Excerpt from: ***Recht en Slecht in Het Land van Brederode Hendrik Vroon, The Rebel of Vianen:***
Outside the city walls of Vianen was a thimble mill belonging to the respected Willem van Rijssel. Together with his workers, Johannes Verstraete, Claes Valckenaar, Wessel Hermens, Hendrik Manassen and Manas Hendriks, he endeavoured to earn a living. When his day's work was done, he sat under the fruit trees in the courtyard, which stretched from his house and factory to the Eikelendreef. It also bordered the Varkensweide and the old orchard on the Gemeenteweg. Willem van Rijssel was a rich man and he was proud of his possessions.

But on a particular Sunday in 1698, it happened!

His neighbour was Elsie Vroon who, together with her husband, Hendrik Vroon, owned a small farm and a few houses in the City. They were simple people, but also what you would call 'well off'. Elsie worked hard, but apart from milking cows and making cheese and butter, she was also abnormally inquisitive. One Sunday morning all was still as everyone had gone to church, including her husband and the van Rijssel family. Elsie looked across at the thimble mill and at her neighbour's house. She had never been inside. It was true to say that the van Rijssels always passed the time of day, but they were extremely 'posh'. Their house must also be very beautiful inside. Elsie was curious and wanted badly to see the luxury for herself. When she could resist no longer, she sneaked to the van Rijssel's house and looked through the kitchen window. The door was locked, but through a small open window Elsie managed to open the door. She could hear the singing in the church and knew that she would not be disturbed for a while. She crept inside, picking up a few luxury items to take a better look at them. But unfortunately for Elsie she was not alone! The maid had not gone to church and was sitting in the cellar taking a secret taste of the wine. She heard noises, and knowing that the house had been empty, thought that the family had returned from church. She quickly mounted the steps and caught Elsie red-handed. The two women were shocked and started shouting at each other. Elsie managed to escape back to her own house.

When the thimble maker Willem van Rijssel returned home, the maid told him what had happened. It looked like burglary and Willem went to the Sheriff. There was only one witness, and therefore Willem van Rijssel demanded that a second witness be used – the rack. The Sheriff picked Elsie up from her home and although she suffered a terrible ordeal on the rack, she did not confess to theft. She hadn't told her husband of her visit to the neighbour's house, but when she arrived home bruised and black and blue, she had no alternative. Her husband, Hendrik, was angry about the accusations of the thimble maker, because he believed his wife. Admittedly Elsie was unnaturally curious, but she was no thief!

He had an idea – what the thimble maker could do, he could do too! He went to the Sheriff and told him that the thimble maker had broken into his house. He too, only had one witness and demanded that the thimble maker be laid on the rack. The Sheriff refused. Elsie's husband, Hendrik, was beside himself at this injustice and swore to take his own revenge. During the night of 2nd July 1698 Hendrik and his family set fire to Willem van Rijssel's house. Both the house and the thimble mill burned to the ground. Hendrik and Elsie did not wait for an opinion of the law, and fled the same night to Amsterdam.

The Lady of Vianen, her excellency The Countess Douairiere Emilia van der Lippe-Dohna, wrote to her secretary: 'The good van Rijssel and his wife have my deepest sympathy in connection with the accident and I recommend a hard punishment be given, setting an example to all.'

This story provides a few details from the rich Dutch thimble history. We now know the names of a number of workers, the people who actually made the thimbles. The story also outlines the high social status of the thimble makers. Willem van Rijssel was an Alderman, he was rich and had friends amongst the nobility. The story also indicates that Willem van Rijssel owned a thimble mill in Vianen and gives a good reason why his previous factory in Amsterdam resumed business in 1703. The story also tells us where the Vianen factory was situated.

Further searches on the site of the van Rijssel thimble mill in the 1970s revealed an exciting discovery. A quantity of about thirty brass thimbles, in various stages of manufacture, and all in unfinished condition, were uncovered (Plate 31). The cast thimbles seem to have been partly turned on a lathe. Brass was expensive and any waste could be re-melted and used again. Considering the story above, it is nice to think that these thimbles survived the fire which destroyed the van Rijssel thimble mill.

Thimbles displaying a squatter shape and a waffle top, shown in Plate 32, are typical of those made by the monopoly. The shape of these thimbles, made in the late seventeenth and early eighteenth century, has changed compared to the earlier thimbles, such as the one possibly made in Mariken Peters' thimble mill (Plate 22). During the period 1687 to 1740 the monopoly made other types of thimbles, such as sewing rings, lined thimbles and the so-called 'French' thimbles (Plates 33 and 34).

Tiny fingers also needed the protection of thimbles. Children sewing for a pittance was not an uncommon occurrence and thimbles were accordingly made in small sizes. Those shown in Plate 35 indicate the variation in sizes.

Brass thimble making continued in Holland until around 1798, when the last thimble mill stopped its waterwheel, due to lack of renovation and enterprise, complacency and murderous competition from England and Germany.

31

32

33

34

Plate 31
Thimbles in various stages of manufacture, all unfinished. Found on the site of Willem van Rijssel's thimble mill in Vianen. The mill burned down on 2nd July, 1698.   KAY SULLIVAN ANTIQUES

Plate 32
Thimbles with waffle top typical of those made by 'the Monopoly', c.1675-1725. 2.2cm, 2.1cm and 2cm (⅞in, ¹³⁄₁₆in and ¾in) high.   KAY SULLIVAN ANTIQUES

Plate 33
So-called 'French' thimbles, c.1675-1750. 2.2cm, 2.5cm and 2cm (⅞in, 1in and ¾in) high.   KAY SULLIVAN ANTIQUES

Plate 34
Sewing rings, c.1700. 1.1cm, 1.3cm, 1.2cm and 1.4cm (⅜in, ½in, ⁷⁄₁₆in and ⁹⁄₁₆in) high.   KAY SULLIVAN ANTIQUES

Plate 35
17th and 18th century thimbles, including two children's sizes. 1.2cm, 2.6cm and 1.5cm (⁷⁄₁₆in, 1¹⁄₁₆in and ⅝in) high.   KAY SULLIVAN ANTIQUES

Late eighteenth and early nineteenth century thimbles

In the eighteenth century, in well-to-do circles, it was the custom for a gentleman to pay attention to a lady by presenting her with a trinket or charm, as according to the etiquette of the day, an expensive piece of jewellery would have been considered quite inappropriate. In the French, and also the Dutch languages, these items were called *galanterieën* and in England they were referred to as toys. Toys were made not for practical use, but as keepsakes to be admired. Some of the most collectable thimbles today date from this period. The porcelain thimbles from Meissen in Germany, the enamelled thimbles from Bilston and London in England and the beautiful mother-of-pearl thimbles made in the Palais Royal in Paris, are all good examples of *galanterieën*.

This fashion had an important influence on the style of gold and silver thimbles made late in the eighteenth and early in the nineteenth centuries. As gold and silver became more accessible due to worldwide discoveries of available raw materials, these commodities were used more often for the making of thimbles. Although an occasional eighteenth century Dutch gold thimble is found, this is more the exception than the rule and it was only at the beginning of the nineteenth century that gold thimbles began to appear with any frequency. The Dutch gold and silversmiths were undoubtedly influenced by their foreign counterparts and their designs are often similar to French gold thimbles of this period, using two or even three different colours of gold. Only close scrutiny of the marks stamped in the thimble will reveal the true story. The gold thimble in Plate 36 was probably made just before the turn of the nineteenth century.

An important fact, which can sometimes help us to date Dutch gold thimbles, is that early gold thimbles were made of 18, 20 or even 22 carats. It was not until 1853 that 14 carat became a legal gold standard. Although 14 carat was introduced at this time, the higher carats continued to be used. Two 20 carat gold thimbles are shown in Plates 37 and 38. The design of the thimble made by David van 't Sandt of Haarlem (Plate 37) bears a close resemblance to that by Willem van Oosterwout of Amsterdam (Plate 38), contained in its original case.

Plate 36
Gold thimble, c.1780-90. Three-tier band decorated with palmettes and wavy lines, and vacant shield. 2.8cm (1⅛in) high.
PRIVATE COLLECTION

Plate 37
Assay mark Kingdom Holland 1807-12. Year letter 17.12.1810 - 01.03.1812. Later assay mark for 20ct. gold. Maker's mark: rabbit. David van 't Sandt, Haarlem. 2.7cm (1¹⁄₁₆in) high.
PRIVATE COLLECTION

Plate 38
20ct. gold thimble. Marks: 20ct. gold 1806-10. Year letter for 21.12.1809 till 17.12.1810. Amsterdam city mark 1806-10. Maker: Willem van Oosterwout, Amsterdam (1805-12). Thimble 2.6cm (1¹⁄₁₆in) high. Case 3.9cm (1⁹⁄₁₆in) long, 3cm (1³⁄₁₆in) high. KAY SULLIVAN ANTIQUES

Plate 39
18ct. gold thimble, c.1825 with decorative two-colour gold band of flowers and leaves. Possibly made as a wedding gift. Maker's mark: Bernardus Gillis, 's-Hertogenbosch (1822-30). Later French import mark, 1864.

KAY SULLIVAN ANTIQUES

Plate 43
Silver thimble with pelican engraved in top, c.1830. Maker's mark: Cornelis Wendels, Middelburg (1828-49).

PRIVATE COLLECTION

Plate 40
18ct. gold thimble, c.1820-40. Band of scrolled leaves and flowers, possibly a wedding gift. Dutch assay mark 1814-1905. Maker's mark indistinct.

PRIVATE COLLECTION

Plate 44
Silver thimble, c.1820. Dutch assay mark 1814-1905. Maker's mark indistinct. 2.1cm (1¾in) high.

PRIVATE COLLECTION

Plate 41
18ct. gold thimble, c.1820, decoration of leaves and shield for initials. Dutch assay for gold 1814-1905. Maker: Willem Littel, Schoonhoven (1814-61).

PRIVATE COLLECTION

Plate 45
Silver thimble, c.1840. Maker's mark: Dirk Hendrik Greup, Schoonhoven (1828-64).

PRIVATE COLLECTION

Plate 42
Gold thimble with silver lining, c.1820-40. Probably a unique piece. Unmarked.

PRIVATE COLLECTION

Plate 46
Left: Silver thimble c.1790-1810. Maker unknown. Right: Silver thimble c.1840-50 with 'palmette' band. Maker unknown.

PRIVATE COLLECTIONS

Plates 39 and 40 illustrate decorative thimbles with a band of two-colour gold, the so-called wedding band. This type of thimble was probably made as a wedding gift and is the most decorative of Dutch gold thimbles. In contrast, the early nineteenth century thimble featured in Plate 41 is much less ornate and at the same time of a more elegant design.

What can only be described as an ungainly thimble is shown in Plate 42. It is probably unique and was possibly made to a special order. A strange-looking object, it is heavy to the touch and made of gold with a silver lining. Perhaps the user had her gold thimble lined with silver to make it durable, or perhaps the thimble was received as a gift and being too large for the recipient was given a silver lining to fit the smaller finger.

In his publication about the Dutch thimble industry, G. van Klaveren mentions a number of cases in which silversmiths were using silver to make thimbles on an industrial basis early in the nineteenth century. One silversmith delivered two dozen silver thimbles for an exhibition in Utrecht in 1808, whilst other documents refer to instruments on which silver thimbles were made. Silver thimbles of this period are rare. Plate 43 features a silver thimble made in Middelburg. In the top is an engraved pelican. Plates 44, 45 and 46 illustrate silver thimbles from the first half of the nineteenth century.

In 1803 there were still two thimble factories in operation, one in Amsterdam and one in Helmond. The thimble with a waffle top shown on the left in Plate 46, was probably made in one of these factories and features the style of the past and next century.

The complicated, and often difficult to decipher, marks found on gold thimbles can be a headache for the researching collector. To confuse matters even more, some Dutch thimbles can bear a remarkable resemblance to French thimbles of the same period. The author had at one time two identical thimbles, both with a French appearance, one bearing gold marks for Paris c.1830 and the other bearing Dutch assay and maker's marks. This latter thimble is illustrated in Plate 47

A rare wooden thimble with a silver cap in the style of a *Zeeuwse knoop* (Zeeland button) is illustrated in Plates 48a and 48b. The rim is trimmed with silver and the thimble has a carved decoration and the lettering 'B. v. Wuffes', presumably the name of the owner.

Plate 47
18ct. gold thimble, c.1830. Dutch assay mark for 18ct. gold 1814-1906. Maker's mark: Dirk Hendrik Greup, Schoonhoven (1828-64). Mark used: 1828-34.
PRIVATE COLLECTION

Plate 48a
Dark hardwood thimble with silver top and rim, mid-19th century. Partly carved decoration and lettering 'B.v.Wuffes'.
PRIVATE COLLECTION

Plate 48b
The silver top resembles a *Zeeuwse knoop* (Zeeland button).

Finger guards

In the first half of the nineteenth century, silver finger guards were made. A shield was worn on the first finger of the hand on which the material was laid, to protect it from the constant pricking of the sharp needle. Dutch finger guards are almost always decorated with fine horizontal ribbing. Schoonhoven seems to have specialised in finger guards, as most examples found today bear marks of silversmiths from this town (Plates 49-51). An exception is the guard with vertical ribbing in Plate 52. This guard is of slightly later manufacture and was not made in Schoonhoven, but in Hoorn. The existence of at least one gold finger guard is known to be in a private collection, bearing the mark of the Amsterdam goldsmith Bennewitz.

Evidence of child labour is again apparent in Plate 53, which shows a rare child's finger guard. The fact that this guard is unmarked could lead us to believe that it was a one-off made to special order. Plate 54 shows an unusual (half) finger guard, perhaps made in the style of the English guards from this period.

Plate 49
Silver finger guard with horizontal ribbed design. Schoonhoven, c.1850. Dutch assay mark: 1814–1905. Maker's mark: Cornelis Monteban, Schoonhoven (1843–80).
PRIVATE COLLECTION

Plate 50
Silver finger guard with horizontal ribbed design. Schoonhoven c.1850. Dutch assay mark: 1814–1905. Maker's mark: Pieter Kuilenburg, Schoonhoven (1818–57).
PRIVATE COLLECTION

Plate 51
Silver finger guard with horizontal ribbed design. Schoonhoven, c.1830. Dutch assay mark: 1814–1905. Maker's mark: Adrianus Kooiman, Schoonhoven (1807–40).
KAY SULLIVAN ANTIQUES

Plate 52
Silver finger guard with vertical ribbing, c.1860. Dutch assay mark 1814–1905. Maker's mark: Johan Rozendaal, Hoorn (1833–74).
PRIVATE COLLECTION

Plate 53
Rare child's finger guard, c.1820-40. Unmarked. (Beside full-size thimble to show scale)
PRIVATE COLLECTION

Plate 54
Silver half thimble guard, c.1820–40. Dutch assay mark: 1814–1905. Maker's mark indistinct.
PRIVATE COLLECTION

Later nineteenth to early twentieth century thimbles

Thimbles made in the mid-nineteenth to early twentieth century seem to have had a better survival rate. Although certainly not plentiful, they are regularly encountered on today's antique marketplace. Gold thimbles were often saved as keepsakes, perhaps received as gifts and not very well-fitting. This would explain why gold, as opposed to silver thimbles, are regularly found in immaculate condition. Dutch gold thimbles set with precious stones are almost non-existent. The gold thimble with a band of tiny turquoise stones and half pearls is a rare exception (Plate 55) and the only one the author has ever come across.

A selection, showing the diversity of thimbles made during this period, is illustrated in Plates 56-74. A particularly noteworthy top decoration is illustrated in Plates 62-68. Although a maker's mark is almost always absent, or indistinct, from marks found on various thimbles with this spiralling design, it has become apparent that they were made in Amsterdam and Rotterdam. Many bear the

Plate 55
14ct. gold thimble c.1870-90. Small band with rectangular cartouche surrounded by alternating tiny turquoise and half pearls in a scrolled border. Assay mark: 1853-1905. Maker's mark indistinct.

PRIVATE COLLECTION

Plate 56
Silver, c.1840. Maker: Willem Littel, Schoonhoven (1814-61). Assay mark: 1814-1905.

PRIVATE COLLECTION

Plate 57
18ct. gold, c.1840. Maker: Wed. B. Gilles, 's-Hertogenbosch (1833-59). Assay mark: 1814-65.

PRIVATE COLLECTION

Plate 58
18ct. gold, c.1840. Maker's mark indistinct. Assay mark: 1814-1905.

KAY SULLIVAN ANTIQUES

Plate 59
18ct. gold, Amsterdam, c.1840. Maker: Jean Louis Roch Nez and Charles Julien Nez (1831-46). Assay mark: 18ct. 1814-1905. Traces of blue and white enamel.

KAY SULLIVAN ANTIQUES

Plate 60
14ct. gold, Rotterdam, c.1860. Assayer mark: Jacobus F. Lameer, Rotterdam (1849-85). Assay mark: 14ct. 1853-1905. Eight-sided faceted band.

PRIVATE COLLECTION

Plate 61
14ct. gold, Amsterdam, c.1860. Maker: Cornelis B.H. Canté, Amsterdam (1852-70). Assayer mark: Hendrik W. van Riel, Amsterdam, (1854-80). Assay mark: 14ct. 1853-1905.

PRIVATE COLLECTION

Plate 62a
14ct. gold c.1860-70. Maker unknown. Assayer mark: Hendrik W. van Riel, Amsterdam (1854-80). Assay mark: 14ct. 1853-1905. Spiralling top design.

PRIVATE COLLECTION

Plate 62b
Detail of spiralling top design.

Plate 63
18ct., c.1860. Maker unknown. Assayer mark: Hendrik W. van Riel, Amsterdam (1854-80). Assay mark: 18ct. 1814-1905. Spiralling top design.

PRIVATE COLLECTION

Plate 64
14ct. gold, c.1865. Maker: Christiaan van Egmond, Amsterdam (1862-69). Dolphin tax mark: 1859-93. Spiralling top design.

PRIVATE COLLECTION

Plate 65
14ct. gold, c.1860-80. Assay mark: 14ct. 1853-1905. Maker's mark indistinct. Spiralling top design.

PRIVATE COLLECTION

Plate 66
14ct. gold, c.1875. Assay mark: 14ct. 1853-1905. Maker's mark indistinct. Spiralling top design.

PRIVATE COLLECTION

Plate 67
18ct. gold, c.1850-70. Maker's mark indistinct. Assay mark: 1814-1905. Spiralling top design and heart-shaped cartouche.

PRIVATE COLLECTION

mark of H.W. van Riel, who was registered as Assayer, testing gold and silver standards. (See Chapter 11.) The indentations of the top spiral in a honeycomb design, meeting in the centre in a small rosette. These quality thimbles demonstrate a high degree of craftsmanship.

An unusual occurrence on gold thimbles made in Holland is the use of enamel as decoration. Plate 59 illustrates a thimble with traces of an enamelled band design bearing the maker's mark of Jean Louis Roch Nez and Charles Julien Nez. These brothers worked in Amsterdam from 1831-46.

Plate 68
18ct., c.1840–70.
Maker's mark indistinct.
Assay mark: 1814–1905.
Spiralling top design.
KAY SULLIVAN ANTIQUES

Plate 69
14ct., c.1860. Maker:
J. Mirani, Rotterdam.
Assay mark: 14ct. 1853–
1905.
KAY SULLIVAN ANTIQUES

Plate 70
Silver, c.1860–70.
Maker's mark indistinct.
Assay mark: 1814–1905.
Simple fantasy flower
design.
PRIVATE COLLECTION

Plate 71
18ct. gold, c.1892–95.
Maker: Eva Groen,
Amsterdam (1892-95).
Assay mark: 1814–1905.
PRIVATE COLLECTION

Plate 72
18ct. gold, c.1870–90.
With finely engraved
flower pattern. Assay
mark: 1814–1905.
Maker's mark indistinct.
PRIVATE COLLECTION

Plate 73
Silver thimble with
quartz top. Maker: Jan
Hendirik van
Denderen, Wildervank
(1878-91). Assay mark:
1814–1905. Heart-
shaped cartouche and
monogram 'A.S.'
PRIVATE COLLECTION

Plate 74
14ct. gold, c. 1915.
Made by or for Roelof
Citroen (1911-20).
Kalverstraat 1,
Amsterdam. Assay
mark: 14ct. 1906-53.
PRIVATE COLLECTION

Their parents came from Ivry-La-Bataille in Normandy, which helps to explain the French influence in their work.

Dutch thimbles with a stone top are not known by the author. The thimble featured in Plate 73 is in fact German, probably from the Gabler factory. The contribution by the Dutch silversmith Jan Hendrik van Denderen is probably only the addition of the heart-shaped cartouche and the presentation of the thimble to the Dutch assay office, after marking it as being his own work.

Thimbles ... not made in Holland

Unsurprisingly, silver thimbles with a Dutch text in the band are often assumed to be of Dutch manufacture. This is not necessarily the case, as indicated by those shown in Plates 75-78. By the twentieth century, the thimble industry in Holland had virtually disappeared and the still very active factories in neighbouring countries, such as Germany, France, Austria and England, took the opportunity to fill the need when thimbles were required. Therefore, most thimbles of this period found with a Dutch text were in fact made elsewhere, for export to Holland, and those made of silver are usually found with an import mark.

Plate 75
Silver, c.1920–30.
VINGER IN DEN HOED (Finger in the hat). Probably German.
BOYMANS VAN BEUNINGEN, ROTTERDAM

Plate 76
Silver, c.1900. *ONS HUIS* (Our House). Dutch import mark: 1893-1905. Maker: Probably Gabler, Germany.
PRIVATE COLLECTION

Plate 77
Silver, c.1920–30.
VERGEET MIJ NIET (Forget me not). Possibly German.
PRIVATE COLLECTION

Plate 78
Silver, c.1920–30.
WANDELT OP ROZEN (Walk on roses). Maker: Gabler, Germany.
PRIVATE COLLECTION

Plate 79
Brass, c.1900–20.
GERZON. Fashion department store advert.
Probably German.
PRIVATE COLLECTION

Plate 80
Aluminium, c.1920–30.
STOUTENBEEK. Furniture advert on yellow band.
German or Austrian.
PRIVATE COLLECTION

Plate 81
Aluminium, c.1920–30.
JACOBUSVERF. Paint advert on blue band. German or Austrian.
PRIVATE COLLECTION

Plate 82
Aluminium, c.1920–30.
WIJSMAN BOTER EN KAAS (Butter and Cheese) on a blue band.
German or Austrian.
PRIVATE COLLECTION

Advertising thimbles were made in abundance, a number bearing a message in the Dutch language. As with the silver thimbles, these were not made in Holland either. Thimble makers in Germany, including the famous Gabler factory, as well as Settmacher in Vienna, Austria and Charles Iles in Birmingham, England, were extremely active in this field. A vast variety of advertising texts were displayed on thimbles of different materials, many of which can still be encountered today (Plates 79-85).

Plate 83
Left to right: Brass, nickel-plate, aluminium, c.1920–30. German or Austrian.
- *Gebouw v. Chr. Belangen te Kolham* (Building for Christian Society).
- *Levensv. My. R.V.S.* (Insurance advert)
- *Levensv. My. R.V.S.* (Insurance advert on yellow band)
Private collection

Plate 84
Left to right: Brass, zinc, brass, brass c.1900–30. From Germany and Austria – four sewing machine adverts:
- *ANKER NAAIMACHINE – MACHINES A COUDRE*
- *ERRES NAAIMACHINES* – green band
- *LEWENSTEIN'S NAAIMACHINES* – red band and glass top (Settmacher, Austria)
- *LEWENSTEIN'S NAAIMACHINES*
Private collection

Plate 85
Left to right: Aluminium, brass, aluminium, aluminium, c.1900–30. German and Austrian. Various advertising texts:
- *DRINKT BRANDSMA'S THEE* – tea advert
- *GEBRUIKT BUISMAN'S G.S.* – coffee enhancer advert
- *GLOBUS ROLMOPS* – blue band and glass top, herring advert (Gabler, Germany)
- *CACAO 'PAX'* – red band, cocoa advert
Private collection

Woman sewing by candlelight (1650-55), follower of Ludolph de Jonge.

Needle and Bodkin Cases
needles, bodkins and stilettos

A little background

To make holes in leather and textiles, a needle, bodkin or stiletto is needed. These early implements, made of bone, wood, brass or iron, are the tools of a large number of different trades and crafts. Until the eighteenth century the terms were used simultaneously, but generally speaking the stiletto has a coarser shape and is found with and without an eye. The eye was used to hang the stiletto up when not in use, or to suspend it from a belt. During excavations in Amsterdam, needles, bodkins and stilettos were found dating from the fourteenth to the seventeenth centuries. These were used by tailors, boot and shoemakers, sailmakers, saddlemakers and candlemakers, for the fabrication of packaging materials, and by the medical trade. These finds now belong to the collection of the Amsterdams Historisch Museum.

Needles

Little is known about the origins of the steel needle, except that it was brought in Medieval times from Islamic countries to Spain, from where it slowly filtered into the rest of Europe. From records we know that needlemakers were registered in Vienna, Austria as early as 1295. Nuremberg in Germany was making steel needles by 1370 and Queen Elizabeth I had the steel needle brought to London in 1566. From the end of the sixteenth century Amsterdam had its own needlemaking industry. The craft of making needles was considered a very lowly trade. There were six small alleyways in the Amsterdam folk neighbourhood of De Jordaan where the needlemakers had their workshops. In towns and cities throughout Holland, evidence of needlemaking is encountered with street names such as *Naaldenmakersstraat* (Needlemaker's Street), but needlemaking on an industrial scale, as is known to have existed in England and Germany, never happened in Holland. Examples of needles dating from the first half of the fourteenth century are illustrated in Plate 1.

A summary of needlemaking by Jost Amman in his *Book of Trades*, 1568, reads as follows.

The needlemaker cuts the needles from iron wire, files them,
makes eyes and sharpens the points, then strengthens them by heating;
they are purchased in quantity by pedlars.

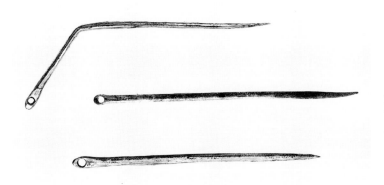

Plate 1
Three brass needles excavated in Amsterdam in the 1970s. First half of the 14th century.
Approx. 6.8cm (2¾in) long.
Bureau Monumenten & Archeologie,
Amsterdam

Bodkins

In Holland during the eighteenth and nineteenth centuries the bodkin was a multi-purpose tool. In some areas it was also used as part of the costume and an important function of this little tool was to lace up the front of the bodice. In the village of Hindelopen in Friesland the bodkin was even worn threaded through the cord of the bodice. A married lady wore her bodkin on the right-hand side of her bodice, whereas an unmarried lady wore it on the left. The main function of the bodkin, however, has always been to thread bands or cords through corsets and other items of clothing. Some bodkins were also used as hair needles. The illustration on page 72, by a follower of Ludolph de Jonge, depicts a woman sewing with a hair needle under her cap. In some areas this also indicated her marital status, depending upon whether she wore the needle on the right or left-hand side of her cap. A multi-purpose bodkin, to be used as a threader as well as a hair needle, bears the initials 'F P' (Plate 2) and the marks

Plate 2a
Rare silver bodkin with a hole for a jewel when worn as hair needle. Primitive design of a hunter with his dog. Hoorn, west Friesland c.1711. Maker unknown. 13.2cm (5¼in) long. PRIVATE COLLECTION

Plate 2b
Detail of marks and initials 'F P'.

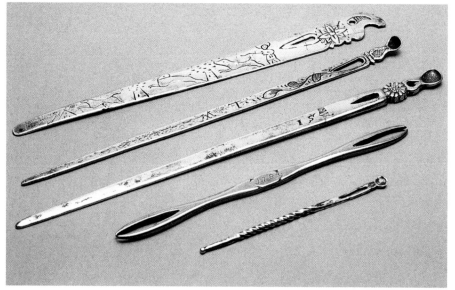

Plate 3
From top to bottom:
Silver bodkin, Hoorn, c.1711 (see Plate 2).
Silver bodkin with ear-spoon. Scrolled design with pineapple motif top. Initials 'L W'. Unmarked, c.1720. 13.1cm (5¼in) long.
Silver bodkin with ear-spoon and daisy motif top. Initials 'I S' or 'S I'. Haarlem, c.1670. 14.1cm (5⅝in) long.
Silver needle for filet work. Unmarked. Dated 1784. 10.2cm (4in) long.
Silver bodkin with ear-spoon. Maker: Pieter Somerwil, Amsterdam (1833-50). 6.6cm (2⅝in) long.

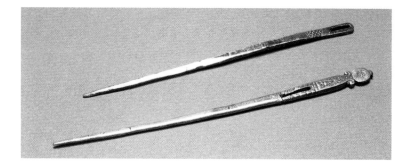

Plate 4
Two silver bodkins: top, with geometric decoration, bottom, with pineapple finial. Friesland, c.1600-1700.

PRIVATE COLLECTION

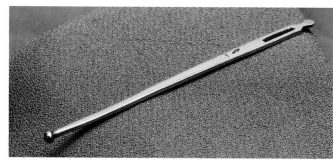

Plate 5
Silver bodkin with ball tip c.1860-63. Assay mark 1814-1905. Maker: Widow Mensje Rond, Schoonhoven (1860-63).

PRIVATE COLLECTION

from Hoorn around 1711. When used as a bodkin, a ribbon or cord can be threaded through the oblong slit. Near the top is a small hole in which to hang a jewel when worn as a hair needle. This bodkin has a primitive design of a hunter with his dog and a sickle-shaped end, often found with hair needles.

Bodkins with an ear-spoon are known from the seventeenth century. The small hollow at the end of the bodkin was used to pick wax out of the ear, which in turn was used for smoothing rough and fraying threads into a usable piece of sewing yarn. A number of early silver bodkins, three of which end in an ear-spoon, are illustrated in Plate 3. Clearly a lot of thought and precision went into making even this smallest tool. Also shown is a double-ended needle used for filet work, a technique used to make fine white netted mesh as a form of lace, and a seventeenth century bodkin made in Haarlem in 1670. Two more early bodkins are shown in Plate 4.

Plate 6
Silver bodkin with ear-spoon. Assay mark 1807-12. Maker not identified.   KAY SULLIVAN ANTIQUES

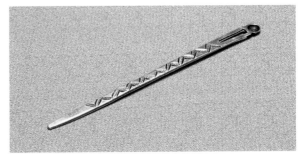

Plate 7
Silver bodkin with ear-spoon with engraved zig-zag design. Assay mark 1814-1905. Maker: Wed. Hindrik Noorman, Nieuwe Pekela, Groningen (1831-32).
PRIVATE COLLECTION

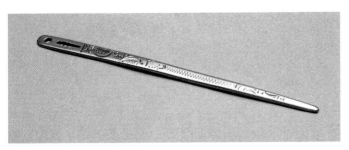

Plate 8
Silver bodkin with chased Biedermeier scrolls/wavy lines, c.1850. Assay mark 1814-1905. Maker: Coenraad Roelof Roelofse, Middelburg/Goes (1801-55).   PRIVATE COLLECTION

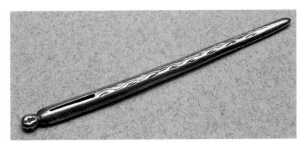

Plate 9
Silver bodkin with rounded shape and wavy design. Assay mark 1814-1905. Maker's mark indistinct, c.1840-70.
PRIVATE COLLECTION

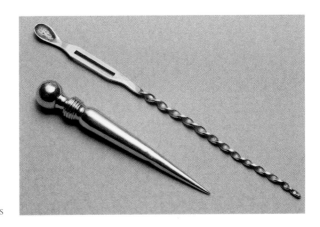

Plate 10
Top: Gold bodkin with ear-spoon. Unusual spiral design. Year letter: Amsterdam 1811-12.
Bottom: Gold stiletto. Assay mark for 18ct. gold. Maker unknown, c.1800-25.   KAY SULLIVAN ANTIQUES

Although the topic of this book is sewing tools and accessories, we can sometimes learn something about the families who made the tools. The strict method of marking gold and silver in Holland over past centuries provides today's collector with a gold mine of information. The bodkin in Plate 5 was made by the widow Mensje Rond from Schoonhoven around 1860. When examining the marks, much was revealed about the maker of this simple little tool. Mensje was born on 11th July, 1790 and married Christiaan Albertus Rond who registered his mark on 3rd May, 1849. He was from Gouda, where he worked as a gold and silversmith. He died on 18th March, 1860 and two weeks later, Mensje continued with her late husband's business. She was then seventy years of age and the oldest silversmith in Schoonhoven. She lived with her son-in-law Teunis Lamoree, who had worked with her husband. Mensje was characterised as 'a simple and capable person, just like her husband'. In 1863 she passed the business on to her son Christiaan Louis Rond and she died on 27th April of the same year

Her son was very different. He deposited his maker's mark on 4th May 1863 and Teunis Lamoree remained with him. However, the young Christiaan was a fickle character, apparently lacking his mother's tenacity. He stopped, and started again, six times. In between he worked as a cow-hand on board ships, as a dock-hand and as a helper in a silver factory. It is possible to tell this story, thanks to only a small, simple, silver bodkin. Such personal details give us an insight into how the early sewing toolmakers lived and worked. It is very easy to find similar information about many other silver and goldsmiths, and this sometimes makes amusing reading. A number of nineteenth century bodkins, simple and decorative, are illustrated in Plates 6-10.

Stilettos

A stiletto, unlike a bodkin, has no slit through which to thread a cord or ribbon. This pointed instrument was used to make a hole in coarse, stiff materials such as canvas, felt or leather to enable the needle to go through more smoothly. For the needlewoman the stiletto was an essential tool. Apart from making holes in fabric, this implement has many uses, amongst which pulling out tacking threads and picking out stitches are just a couple. Stilettos were made in gold and in silver, in many different shapes and designs (Plate 11).

The earliest recorded silver stilettos made in Holland date from the early eighteenth century. The oldest silver stiletto mentioned in this chapter dates from around 1760 (Plate 12). This fine example

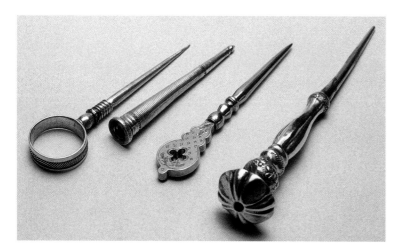

Plate 11
19th century gold and silver stilettos.

PRIVATE COLLECTION

Plate 12
Left: Silver stiletto with pelican design and beaded edge, probably Amsterdam, c.1760. Later assay mark – otherwise unmarked.
Centre: Silver stiletto with beaded ring and sheath, Amsterdam, 1809. Maker: Johannes van Somerwil (1786-1833).
Right: Silver stiletto in sheath with top decoration of a crowned mermaid. The hole in the crown was used as an eye for a chatelaine chain, c.1780. Marks: Crowned 'O' for 1807.

PRIVATE COLLECTION

Plate 13

Silver stiletto in sheath decorated with green-coloured, polished shagreen. The grip decoration is a faceted pearl ring around a central oval. Probably Groningen, c.1775-1800. 9.6cm (3¾in) long.

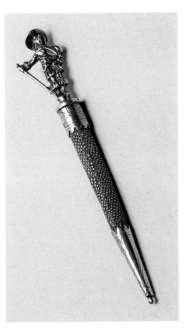

Plate 14

Silver stiletto in a sheath decorated with grey-coloured shagreen, Grip design of a marksman dressed in 17th century costume, c.1770-90. Possibly Amsterdam. 11.5cm (4⅝in) long.

Plate 15

Silver stiletto in sheath with a silver decoration on a mother-of-pearl background, topped with a bow. Possibly Amsterdam, c.1790-1810.

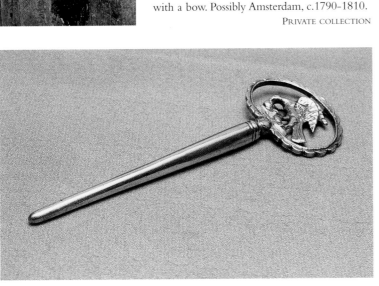

Plate 16

Silver stiletto in a sheath with elaborate decoration of a bird of prey in a surround of leaves, picking at a rabbit, c.1780-90. Maker's mark indistinct. 11cm (4⅜in) long.

is decorated with pelicans on a beaded surround. Another stiletto in the same illustration has a crowned mermaid as decoration, the crown serving as an eye for a chatelaine chain. It is fitted with a silver sheath, as is the nineteenth century stiletto shown beside it.

Shagreen was occasionally combined with silver to decorate sewing tools. Two examples showing the use of this material are illustrated in Plates 13 and 14. Both were made at the turn of the nineteenth century, the latter with a design of a marksman in seventeenth century costume. Plate 15 shows a decorative stiletto with silver on mother-of-pearl.

A good example of craftsmanship in even the smallest tool is the stiletto decorated with a bird of prey, shown in Plate 16. Nineteenth century silver stilettos of varying styles are shown in Plates 17-19. The gold stilettos in Plate 20 are typical of those found in sewing sets.

Stilettos were still made well into the twentieth century when the designs became plainer, leading up to the Art Deco period (Plate 21). They were often found in boxes made of ivory or simple cardboard, as part of a complete set of tools.

Plate 17
Silver stiletto in ribbed sheath with a ball finial. Possibly Schoonhoven, c.1800-25. Maker's mark indistinct.

PRIVATE COLLECTION

Plate 18
Silver stiletto in sheath with eight-panelled eye. Schoonhoven, c.1850. Maker: Andries Jzn. Graves Kooiman 1838-79.

PRIVATE COLLECTION

Plate 19
Silver stiletto in Biedermeier style, with fine engraving and six-panelled sheath, c.1870. Assay mark 1814-1905. Maker's mark indistinct.   KAY SULLIVAN ANTIQUES

Plate 20
Left: 14ct. gold stiletto, c.1860. Biedermeier style with chased design. Assay mark: 1853-1905. Maker's mark indistinct.
Centre: 18ct. gold stiletto, c.1825. Engraved in Louis XV style. Assay mark 1814-65.
Right: Gold stiletto, c.1860 with engraved top decoration. All originally from sewing boxes.   KAY SULLIVAN ANTIQUES

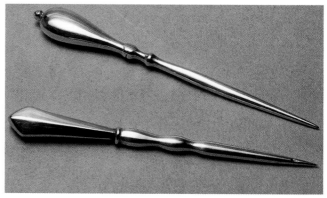

Plate 21
20th century gold stilettos, c. 1910.   KAY SULLIVAN ANTIQUES

Needle and Bodkin Cases

Needle cases appeared with the introduction of metal sewing needles. The needlemaker sold his laboriously-made needles in small quantities to the market stall holder and the pedlar. For those who could not reach the market, it was left to the pedlar to cover the many miles on foot to the scattered cottages and mansion houses in outlying districts. For those living far from the towns, it could be a disaster to lose the only needle they had, especially if the pedlar's visit was not imminent. It was therefore of the utmost importance that the needle was securely stored whilst not in use. Sylvia Groves tells us in her book *The History of Needlework Tools and Accessories* that in England needles were stored in an open-ended needle case, worn hanging from the waist. This type of needle case was made out of a piece of wood or bone, hollowed out so that it could move freely up and down on the cord. On the end of the cord was a piece of material onto which one or two needles could be fastened, and over which the tube could be slid, covering the needles to keep them safely until the next time they were needed. As far as the earliest needle cases used in Holland are concerned, we have no reason to believe that the situation would have been any different to that sketched by Sylvia Groves. The pewter needle case in Plate 22 is one of the earliest metal needle cases to have been uncovered during excavations and dates from the fifteenth century.

For home crafts, wood was an ideal material to use for an inexpensive needle case. The simple wooden case shown in Plate 23 was excavated in Amsterdam. Half of a pewter needle case from the seventeenth century was found in Middelburg (Plate 24). This was fitted with rings for a chain or cord to hang it from the belt.

Plate 22 (above left)
Pewter needle case, Friesland c.1450-75. 7.7cm (3in) long.

PRIVATE COLLECTION

Plate 23 (above right)
Wooden needle case, c.1600-50. Excavated in Amsterdam, 1970s.

PRIVATE COLLECTION

Plate 24
Pewter needle case (top missing), c.1600-50. Excavated in Middelburg, 1986.

PRIVATE COLLECTION

An interesting collection of early needle cases, displaying the different materials used, is in the collection of Museum Boymans van Beuningen, Rotterdam. A number of these needle cases are fitted, not with a ring, but with a small tube of brass through which to thread the cord or string (Plate 25).

Some say that the tulip originated in the Orient and others that it came originally from China, Turkey or Greece. Whichever is true, the tulip is recorded at various places in Western Europe in the mid-sixteenth century. The enthusiasm of flower-lovers in Holland for this pretty flower was so extreme that it resulted in 'tulip mania'. Astronomical prices were paid for a tulip bulb and tradesmen even bought and sold bulbs that they had never possessed, rather on the basis of stocks and shares today. The silver needle case in Plate 26 is thought to be one of the oldest Dutch silver examples in existence. It is of a similar shape to the case in Plate 24, and also has rings for a chain. The design, together with the tulip pattern, would indicate that this needle case was made just before the crash of the tulip trade in the first half of the seventeenth century.

By the early eighteenth century, many more needle cases made of silver came into use. The silver needle case in Plate 27, dated 1713, is still of a similar shape to those seen in Plates 24 and 26. The top section of this needle case slides up and down on the chains, rendering the needles easily accessible when needed. The decoration is of Chinese figures and it was probably once part of a chatelaine. A similar needle case without rings for chains was made in Amsterdam in 1737 in the romantic style of Louis XV (Plate 28).

An important needle case-cum-thimble holder, the 'thimble house', is seen in Plate 29. The long pointed shape is still in evidence and the body of the case has a relief design of a study of sheep.

The second half of the eighteenth century produced a diversity of styles, one of which was especially prominent. The long pointed shape was replaced by a straighter, tapering design with screw-top fitting and flat ends, of which at least one end could be used as a seal. Family crests, monograms, dates and initials were engraved into the flat end, making the needle case exclusive to

Plate 25
Brass and pewter 16th and 17th century needle cases with rings and tubes for a cord.

MUSEUM BOYMANS VAN BEUNINGEN, ROTTERDAM

Plate 26
Silver needle case from a chatelaine, finely decorated with tulips. Unmarked, c.1635. 6.6cm (2⅝in) long.   PRIVATE COLLECTION

Plate 27
Silver needle case on chain. Marks: Year letter 'P' for 1713. Maker: Pieter Haselbeek, The Hague (1712-17). 8.5cm (3⅜in) long.   PRIVATE COLLECTION

Plate 28
Silver needle case in romantic Louis XV style. Marks: Amsterdam city mark and year letter 1737.
PRIVATE COLLECTION

Plate 29
Silver needle case-cum-thimble holder, so-called 'thimble house' with study of sheep. Friesland, c.1775-1800. Maker's mark indistinct. 10.1cm (4in) long.
PRIVATE COLLECTION

the user. A number of needle cases with an engraved family crest, to be used as a seal, have turned up bearing the mark of silversmith Carolus ten Ham, who worked in Amsterdam between 1743 and 1793 (Plate 30). This design was especially popular in the eighteenth century and continued to be made until the middle of the nineteenth century. Decorations often depict farming scenes, for example the needle case in Plate 34, showing a milkmaid milking cows. The needle case shown in Plate 35 has a ring in the flat end, presumably to suspend it from the waistband, most likely as part of a chatelaine. Pastoral and religious themes are also frequently encountered, as well as angels and cherubs, flowers and birds. Upon examining the marks on tapering needle cases, it comes to light that the majority were made in Amsterdam (Plates 32-35).

Two needle cases from early in the second half of the eighteenth century differ greatly from those already mentioned. One rare example (Plate 36) of a twisted pedestal design was made in Friesland and has two different and elaborate crested seals, top and bottom. Another needle case of simple design was made in Dordrecht around the same time (Plate 37).

A curious silver knitting sheath with a compartment in the middle for sewing needles dates from the second half of the eighteenth century (Plate 38).

A temporary revival of the pointed needle case manifested itself late in the eighteenth century in the shape of an umbrella. This popular theme has been used in past centuries for needle cases made of all sorts of materials including ivory, bone, wood, celluloid and plastic. The silver umbrella needle

Plate 30
Silver needle case with flower design and intricate family crest to be used as a seal, c.1760–70. Maker: Carolus ten Ham, Amsterdam (1743–93).

PRIVATE COLLECTION

Plate 31
Silver needle case in Louis XV style with birds and small figurines. Hoorn, west Friesland c.1780. Maker : Dirk Hoep, Hoorn (1735–1813). 9.1cm (3⅝in) long.

PRIVATE COLLECTION

Plate 32
Silver needle case with scene of 'Jesus and Peter walking on the water' (Matthew 14:22-33). Windmill seal with initials 'MBM', c.1800. Marks: Amsterdam city mark. Maker: Cornelis van Hoek, Amsterdam (1786–1813).

PRIVATE COLLECTION

Plate 33
Silver needle case with family crest as seal. Amsterdam, 1775. Marks: Amsterdam city mark and year letter for 1775. Maker: Carolus ten Ham (1743-93). 9.1cm (3⅝in) long.

Plate 34
Silver needle case with decoration of a milkmaid with her cows. Amsterdam, c.1796. Maker: Dirk Goedhart (1782-1816). 10cm (4in) long.

Plate 35
Silver needle case with figures, scrolls and flower design and ring to hang from a chatelaine. Amsterdam, c.1770-90. Maker's mark indistinct. 10.2cm (4¹⁄₁₆in) long.

Plate 36
Silver needle case designed as a pillar with screw cap and seals top and bottom. Bolsward, Friesland, c.1750-60. Top seal: Engraved with bearded man with a book.
Bottom seal: Engraved coat of arms of Friesian family of nobility. 8.6cm (3⅜in) long.

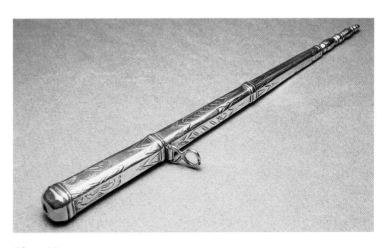

Plate 37
Round silver needle case with no decoration. Dordrecht c.1760. Marks: Dordrecht Rose – mid–18th century. Maker unidentified. 10.6cm (4¼in) long.

Plate 38
Rare silver knitting sheath with Louis XIV engraving and middle compartment for sewing needles. Leeuwarden, c.1780. Maker: Hendrik Dauw (1764-1807). 16.8cm (6¾in) long.

case, with a design simulating the folds of an umbrella, became popular in Holland late in the eighteenth century. Umbrella needle cases were also engraved with a fine design. Two versions are illustrated in Plates 39 and 40.

Small items, including needlework tools, were made of filigree silver in the eighteenth and early nineteenth centuries. A fine example is the needle case in the shape of a carp (Plate 41), made in Leeuwarden, Friesland in 1794.

Plate 40
Silver needle case with finely engraved wavy lines, simulating a folded umbrella. Maker: J. van Gelder, Utrecht (1807-12). 10.2cm (4¹⁄₁₆in) long.

PRIVATE COLLECTION

Plate 39
Silver needle case simulating a folded umbrella. Probably Amsterdam, c.1790-1800. 10.2cm (4¹⁄₁₆in) long.

PRIVATE COLLECTION

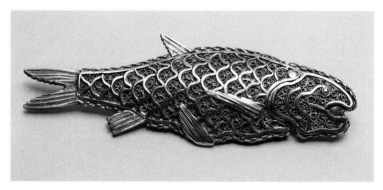

Plate 41
Silver filigree needle case shaped as a fish. Leeuwarden, Friesland, c.1794. Maker: Nicolaas Swalue (1775-1812). 8.2cm (3¼in) long.

PRIVATE COLLECTION

The Silver City of Schoonhoven

Many Dutch needlework tools come from the silver city of Schoonhoven, which specialised in thimbles in the seventeenth century. In 1425 it was already an important centre and in such a city, at least one or more gold and silversmiths could be found. In the cities gold and silversmiths were originally registered in a Guild together with blacksmiths, brass and pewter smiths. Only when there were five to ten gold and silversmiths was it considered justified to form a separate Guild. In all probability, this did not come about in Schoonhoven until 1638, when the Guild had ten members. As early as the seventeenth century, Schoonhoven was mass-manufacturing small gold and especially silver articles. By the eighteenth century the Guild had grown, having twenty-seven members in 1745, rising to forty by 1798. This was a prestigious number compared to other, larger cities in the same year. Delft had forty Guild members, The Hague forty-six, Rotterdam seventy-eight and Amsterdam 286.

Even today, Schoonhoven is still a centre producing small silver items, mostly for tourists as souvenirs of this important historical and picturesque place. Until recently there was still a school in Schoonhoven for training gold and silversmiths.

Although the making of silver thimbles was a speciality in the seventeenth century, at the end of the eighteenth century, the speciality in Schoonhoven had shifted to the making of all sorts of small articles such as snuff boxes, vinaigrettes, smoking articles, costume accessories and sewing tools. Many needle cases can be attributed to silver and goldsmiths from this city.

The popularity of the needle case continued throughout the nineteenth century. Plates 42-49 give a broad view of the varying styles and decorations used throughout this period. The influence of the French style at the end of the eighteenth century is evident, with the two-colour gold needle case made in Schoonhoven c.1795 (Plate 42).

Plate 42

Eight-sided tapering 18ct. gold needle case in two-colour gold. Schoonhoven, c.1795. Maker: Gysbert Lameer (1779-1809). 9cm (3⅝in) long. PRIVATE COLLECTION

Plate 43

Silver needle case on chain to hang from waistband with fine engraved flower pattern. Probably Schoonhoven, c.1775. Maker's mark indistinct. 9.5cm (3¹³⁄₁₆in) long. PRIVATE COLLECTION

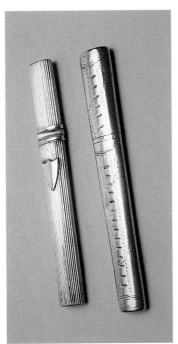

Plate 44

Left: Silver needle case with fine ribbed pattern and shield for monogram. Schoonhoven, c.1840-60. Maker: Andries Graves Kooiman, Schoonhoven (1838-79). 9.4cm (3¾in) long.
Right: Silver needle case with fine engraved pattern. Schoonhoven, year letter 'C', 1809-10. Assay Office, Utrecht 1807-12. Maker: Pieter Geyskes, Schoonhoven (1788-1832). 10.2cm (4in) long.
PRIVATE COLLECTION

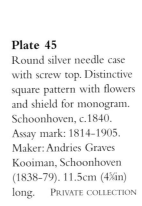

Plate 45

Round silver needle case with screw top. Distinctive square pattern with flowers and shield for monogram. Schoonhoven, c.1840. Assay mark: 1814-1905. Maker: Andries Graves Kooiman, Schoonhoven (1838-79). 11.5cm (4⅝in) long. PRIVATE COLLECTION

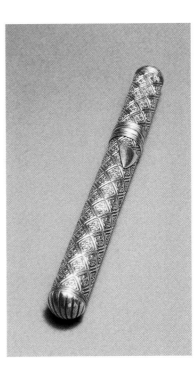

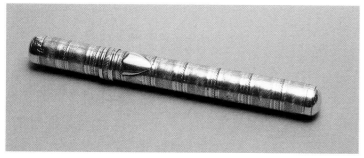

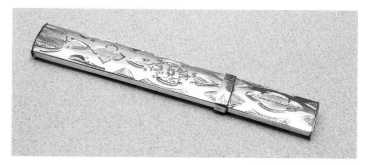

Plate 46
Round silver needle case with finely engraved pattern and screw top.
Schoonhoven c.1840. Assay mark: 1814-1905. Maker: Dirk Hendrik Greup,
Schoonhoven (1828-64). 11.2cm (4½in) long.

Plate 47
Silver needle case engraved and with monogram and date 27.2.'65.
Schoonhoven, c.1865. Assay mark: 1814-1905. Maker's mark: Gerrit
Kuylenburg, Schoonhoven (1854-71). 9.5cm (3¹³⁄₁₆in) long.

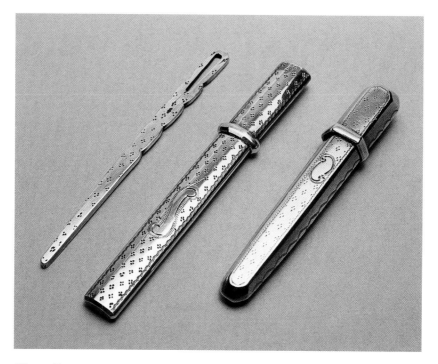

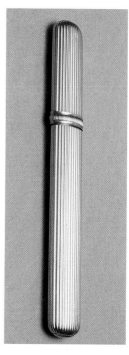

Plate 48
Left: Silver needle case with
ribbed design. Schoonhoven,
c.1840-60. Assay mark: 1814-
1905. Maker's mark indistinct.
9.4cm (3¾in) long.
Right: Silver needle case with
engraved design.
Schoonhoven, c.1860-75.
Assay mark: 1814-1905.
Maker: Johannes Gaillard,
Schoonhoven (1852-1910).
9.6cm (3⅞in) long.

Plate 49
Left: Silver needle case containing silver bodkin. Schoonhoven, c.1880-90. Assay
mark: 1814-1905. Maker's mark: Gerrit van der Dussen, Schoonhoven (1867-1912).
8.4cm (3⅜in) long.
Right: Small silver needle case with stipple engraving and space for a monogram.
Assay mark: 1814-1905. Maker's mark: Jan van Kassen, Schoonhoven (1883-85). 7cm
(2¾in) long.

Plate 50
18ct. gold needle case
with ribbed design in
Schoonhoven style
c.1825-40. Assay mark
1814-1905. Maker's
mark: Christiaan Straater,
Amsterdam (1816-46).
8cm (3¼in) long.

Plate 49 shows a needle case which is also used to store a silver bodkin. This combination is mostly encountered with cases of a flat design. Occasionally one will be discovered with a matching bodkin, indicating that the case was made for this purpose (Plate 51). Needlework tools with a ribbed design were made during most of the nineteenth century. Early in the century a broad rib was most common, whereas needle cases of a later date tended towards a finer rib.

Although the origins of many needle cases encountered today can be traced to the silver city of Schoonhoven, this was only one of many places responsible for making needlework tools in the nineteenth century. Throughout Holland there were centres where gold and silversmiths competed to make their product more attractive than that of their counterparts (Plates 52-57).

An important needle case is that made in the shape of a baby in swaddling clothes (Plate 58). This old theme, originally used in the early eighteenth century by the porcelain factory in Meissen, Germany, was revived nearly two centuries later by the enterprising Dutch silversmith who made this version of a swaddling babe in silver.

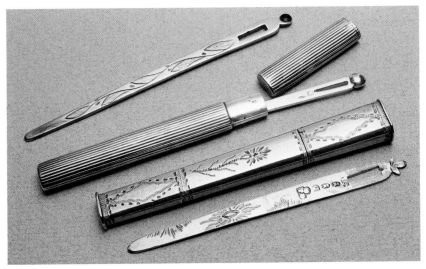

Plate 51
Top: Silver bodkin with ear-spoon. Middelburg, c.1825. Assay mark: 1814-1905. Maker: D.H. Weessich, Middelburg (1822-28). 8.5cm (3⅜in) long.
Centre: Silver bodkin case with silver bodkin. Assay mark: 1814-1905. Maker, bodkin: Pieter du Croix, Leiden (1835-64). 9.4cm (3¾in) long.
Bottom: Silver bodkin case with original bodkin. Schoonhoven/Middelburg. Both pieces bear a year letter for 1807. 9.5cm (3¹³⁄₁₆in) long.   Private collection

Plate 54
Silver needle case with engraved ovals and dots c.1820-40. Assay mark: 1814-1905. Maker's mark indistinct. 8.5cm (3⅜in) long.   Private collection

Plate 52
Small silver needle case with Biedermeier engraving. Amsterdam, c.1850. Assay mark: 1814-1905. Maker's mark: Martinus van Leeuwen, Amsterdam (1830-66). 8cm (3¼in) long.   Private collection

Plate 53
Silver needle case with Biedermeier engraving. Schoonhoven, c.1880. Assay mark: 1814-1905. Maker's mark: Widow Teuntje van Halteren (1863-1895). 9.5cm (3¹³⁄₁₆in) long.   Private collection

Plate 55
Small gold needle case. Assay mark 1853-1905 for 14ct. gold. Maker unknown, c.1860. 7cm (2¾in) long.   Private collection

A woman reading a letter, Gabriel Metsu (1660–65).

THE NATIONAL GALLERY OF IRELAND, DUBLIN

CHAPTER 5

Pincushions and Containers

The Pin

The pin is probably the least considered tool in the household. It is almost certainly one of the oldest. Used by tailors, dressmakers, lacemakers and housewives for centuries, the honest little pin is indispensable and for the most part taken shamefully for granted.

The history of the pin goes back to prehistoric man who devised a simple implement to join animal skins to form some sort of covering for the body in cold climates. The first pins were made from thorns or fish and animal bones, to be replaced in the Bronze Age by pins of metal. At least as early as the fourteenth century, simple pins for sewing and fastening articles of clothing were made by Guilds and in monasteries throughout Europe. Towards the end of the fourteenth century France, Germany and England had large pin-making industries and it is likely that pins used in Holland at this time came from these sources. At one time the pin was made completely by hand and was an expensive commodity, even for the well-to-do. For the poor they were a luxury. Pins were therefore a very acceptable gift for any woman, whatever her status.

In the sixteenth and seventeenth centuries, pin making in Amsterdam was a typical home industry. In later centuries, pin making took place in small workshops in the cities. In the city of Gouda, known for its cheese making, the *Speldenmakerssteeg* (Pin Maker's Alley) still exists today.

In 1613 a Pin Makers' Guild was founded in Gouda, The Guild had female members and also admitted boys and girls from the orphanage as apprentices. At this time their pins were exported to countries across the border, as well as to Spain and Portugal. The day before the pins were to be sold, they were controlled for weight by an inspector. If they were considered below the required quality, the city crest on the packaging was blackened out and they were sold for a lower price. In some cases, the pins were under the required weight and the pin maker compensated for this by making the packaging heavier. An end came to this deception in 1616 when maximum weights for the packaging were established. The Pin Makers' Guild in Gouda existed until 1656, by which time there was so little work that the Guild disappeared.

As was the case with needle making, pin making was considered a very lowly form of trade and like the needle makers, many had their workshops in the alleyways of the Jordaan area of Amsterdam (Plate 1).

Plate 1

De Speldemaaker (The Pin Maker). Workshop in Amsterdam, 1694.
Het Menselijk Bedrijf. Johannes en Caspaares Luiken.

In Amsterdam in 1585 there were approximately 3000 citizens registered for taxation. Of these 3000, the professions of about 1400 are registered, of whom only three were pin makers. It would appear that the pin makers Quyrijn and Pieters, both resident in Amsterdam, each paid one Guilder tax, whereas the needle maker Meynert paid the costly sum of two Guilders.

During excavations in Amsterdam, both large and small pins were found. The oldest, a pin with a fancy head used presumably for fastening clothing, dates from the first half of the fourteenth century and can be seen in the Amsterdams Historisch Museum (Plate 2). Larger pins were used to fasten clothing. These could be very decorative and were worn as accessories to the costume in various parts of the country. Smaller pins were probably used for sewing and lace making. The most common method of making a pin was to take a length of metal wire of an appropriate thickness, and cut it into pieces, adding the round knob top separately. This was made from a length of brass wire, twisted several times to form a ball which was then attached to the top of the shank of the pin. Until the eighteenth century pins had this rounded knob-type top, to be replaced later by the flat top. Pins were made by hand until the nineteenth century. Pins dating from the fifteenth to eighteenth centuries are illustrated in Plates 4 and 5, together with other sewing items excavated at the same time.

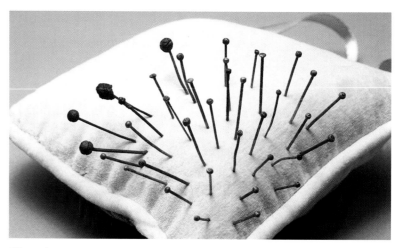

Plate 4
Hand made brass pins, 15th-18th century. Excavated in Gouda.

PRIVATE COLLECTION

Plate 2 (above left)
Large fancy pin for fastening clothing. The pin head is a lead knob with a brass cap, 4.1cm (1⅝in) long. First half of the 14th century. Excavated in Amsterdam.

BUREAU MONUMENTEN & ARCHEOLOGIE, AMSTERDAM

Plate 3 (above right)
Large brass pin for fastening clothing, c.1450-1550. 6.4cm (2¹⁄₁₆in) long. Excavated in Amsterdam.

BUREAU MONUMENTEN & ARCHEOLOGIE, AMSTERDAM

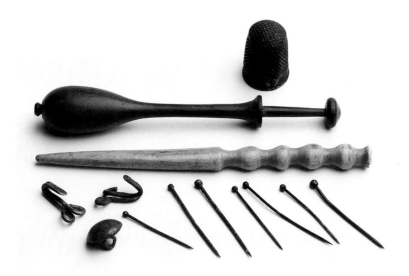

Plate 5
15th to 18th century pins excavated in Amsterdam, together with a lace bobbin, stiletto, thimble, a button, and hooks and eyes.

PRIVATE COLLECTION

Seventeenth century pin trays and boxes

There were various ways to store pins. One method in the seventeenth century, for those who could afford such a luxury, was a little silver pin tray. Although these are now virtually non-existent, a beautiful example, decorated with flowers and a cherub with his foot on a flask, playing a flute, can be found in the Catharina Gasthuis museum in Gouda (Plate 6). It was made by Johannes van Oyen, who worked there from 1675 until his death in 1725. He was the most important silversmith in Gouda at that time and was on the board of governors of the Guild of Silversmiths – the St. Eloysgilde. Multi-purpose boxes were also made to contain pins and needles, and were equally popular for storing snuff.

Pincushions and pin books

In the seventeenth century large pincushions, often mounted on silver bases, were used for storing pins. Such pincushions were standard components of dressing table sets, along with glass pots and jars containing necessary daily requisites. Earlier ones were circular and were often incorporated into the lid of a powder pot. These pincushions were used primarily for the large decorative pins which held articles of clothing together.

The painting illustrated on page 90 is called *Brief lezende vrouw* (Woman reading a letter). The woman in question may at that moment be reading a letter, but before the letter arrived, she was obviously engaged in sewing. She has a cushion on her lap on which threads are laid and her thimble has rolled away on the floor, to the corner of the picture. This picture also provides an insight into the domestic situation in the seventeenth century. The woman sits on a wooden platform, as at that period, with little heating, it was too cold to be seated with one's feet resting on a stone floor for any length of time. She sits by the window to take advantage of the light needed for her sewing, as it was the custom to place furniture against the wall, away from the window. She therefore has no table on which to put her sewing tools. In this case, the cushion is something on which to rest her work and lay her small tools whilst sewing.

In the eighteenth century, for those with the means to engage in an expensive hobby, the collecting of small silver miniatures became a popular pastime. These 'toys' were mostly made to resemble household articles and furniture for doll's houses, windmills and figures. It is unusual to find one of these miniatures with a function, as is the case with the small silver filigree sleigh with velvet pincushion seen in Plate 7.

Plate 6
Silver pin tray with corner decoration of flowers, a cherub, a flask and a flute. Maker: Johannes van Oyen (Gouda 1675-1725). Six star city mark for Gouda. Year letter 'K' – 1691. Crowned lion – provincial mark.
CATHARINA GASTHUIS, GOUDA

Plate 7
Silver filigree miniature sleigh with a blue/green velvet pincushion. Probably Friesland c.1750-1800. Unmarked. 5.5cm (2¼in) long.
PRIVATE COLLECTION

As well as a pincushion, a pin book could be used. The thin layers of cotton or linen used for the 'pages' in which the pins were stored, have in most cases not survived the centuries. One exception is the luxury book with a cover of mother-of-pearl and a silver hinge and clasp (Plate 8).

Plate 8
Rare pin book with mother-of-pearl cover and silver hinge and clasp. Cloth 'pages' for pins. Unmarked, c.1740. (Tax marks for 1807 and 1812.) 6.2cm (2½in) long.

Chatelaine pincushions

In the seventeenth century in the northern parts of Holland, in Friesland and Groningen, a pincushion would have been worn hanging from the belt or apron strings as part of the costume. The pincushion sometimes formed part of a chatelaine. Few of these early pincushions have survived. A chatelaine pincushion was invariably encased in a silver mount with a silver ring through which a chain, ribbon or string could be threaded. In some cases the silver marks on the mount will help us to accurately date the pincushion. However, when the silver was below a minimum weight, it was not compulsory to have the item marked. Some indication as to the date can also be obtained from the shape. Generally speaking, seventeenth and early eighteenth century pincushions were almost always round. At the end of the eighteenth century, the round shape was replaced by an oval mount and a little later it became heart-shaped.

The round pincushion in Plate 9, originally part of a Friesian chatelaine, has a design of peacocks and foliage and dates from the first half of the eighteenth century. Peacocks and designs incorporating other birds are often encountered in sewing tools made in the Friesian area of Holland (Plate 10b).

The mount of a chatelaine pincushion can tell its own story. They are frequently very decorative and sometimes show pictorial scenes with figures. As a silver chatelaine would have belonged in many cases to a well-to-do family, maybe to the wife of a country squire, a farming scene or figures are often found. This is the case with the eighteenth century chintz pincushion with an impression of a farming woman on the oval silver mount (Plate 11). Plates 12-14 show early nineteenth century pincushions in heart-shaped mounts, Plate 13 depicting the figures of a farmer and his wife.

Plate 10a
Brown velvet pincushion in round silver mount. Friesland, early 18th century.

Plate 10b
Detail of cushion mount featured in Plate 10a, showing design with flowers and a bird. 4cm diameter.

Plate 9
Silver mount decorated with peacocks, leaves and scrolls surrounding a blue velvet pincushion. Unmarked. Friesland, early 18th century. 5.3cm (2⅛in) diameter.

Plate 12
Black velvet pincushion in heart-shaped silver mount. Friesland, c.1807.

Plate 13
Blue velvet pincushion in a heart-shaped silver mount showing a farmer on one side and on the other his wife. Friesland, year letter 1824.

Plate 11
Pincushion of chintz in a silver mount depicting a farmer's wife. Friesland, late 18th/early 19th century.

Plate 14
Brown velvet pincushion in silver, heart-shaped mount. Friesland, early 19th century. 8cm (3¼in) long.

Other pincushions

In the eighteenth and nineteenth centuries, sewing thread was uneven and prone to fraying. To smooth the thread and make it supple enough to work with, it would be pulled several times over a small block of wax. A rare pedestal pincushion (Plate 15), incorporating a block of wax in the base, was made in Amsterdam in 1830. Little wax blocks were normally kept in small boxes or were sometimes mounted between two discs of silver or gold. This latter type of wax spool was usually part of a sewing set (Plate 16). The dual-purpose pin box-cum-pincushion in Plate 17 was made by silversmith Pieter Kuilenburg, known as a maker of small boxes. The pins were stored in the ribbed silver box which has a pincushion fitted into the lid. The rings on the side of the box indicate that it was intended to hang on a chain, as part of a chatelaine.

A pincushion on top of a sewing box, also described in Chapter 1, could be used by rich and poor alike. Such a box might contain a fully fitted set of tools made of gold, silver or ivory, or simple implements of bone, wood or metal (Plate 18).

Friesian wood carving was especially popular in the nineteenth century. An example of this home craft is the pincushion in a small wooden shoe shown in Plate 19.

Plate 15
Rare green velvet pincushion on silver pedestal with waxer in base. Amsterdam, c.1830. Maker: C. Preyers, Amsterdam (1822-34). 4.9cm (2in) high.
PRIVATE COLLECTION

Plate 16
Small silver wax holder, c.1825. Maker: Johannes Renkhoff, Amsterdam (1824-28). 3cm (1¾in) diameter.
PRIVATE COLLECTION

Plate 17
Blue velvet pincushion and pin box with rings for chain, c.1835. Marks: Assay mark 1814-1906. Maker: Pieter Kuilenburg, Schoonhoven (1818-57). 4cm (1⅝in) high.
PRIVATE COLLECTION

Plate 18
Wooden sewing box with green pincushion, c.1825-40.
COURTESY OF INEZ EIKELENBOOM/MRS. OAKTREE

Plate 19
Miniature shoe decorated with Friesian wood carving, containing a blue velvet pincushion. 7cm (2¾in) long. Late 19th century.   PRIVATE COLLECTION

Pincushions with sewing clamps

Sewing clamps with pincushions were very popular in the nineteenth century. They were fastened with a screw fitting to to the edge of a table, or to the arm of a chair. A rare wooden clamp with hand-painted design (Plate 20), traditional to the Friesian town of Hindelopen, has a built-in mirror on one side for extra light. This clamp can be found in the Fries Museum, Leeuwarden. In the nineteenth century sewing clamps were frequently made of silver. Although occasionally a clamp is found which was made in another part of the country, most examples come from Amsterdam. Silversmith Harmanus Lintvelt, who worked in Amsterdam between 1797 and 1833, appears to have made something of a speciality in these sewing clamps, as many found today bear his mark. Two of his clamps are featured in Plates 21 and 22. A third example, Plate 23, was made in Amsterdam by Dirk van Maarseveen Sr.

  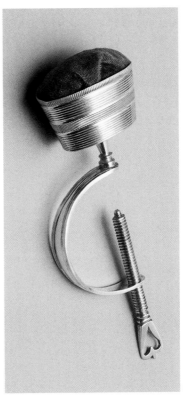

Plate 20 (above left)
Hand-painted wooden sewing clamp with built-in mirror for extra light and blue velvet pincushion. Hindelopen, Friesland, 19th century. 16cm (6⅜in) high
FRIES MUSEUM, LEEUWARDEN

Plate 21 (above centre)
Silver sewing clamp with brocade pincushion. Year letter: 1827. Maker: Harmanus Lintvelt, Amsterdam (1797–1833). 11.5cm (4⅝in) high.   KAY SULLIVAN ANTIQUES

Plate 22 (above right)
Silver sewing clamp with blue velvet pincushion. Year letter 1831. Maker: Harmanus Lintvelt, Amsterdam (1797–1833). 10.5cm (4¼in) high.   KAY SULLIVAN ANTIQUES

Plate 23 (left)
Silver sewing clamp with red velvet pincushion. Amsterdam, year letter 1839. Maker: Dirk van Maarseveen Sr., Amsterdam (1816–40). 11.2cm (4⅖in) high.   PRIVATE COLLECTION

Textile pincushions

Many early pincushions were made by hand. Evidence of the type of sewing tools used in past centuries can often be seen in old paintings. The painting by David A.C. Artz (Plate 24) shows an interior of the orphanage at Katwijk-Binnen, with three industrious girls sewing under the watchful eye of a governess. The tools on the table include a pair of scissors, cotton reels and an embroidered pincushion.

Few of these pincushions remain, due to the frail materials from which they were made. A small collection of hand made textile pincushions of varying materials and handwork techniques belongs to the collection of the Nederlands Openluchtmuseum in Arnhem (Plates 25-29). Although we cannot see the colours on these old black and white photographs, with a little imagination we can visualise the glorious effects achieved when these pincushions were first made.

Plate 24
Orphanage in Katwijk-Binnen,
David A.C. Artz (1837-1890).
On the table are a textile
pincushion and other sewing
tools (see detail).
RIJKSMUSEUM, AMSTERDAM

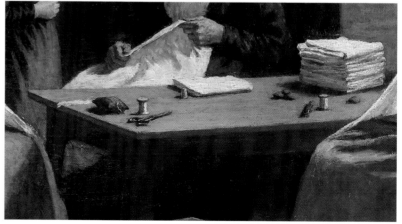

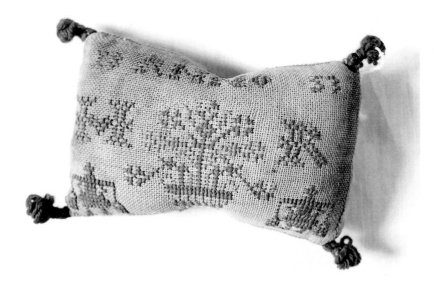

Plate 25

Canvas pincushion with cross-stitch embroidery in wool. Design of a flower basket, initials 'H R' and text 'Anno 1853'. 11cm x 17cm (4⅜in x 6¾in).

NEDERLANDS OPENLUCHTMUSEUM, ARNHEM
ON LOAN: HET ADMIRALITEITSHUIS, DOKKUM

Plate 26

Canvas pincushion with cross-stitch embroidery in wool, worked in a sampler design and dated 1860. 12.5cm x 16.5cm (5in x 6⅝in).

NEDERLANDS OPENLUCHTMUSEUM, ARNHEM

Plate 27

White linen pincushion with cotton fringe. *Zaans stikwerk* (Zaans stitchery). 19th century. 10cm x 17cm (4in x 6¾in).

NEDERLANDS OPENLUCHTMUSEUM, ARNHEM

Plate 28
Purple damask pincushion with embroidered highlights in pink, beige and ivory
colouring. The cushion is filled with sawdust. Early 19th century. 13cm x 18cm
(5¼in x 7¼in).
NEDERLANDS OPENLUCHTMUSEUM, ARNHEM

Plate 29
Dark red-brown satin pincushion with cross-stitch embroidery.
19th century. 17cm x 17cm (6¾in x 6¾in).
NEDERLANDS OPENLUCHTMUSEUM, ARNHEM

Plates 25 and 26 are canvas cushions worked in cross-stitch with fine woollen thread. Both cushions
have designs which are comparable to miniature samplers. Plate 27 shows a pincushion of white linen
decorated in *Zaans stikwerk* (Zaans stitchery). This handwork technique was often used to decorate
slits, collars and cuffs of shirts. Plates 28 and 29 illustrate pincushions with embroidered designs.

Pin boxes

In the second half of the nineteenth century pin boxes had a short revival. These differed from the
seventeenth century square and oblong snuff box type, as they were now of a cylindrical shape. The
two examples shown here (Plates 30 and 31) were both made in Schoonhoven.

Plate 30
Small silver cylinder-shaped pin box,
c.1870. Marks: Assay mark 1814-1905.
Maker: Arie de Jong, Schoonhoven
(1865-73). 4.1cm (1⅝in) long.
PRIVATE COLLECTION

Plate 31
Small silver cylinder-shaped pin box,
c.1875. Marks: Assay mark 1814-1905.
Maker: Gerrit van der Dussen,
Schoonhoven (1866-1912). 4cm (1⅝in)
long.
PRIVATE COLLECTION

20th century pincushions

By the twentieth century, souvenir and advertising items began to appear in large numbers. On the delightful pair of wooden shoes, with original silk pincushions (Plate 32), the artist has painted two different boats at sea. The text on the side of one shoe tells us that it was a souvenir from Scheveningen. This select seaside town near the Hague, on the North Sea coast, was very popular at the beginning of the twentieth century. Sewing items were often used for advertising messages. The metal pincushion illustrated in Plate 33 also functions as a pin box. The advertiser hoped to encourage the consumer to use lignite coal – *Stookt Bruinkool Briketten*. He claims that *Bruinkool* was not only the cleanest, but also the cheapest fuel to use. The German thread manufacturer Gütermann also advertised his silk thread on the Dutch market. A pincushion on metal base is illustrated in Plate 34. The latter two pincushions were probably made in Germany for export to Holland.

The charming girl of bisque porcelain (Plate 35) has been incorporated into a double pincushion, probably made in a nunnery in the south of Holland. This complex creation is edged with roped cord and gold embroidered thread, and has a tiny drawer at the bottom for storing pins or threads.

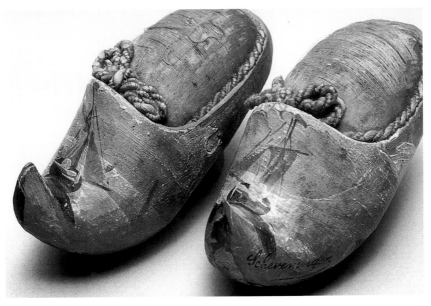

Plate 33
Metal pincushion and pin box with advertising message: *Stookt Bruinkool Briketten, Zindelijkste en Goedkoopste brandstof.* Early 20th century.

PRIVATE COLLECTION

Plate 32
Wooden shoes with hand-painted boats at sea. Text: *Scheveningen*. Pink silk pincushions and braiding. c.1900.

PRIVATE COLLECTION

Plate 34
Red velvet pincushion on metal base with advertising message for *Gütermanns Naaizijde*. Early 20th century.

KAY SULLIVAN ANTIQUES

Plate 35
Hand made standing pincushion with a bisque porcelain figure of a girl leaning against a wall. Pincushions of brown felt edged with gold braid and roped cord. Small drawer for pins or threads. Nunnery work from Limburg, c.1900.

KAY SULLIVAN ANTIQUES

The Young Mother, 1658, Gerard Dou (1618-1675).

CHAPTER 6
Scissors

A little history

Scissors are such an essential household item that life without them would seem almost impossible. There are two main types, the oldest form being those with a spring action, made in one piece and now commonly called shears, and the other type, made in two parts with pivoted blades and called scissors, still in use today. Fourteenth to seventeenth century iron shears are illustrated in Plates 1 to 4. From the sixteenth century, shears and scissors were used for some time alongside each other for professional and household purposes. After the seventeenth century shears fell out of use, except for specific outdoor jobs such as cutting hedges or shearing sheep. The young mother in Gerrit Dou's painting, opposite, dated 1658, has a sewing cushion on her lap and is holding a pair of shears in her hand.

Plate 1
Iron shears, c.1300–50. Excavated in Amsterdam. 15.3cm (6⅛in) long.
BUREAU MONUMENTEN & ARCHEOLOGIE, AMSTERDAM

Plate 2
Iron shears, c.1450–1500. Excavated in Amsterdam. 19.5cm (7¾in) long.
BUREAU MONUMENTEN & ARCHEOLOGIE, AMSTERDAM

Needlework scissors and cases

Only one pair of scissors, dating from the seventeenth or eighteenth century, was found during excavations in Amsterdam. This small, decorative pair (Plate 7) was almost certainly intended for needlework. Scissors made in two parts, with blades of steel and silver handles, first came into use during the seventeenth century. Cornelis Bormeester made needlework scissors early in the eighteenth century. This silversmith worked in Amsterdam from 1730-85. An example of his work can be seen in Plate 8, illustrating a small pair of needlework scissors from around 1730, together with other small scissors and one example from a chatelaine.

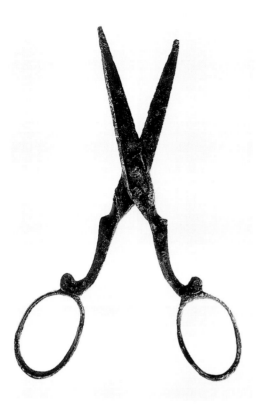

Plate 7

Iron needlework scissors, late 17th or early 18th century. Excavated in Amsterdam.

BUREAU MONUMENTEN & ARCHEOLOGIE, AMSTERDAM

Plate 8

From top to bottom:
Scissors from a chatelaine, Schoonhoven, c.1840.
Silver needlework scissors, c.1840. Maker: Jacobus Simonis, The Hague (1839-44).
Silver needlework scissors, Schoonhoven, c.1860.
Silver needlework scissors, c.1730. Maker: Cornelis Bormeester, Amsterdam (1730-85).

KAY SULLIVAN ANTIQUES

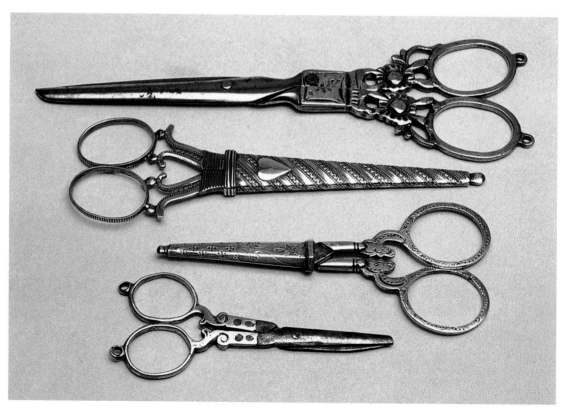

Cases in which a pair of iron scissors would have been kept were in use early in the seventeenth century, and on the rare occasions that they are found are almost always without scissors. These little cases were often suspended from chatelaines. Plates 9 and 10 illustrate silver cases for scissors, both of which once formed part of a chatelaine. A number of gold chatelaines from the seventeenth and eighteenth centuries, illustrated in Chapter 2, include scissors cases. Plate 11 shows one of these gold cases.

Amongst the upper classes in the eighteenth century it was customary for the lady of the house and her daughters to be able to darn stockings, knot purses, embroider slippers and generally produce a fine piece of embroidery. It was fashionable for friends to do their handwork together and suitable tools, small enough to fit into a small bag, were made for this purpose. An extravagant, not to mention costly, scissors case was an ideal item with which to win admiration and to create conversation during the sewing session.

Plate 9
Silver scissors case decorated in Renaissance style with fauns' heads, flowers and leaves, c.1630. Marked with swan in oval. 7cm (2¾in) long.

PRIVATE COLLECTION

Plate 10
Scissors case in filigree silver, c.1650-75, decorated in Renaissance style with cherubs and flowers. Unmarked. 7cm (2¾in) long.

PRIVATE COLLECTION

Plate 11
Gold case for scissors from chatelaine, c.1725-50. 9cm (3⅝in) long.

FRIES MUSEUM, LEEUWARDEN

The name of Jan Borduur is regularly encountered in connection with sewing tools. His name, translated into English, is 'John Embroidery'. This would seem particularly appropriate when considering an extraordinary pair of needlework scissors made by him (Plate 12). The silver scissors are made in the shape of a jester, with a red garnet in his hat and bear a year letter for 1736. Jan Borduur is known to have made other sewing tools as well as silver doll's house miniatures.

A selection of small needlework scissors in gold and silver is shown in Plates 13-18. Various styles are represented, including Rococo, Biedermeier and the familiar ribbed design. It is noticeable that most of the small scissors, as well as the slightly larger nineteenth century examples seen in Plates 19, 20 and 21, are contained in a protective sheath. The sheath of the scissors in Plate 19 has a design of diagonal lines with dots, which is a regularly recurring pattern, typical of silver made in Friesland.

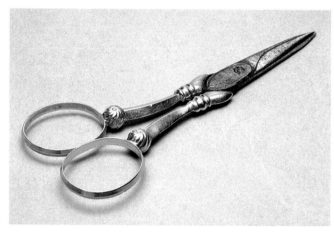

Plate 13
18ct. gold needlework scissors, c.1825-40. Assay mark 1814-1905. 8cm (3⅛in) long.
COURTESY OF INEZ EIKELENBOOM/MRS. OAKTREE

Plate 14
Silver needlework scissors in sheath with ribbed design, c.1820-35. Assay mark 1814-1905. 8.5cm (3⅜in) long.
PRIVATE COLLECTION

Plate 12
Silver scissors in the shape of a jester with a red garnet in his hat. Maker: Jan Borduur, Amsterdam (1731-66). Year letter: Amsterdam 1736. 8.7cm (3½in) long.
PRIVATE COLLECTION

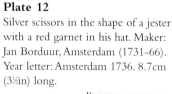

Plate 15
Silver needlework scissors in sheath with Biedermeier decoration. Schoonhoven, c.1860. Maker: Laurens van Gelderen, Schoonhoven (1834-73). 8.5cm (3⅜in) long.
PRIVATE COLLECTION

Plate 16
14ct. gold needlework scissors in sheath in Biedermeier style, c.1860. Assay mark 1853-1905. 9cm (3⅝in) long.

Plate 17
14ct. gold needlework scissors in sheath, c.1875. Maker: Cornelis Kouwenberg, Breda (1858-1901). 9cm (3⅝in) long.

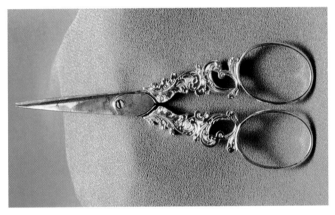

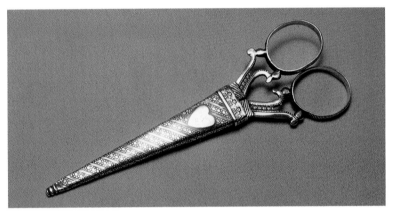

Plate 18
14ct. gold needlework scissors in Rococo style, c.1860. Assay mark 1853-1905. 8.5cm (3⅜in) long.　

Plate 19
Silver scissors in sheath in Empire design. Sneek, Friesland, c.1849. Laurens van Manen (1844-71). 12.5cm (5in) long.　

Plate 20
Silver scissors in sheath, c.1870. The space between the handles resembles a heart. Maker: Johannes Schijfsma Jz., Woudsend (1848-1902). 17cm (6¾in) long.

Plate 21
Silver scissors in sheath with ball mounts to eyes. Handles with flower design. Sheath with diagonal bands and stars on reeded ground, c.1840. Marks: Assay mark 1814-1905. Maker: Jacobus Simonis, The Hague (1839-44). 15cm (6in) long.

Chatelaine scissors

The tools found on old chatelaines have usually been acquired, replaced and added to over a long period of time. Every chatelaine therefore carries its own individual array of tools, nearly always including scissors, one of the most important items of sewing equipment (Plate 22).

Chatelaine scissors have iron or steel blades and mostly have silver handles. The handles are almost always cast in one piece and were an invitation for the silversmith to show his skill. Decorations on chatelaine scissors cover a wonderful array of designs on a diversity of subjects, ranging from animals, birds, flowers and figures to religious and symbolic designs. The design can sometimes help us to identify the origins of the scissors. Those made in Friesland or Groningen often have a decoration which includes flowers, leaves or birds. A distinguishing characteristic to help us identify scissors made in Schoonhoven is a rectangular shape with a simple flower or star in the centre at the connecting piece where the blades are joined to the silver handle (Plate 29).

Plate 22
Early 19th century silver chatelaine with pincushion, needle case and scissors, worn with folk costume from the Zaanstreek. The apron is tambour lace on tulle.

ZUIDERZEEMUSEUM, ENKHUIZEN

Plate 23
Silver chatelaine scissors with chain typical for Groningen, c.1770-1800. Handles with crowned doves (see detail). Marks: Dolphin for old silver 1859-93. Maker's mark indistinct. 16cm (6⅜in) long.

PRIVATE COLLECTION

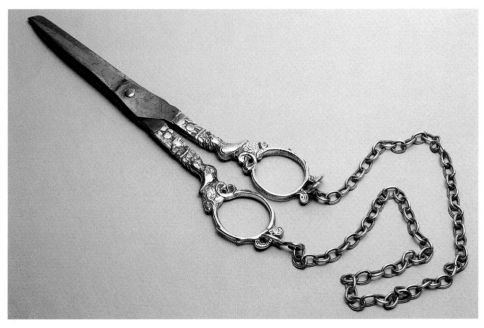

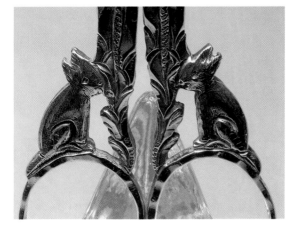

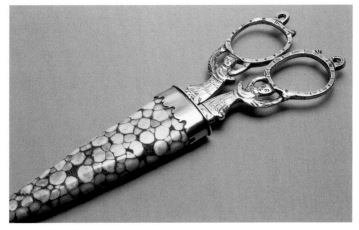

Plate 24

Silver chatelaine scissors on chain, c.1794. Design with two doves. Marks: Year letter Haarlem 1794. Maker's mark indistinct. 18.4cm (7⅛in) long.

Plate 25

Silver scissors from a chatelaine, Amsterdam c.1812-18. Small animal incorporated in handles (see detail). Maker: Josephus Servatius Anderlee, Amsterdam (1782-1818). 15.2cm (6in) long.

Plate 26

Silver scissors in sheath covered in shagreen. Friesland/Groningen, c.1815–25. Handles shaped as angels (see detail). 12.3cm (4¹⁵⁄₁₆in) long.

Plate 27a and b
Silver chatelaine scissors on hook, each handle has an impression of a man sitting, one on a barrel. On the other side, the handles are decorated with two women, one holding flowers, the other sitting in front of a fire. Chains are attached to a silver hook, made from a bible clasp. Friesland c.1830. Maker: Rein Sipkes Zijlstra, Drachen (1818-61).

PRIVATE COLLECTION

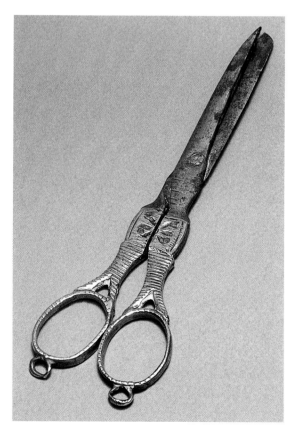

Plate 28
Silver chatelaine scissors on chain, c.1805. Handles with an elaborate design of wings. City mark: Schoonhoven 1805. Maker: Gerrit Lazonder, Schoonhoven (1796-1824). 14.4cm (5¾in) long.

KAY SULLIVAN ANTIQUES

Plate 29
Silver scissors from chatelaine, c.1835. Handles with horizontal ribbed and square centre design. Maker: Laurens van Gelderen, Schoonhoven (1834-73). 14.5cm (5¹³⁄₁₆in) long.

KAY SULLIVAN ANTIQUES

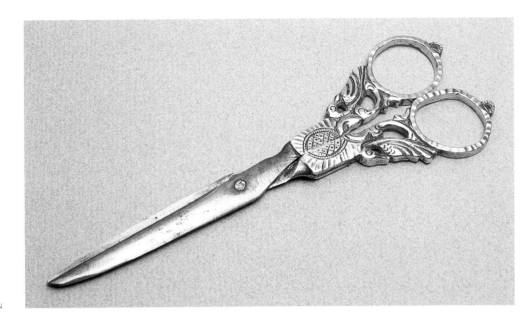

Plate 30

Silver scissors from a chatelaine with a handle decoration of parrots, c.1825. Maker: Willem Hermanus Weenink, Zwolle (1818–47). 16.7cm (6¹¹⁄₁₆in) long.

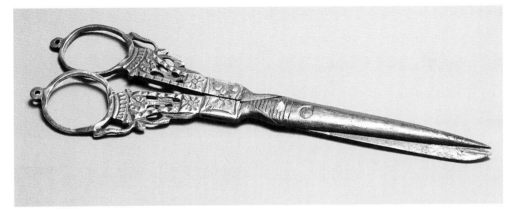

Plate 31

Silver chatelaine scissors with flower basket decoration to handles. Schoonhoven, early 19th century. Marks: Assay mark 1814–1905. Maker's mark indistinct. 16.5cm (6⅝in) long.

Plate 32

Silver chatelaine scissors, c.1835. Handle design of sunflowers in baskets (see detail). Maker: Egidius J. Wientjes, Ootmarsum (1807-56). 16.3cm (6½in) long.

We know much about the lives of the gold and silversmiths working in past centuries, thanks to the method of registration and the accurate marking of gold and silver. Many businesses were passed down through generations of fathers and sons, and from records we know that nephews, sons-in-law and other family members were often working together in the family business. The scissors seen in Plate 28 were made by Gerrit Lazonder from Schoonhoven. This silversmith was the founding father of the Schoonhoven silver dynasty, Lazonder-Haalbos. Gerrit's son Johannes Marinus was a goldsmith and was related by marriage, more than once, to the Greup family of silversmiths, a name often encountered in connection with sewing tools. Johannes Marinus's brother, Adrianus Haalbos Lazonder, was also a gold and silversmith. Johannes Marinus was well-to-do and in 1862 his son Gerrit was running the family business.

Another family of silversmiths was that of van Gelderen from Schoonhoven and some of the scissors featured in this chapter can be attributed to different members of this family (Plates 15 and 33). Pieter van Gelderen learned the trade from his father, Jan, and in 1781 was working as an apprentice in his father's business. In 1819 he branched out on his own and his brother Cornelis continued with Jan's business. Pieter extended his workshop to a business with four employees and five apprentices. In 1842 it passed to his son Cornelis who continued until 1873, when he in turn passed it on to his sons, Pieter and Jacob.

Sometimes scissors with a waist plaque and chains did not make up part of a chatelaine with various other tools, but were made as 'scissors chatelaines' in their own right. Early in the twentieth century hooks from old chatelaine bags were often re-used for other tools. An example of such a 'marriage' is the early twentieth century scissors chatelaine with chains suspended from a bag hook, shown in Plate 34.

In the area of Staphorst, scissors hanging on a long leather strap were worn suspended from the waistband as part of the local costume. These distinctive scissors chatelaines were individually made and could be decorated with metal or brass studs. That shown in Plate 35 bears the initials C.K. and Plate 36 features a less elaborate example.

Plate 33
Silver chatelaine scissors, c.1840. Handle design of daisies.
Maker: Pieter van Gelderen, Schoonhoven (1819-42). 16cm (6⅜in) long.

KAY SULLIVAN ANTIQUES

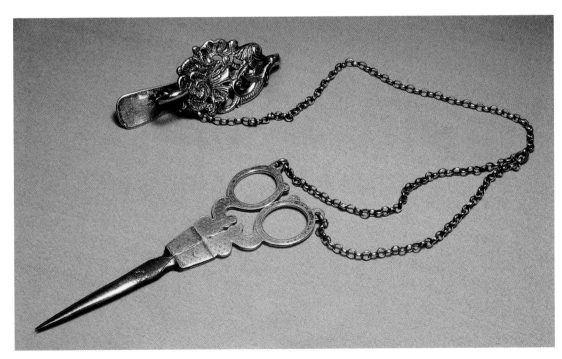

Plate 34
Scissors chatelaines complete with hook and chain, c.1902.
Hook with scrolls, engraved 'T.K. 1902'. Scissors with stippled design.
Marks: Assay mark 1814-1905.
Scissors 15cm (6in) long.
KAY SULLIVAN ANTIQUES

Plate 35
Scissors chatelaine hook with leather strap to hang from the belt. Rouveen, Staphorst, c.1850.
NEDERLANDS OPENLUCHTMUSEUM, ARNHEM

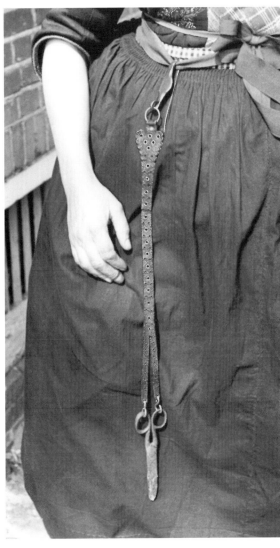

Plate 36
Lady wearing a scissors chatelaine on hook and leather strap. Staphorst, c.1850.
NEDERLANDS OPENLUCHTMUSEUM, ARNHEM

115

Tailor's workshop, 1661, Quirijn Brekelenkam.

CHAPTER 7
Measuring Sticks and Tapes

Measuring sticks

We know that the oldest methods for measuring lengths have parts of the human body to thank for their names. The ell, the foot, the hand palm and the thumb were all forms of measuring. Feet are still referred to today and the expression 'rule of thumb' is a common phrase. An ell was a measure used especially for textiles. The word originates from elbow and is measured from the middle finger to the elbow.

The ell measuring method was already in use in Middle Eastern countries around 650BC. Even at this time the length of an ell was variable, according to where it was used. In later centuries, the ell used in Amsterdam was 0.688m, in England (yard) 0.914m, in Berlin 0.660m, and in Leipzig 0.565m. The famous Wiegersma wooden folk art collection (see Chapter 10) also contained ell measuring sticks, together with the description: 'the ell is derived from the Latin *ulna* and the Gothic *aleina*, is about 68cm long and is made up of four parts. On almost all ells, the thumb is also given as a measure – this is 2.5cm. The ell was in use all over Holland.'

In the eighteenth century, before ready-made clothing was introduced, it was left to the tailor, the dressmaker or the housewife to provide the family with their necessary attire. A measuring stick, called an *ellemaat* in Holland, was therefore an essential household item for measuring fabrics, ribbons, lace, and silk. The housewife would take her measuring stick with her to the door when the travelling salesman came to call, to check that her purchases were of the correct length. These were the circles to which Maria Dircksdochter belonged. Maria was the daughter of a miller from Leiden in the sixteenth century. The making of one's own clothing, alterations and repairs was certainly common practice at that time for someone in her position and Maria's inventory, made in 1579, included a round sewing basket and an ell measuring stick.

That *ellemaaten* were brought into circulation in a wide variety of imaginative designs is clear to see from surviving examples. The *ellemaat* was made in different sizes: a quarter, a half and a whole ell. A fine example of a quarter ell is seen in Plate 1. This is made of mahogany with an alabaster grip and inlaid mother-of-pearl measuring sections. The mother-of-pearl thumbpiece indicates the first point from which to measure, to the end of the stick being a quarter ell, in this case 17.2cm (6⅞in). The same method of measuring applies to the half and whole *ellemaat*, illustrated in Plates 2 and 3.

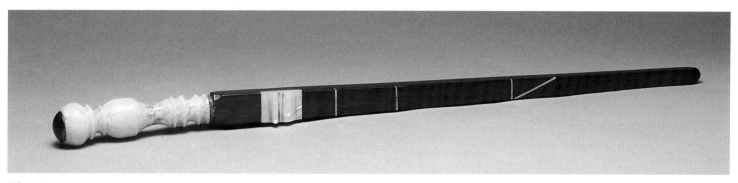

Plate 1
19th century mahogany measuring stick or *ellemaat*, with alabaster grip and inlaid mother-of-pearl thumbpiece and measuring indicator of mother-of-pearl.

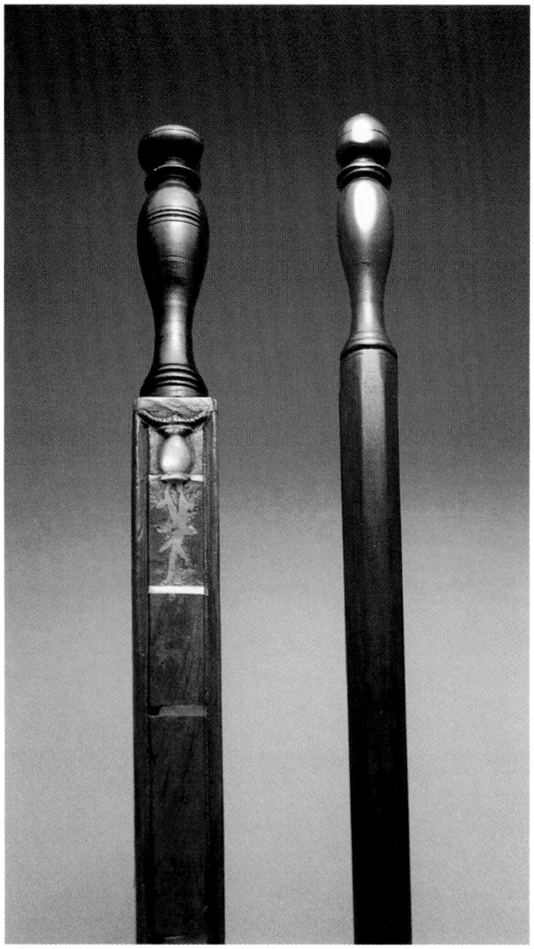

Plate 2
Two wooden 'half *ellemaat*' measuring sticks. Left: mahogany stick, inlaid with mother-of-pearl, with ebony grip. Right: fine, plain wooden stick without decorations. Both mid-19th century.
KAY SULLIVAN ANTIQUES

Plate 3
Two wooden 'half *ellemaat*' measuring sticks. Left: mahogany stick with ebony grip and ivory finial. Metal measuring sections. Right: mahogany stick with carved palm wood grip and ivory measuring indicators. Both mid-19th century.
KAY SULLIVAN ANTIQUES

Tape measures

The *ellemaat* and the tape measure overlapped each other. The measuring stick remained in use throughout the eighteenth and nineteenth centuries. The tape measure came into use in the eighteenth century. Being compact and easy to use, it replaced the measuring stick in many homes, but the measuring stick continued to be used for professional purposes at markets and in fabric shops and haberdashers, as is sometimes still the case today. The *ellemaat* can be found with an official stamp verifying the accuracy of the length.

A fabric tape measure was often contained in a cylinder-shaped holder made of silver or gold. Eighteenth century tapes of this type are rare and exceptional if found with the original tape, sometimes marked out in old ell measures. The earliest date from the second half of the eighteenth century and are mostly unmarked (Plates 4, 5, 6 and 7). Two ball-shaped examples of a similar date belong to the collection of the Fries Museum in Leeuwarden, the smallest having a diameter of only 1.7cm (Plates 8 and 9). The wind-up mechanism varies from a handle with a knob to grip whilst winding, to a small straight knob. The former method is the most practical and is easier to use.

Plate 4
Silver tape measure containing original pink silk tape, c.1750–70. Later assay mark for old and inland work, otherwise unmarked. Diameter 1.7cm (¹¹⁄₁₆in), height 1.1cm (⁷⁄₁₆in).

PRIVATE COLLECTION

Plate 5
Silver tape measure containing original yellow tape, c.1750–70. Maker's mark indistinct. Diameter 1.7cm (¹¹⁄₁₆in), height 1.3cm (½in).

PRIVATE COLLECTION

Plate 6
Silver filigree tape measure containing original green tape, c.1780–1800. Friesland/Groningen. Crowned 'O' mark for old work before 1807. Diameter 1.3cm (½in), height 2.2cm (⅞in).

PRIVATE COLLECTION

Plate 7
Silver filigree tape measure containing original red tape, c.1780–1800 Height 2cm (¹³⁄₁₆in).

FRIES MUSEUM, LEEUWARDEN

Plate 8
Silver ball-shaped tape measure containing original pink silk tape, c.1750–70. Diameter 3cm (1¼in).

FRIES MUSEUM, LEEUWARDEN

Plate 9
Silver ball-shaped tape measure contining original green silk tape, c.1750–70. Diameter 1.7cm (¹¹⁄₁₆in).

FRIES MUSEUM, LEEUWARDEN

119

Plate 11

Silver tape measure of broad ribbed design and original green silk tape, c.1820-40. Maker: Pieter Loopuijt, Hoorn (1820-53) Assay mark 1814-1905. Diameter 1.9cm (¾in), height 2.75cm (1⅛in).

Plate 10

18ct. gold eight-sided tape measure with original blue silk tape, c.1800. Unmarked.

The earliest eighteenth century tape measures are of plain design, but nineteenth century examples are often decorated with pretty engraved patterns. A rare gold example is illustrated in Plate 10. The ribbed design, often used on early nineteenth century sewing tools, is seen in Plates 11 and 12. These charming tape measures, which would have been individually and infrequently made, are very desirable for today's collectors. It would seem that there are no two alike.

Plate 12

Silver tape measure of fine ribbed design and original green tape, c.1820-35. Maker: Pierre Louis Uriot, Amsterdam (1812-62).

Plate 13

Silver tape measure with sawn-out design and original tape, c.1820-40. Maker's mark indistinct. Assay mark 1814-1905. Diameter 1.8cm (¹¹⁄₁₆in).

Plate 14

Silver tape measure of plain design with original red silk tape, c.1830-50. Maker's mark indistinct. Diameter 1.7cm (⅝in), height 3cm.

Plate 15
Silver tape measure with engraved leaf design, c.1830. Probably Schoonhoven. Assay mark 1814–1905. Height 3.35cm (1⅜in).

Plate 16
Silver tape measure of octagonal shape and with original tape, c.1850. Maker's mark indistinct. Diameter 1.7cm (⅝in), height 2.3cm (¹⁵⁄₁₆in).

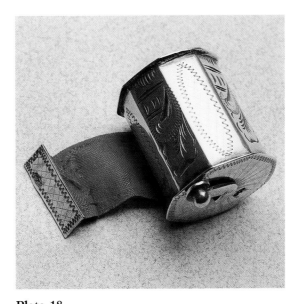

Plate 17
Silver tape measure with dotted pattern design and original red silk tape, c.1860. Diameter 1.7cm (⅝in), height 2.5cm (1in).

Plate 18
Silver tape measure engraved with geometrical designs, waves and leaves and original red silk tape. Schoonhoven, c.1870. Maker: Andries Teunissen (1859–99). Diameter 1.5cm (⅝in).

Plate 19
Silver octagonal tape measure engraved with geometrical and foliage design with original tape, c.1870. Maker: Andries Teunissen (1859–99).

The Spinner, Gerard ter Borch (1617-1681).

WILLEM VAN DER VORM FOUNDATION, MUSEUM BOYMANS VAN BEUNINGEN, ROTTERDAM

CHAPTER 8
Thread Holders

Iedere dag een draadje
is een hemdsmouw in het jaar.

(A thread every day
is a shirt sleeve in a year.)

Old Dutch proverb

A little background

Before we can sew or knit, we need thread or wool. In prehistoric times thread was made from the sinews of animals. Later, it was made by plaiting and twisting reeds and rushes, which led to the beginnings of weaving. It was not long before shepherds became aware of the important properties contained in wool, enabling it to be drawn and twisted into fine yarn. By medieval times thread was an essential commodity, and all clothing, bedlinen and household linens, including floor coverings, were made in the home. Everything was repaired and patched time and time again.

One of the oldest methods of converting wool or flax into a thread is to work with a hand spindle. The spindle consists of a stick, about 15-30cm (6-12in) long, usually thicker in the middle than at the ends, and a spinning stone – called a whorl. Whorls could be made of wood, bone, lead, pottery, glass or stone. By revolving the stick between the fingers the wool or flax was formed into a thread. The skilful task of spinning was carried out in the home by the female members of the family. From finds in the 1970s, it is evident that this craft was practised in medieval Amsterdam and that it ceased to be practised in the seventeenth century. The spinning stick and whorls shown in Plates 1 and 2 were all excavated in Amsterdam.

Plate 1
Spinning whorl and stick, 14th/15th century. Excavated in Amsterdam, 1970s.

PRIVATE COLLECTION

Plate 2
Spinning whorls, 14th and 15th century. All items excavated in Amsterdam.

PRIVATE COLLECTION

Primitive methods of spinning gave way to the spinning wheel, at the same time introducing a pleasant pastime for ladies in well-to-do circles, as spinning was considered a very suitable drawing room occupation. Storing the home-spun thread was always a problem as it tangled easily and, depending upon the skill of the spinner, could be very uneven and prone to break. Simple thread winders, made of pieces of wood, bone or card, were used to keep the thread untangled and tidy.

Silver thread holders

Dutch silversmiths of the past designed extremely inventive containers and holders for thread. One of the earliest known methods of holding thread is the spool knave, used from early in the eighteenth century, and covered in Chapter 9.

Another rare thread holder, and a work of art, dates from around 1750 (Plate 3). It is a covered basket of very fine Friesian wirework made of woven silver. An equally unusual item is a tiny silver container which probably originally formed part of a set of tools belonging to a workbox, dating from around 1800 (Plate 4). This box is so small that it could only have been intended to hold a small quantity of the finest embroidery silk.

Plate 4
Silver thread container, c.1800. Old tax mark. Diameter 1.45cm (⁹⁄₁₆in), height 1.2cm (⁷⁄₁₆in).
PRIVATE COLLECTION

Plate 3
Woven silver wirework typical for Friesland, c.1750. Unmarked. 8.6cm (3⅜in) long.
PRIVATE COLLECTION

Thread baskets and tubs

Towards the end of the eighteenth century little silver baskets and tubs to contain thread were used for various methods of handwork where a continuous supply of thread was required. In Dutch, the little baskets are called *breimandjes*, meaning 'knitting baskets' (with handle) or *breitobbetje*, meaning 'knitting tubs' (without handle). The description is a little misleading, as although the basket or tub was indeed used to hold a small ball of wool while knitting (see Plate 5), it was also used quite extensively for other forms of handwork where cotton or flax thread was needed, such as tambour and crochet work.

With only a few exceptions, these small thread containers were made of silver. They were round or oval-shaped and mostly decorated with an openwork pattern. The lady knitting in Plate 5 would lead us to believe that such baskets were worn hanging over the arm. Although this charming picture sketches a homely scene of the nineteenth century, most silver knitting baskets could not have been worn in this manner as, with a maximum diameter of about 10cm for the handle, this would have been impossible. This handy utensil allowed the thread to flow freely and reduced the risk of tangling, or of the ball of thread falling on to the floor. Two of the earliest silver thread tubs are illustrated in Plates 6 and 7.

Plate 5
Drawing showing a lady knitting with a silver thread basket over her arm. Early 19th century.

Nederlands Openlucht Museum, Arnhem

Plate 6
Boat-shaped silver thread tub in Louis XVI style with beaded top rim. Marks: Amsterdam city mark used 1790-1807. Crowned 'O' for 1807. Engraved text: 'A.M. v. Hillenberg'. 6.5cm (2⅝in) high.

Private collection

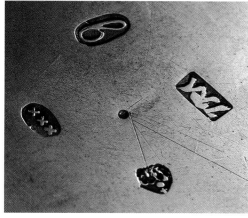

Plate 7a

Silver thread tub of circular shape with open pierced spokes and a border of C-volutes, two making a circle. Amsterdam, year mark for 1809. Maker: Jean Pierre Massee (1809-32; 1844-46). 6.9cm (2¾in) high.

KAY SULLIVAN ANTIQUES

Plate 7b

Detail of marks on silver thread tub. From top and clockwise: 'B': year letter for 1809; 'JPM': Maker's mark: Jean Pierre Massee (1809-12); Crown assay mark 1807-12 for silver of first fineness; Three crosses mark for city of Amsterdam. (Centre): Crown + 'V': 1814-93 tax free census mark used upon invalidation of the hallmarks of Louis Napoleon's Kingdom of Holland and those of the French Empire added in 1816.

Plate 8

Decorative silver bracelet thread or wool container. Filigree work with semi-precious stone in handle. Marks indistinct but typical of Friesland, 1807-12 period. 20.5cm (8¼in) long.

PRIVATE COLLECTION

Unlike the small baskets with handles, another type of basket, with a long handle, was worn over the arm (Plates 8 and 9).

These fragile baskets were mostly made of filigree silver and would have been great show objects for ladies sewing or knitting with friends and quite certainly luxury items, not within everybody's reach.

The wool holder in Plate 9 was thought to have been made in Holland. Very recently however, a nearly identical example turned up marked 'Schott, Frankfurt, Germany'. This new information renders the origins of the one in Plate 9 questionable. That items of silver filigree were made in Holland is certain, a good example being the decorative thread basket made by the brothers Nez in Amsterdam in 1831 (Plate 10).

Plate 9
Silver filigree bracelet-style thread or wool holder, c.1832. Diameter 6.8cm (2¾in), 21.5cm (8⅜in) long.

NEDERLANDS OPENLUCHTMUSEUM, ARNHEM

Plate 10
Oval silver filigree basket with hinged handle. Amsterdam, year letter 1831. Maker: Jean Louis Roch and Charles Julien Nez, Amsterdam (1831-46). 5cm (2in) high, 9.8cm (3⅞in) long.

KAY SULLIVAN ANTIQUES

Plate 11a
Round silver thread tub, c.1810-11. Maker: Hendrik Smits, Amsterdam (1798-1836). Engraved shield 'JFS 1811'. Year letter 17 Dec.1810 - 1 March 1812. 4.1cm (1⅝in) high, diameter 8.3cm (3⁵⁄₁₆in).

PRIVATE COLLECTION

Plate 11b
Detail of marks. Crown: Assay mark 1807-12; three crosses: Amsterdam city mark 1807-12; 'Diemont': retailer's mark; 'H.S.': Hendrik Smits (maker); year letter 'd': 1810-12.

Plate 12
Round silver thread basket with handle. Marks: Assay mark, Rotterdam 1814-1906 and year letter 1821. Maker: Laurens Koster, Rotterdam (1807-28). 4.3cm (1¾in) high, diameter 7.75cm (3⅛in).

PRIVATE COLLECTION

Plate 13
Round gilded silver thread basket with 'counted money' design. Year letter 1826. Maker: J.A. Duncan 's-Hertogenbosch (1815-53). 7.5cm (3in) diameter.
Gilded silver knitting needle protectors. Maker: Gerrit Hendriksz Kleinhout & Jan Jacob Eduard Koene, Amsterdam (1842-46).

KAY SULLIVAN ANTIQUES

Dutch silversmiths were masters in creativity and used the full extent of their skills when making sewing tools, including nineteenth century thread baskets and tubs. The variety in style and decoration is amazing, considering the short period they were made. A selection of these charming little baskets and tubs is illustrated in Plates 11-22. All of those shown here have flat bases. Small baskets of this type sometimes stand on a pedestal foot. These are generally considered to be baskets for sweetmeats but could also have been used for holding thread.

Gilding of silver is not common practice in Holland. The thread basket and knitting needle protectors in Plate 13 are rare exceptions, as both are gilded. The decoration on the basket resembles coins piled upon each other, and this design has therefore acquired the name of 'counted money'.

A little history

Sewing tools sometimes commemorate historical events. The Amsterdams Historisch Museum at one time housed the orphans of the city. A famous story connected with this museum is that of the hero 'van Speyk' (Plate 14). After a chequered upbringing, the young orphan Jan van Speyk joined the Navy, where he did very well. On the 5th February 1831, in battle against the Belgians, rather than let the enemy take over his ship, he descended the stairs to the gunpowder room with a lighted cigar, commanded all the crew to leave the ship, and lit the fuse. Cannon boat no.2 exploded into the air carrying van Speyk and the enemy with it. An exceptional silver thread basket (Plate 15) commemorates this national hero with the text 'De Held J.C.J. van Speyk' (The Hero J.C.J. van Speyk) in pierced letters.

Plate 15
Oval silver thread basket commemorating the national hero, Jan van Speyk. Pierced text: *De Held J.C.J. van Speyk* (The hero, J.C.J. van Speyk). Year letter 1831 (same year as event). Maker: Hendrik Remmers, Amsterdam (1806-47). 7.5cm (3in) long.
PRIVATE COLLECTION

Plate 14
Painting by J. Schoemaker-Doyer (1792-1867).
The former civic orphan van Speyk has achieved, aged 29, the position as Commander of a cannon boat which was brought into action during the uprising of the Belgians. Due to strong winds, van Speyk could not get his ship into the right position, and ended up ashore, allowing the Belgians to climb on board. Rather than surrender, van Speyk blows up the boat, having first warned the ship's boys to 'get off quick'.
AMSTERDAMS HISTORISCH MUSEUM, ON LOAN: SAC-AMSTELSTAD
JEUGDZORG

Plate 16
Oval silver thread basket in Empire style with pierced foliage design and filet borders. Inscribed on base: *Gedachtenis van EK* (In memory of EK). Year letter 1825. Maker: Cornelis de Keijzer Leeflang, Leiden (1820-43). 8cm (3⅛in) long.

PRIVATE COLLECTION

Plate 17
Silver thread basket with cable border and pierced design. Year letter 1829. Maker: Johannes van Leuven Sr., Alkmaar (1807–58). 9.5cm (3¹³⁄₁₆in) long.

KAY SULLIVAN ANTIQUES

Plate 18
Silver thread basket. Marked: Rotterdam year letter 1831. Maker: Jacobus Schalkwijk, Rotterdam (1818-47). 8.6cm(3⅜in) long.

MUSEUM BOYMANS VAN BEUNINGEN, ROTTERDAM

Plate 19
Oval silver thread or wool basket with pierced text *Uit Achting* (With Respect). Year letter 1834. Maker: Widow B. Gillis, 's-Hertogenbosch (1833-59). 7.5cm (3in) long.

PRIVATE COLLECTION

In various chapters in this book we come across sewing tools made by the lady jeweller, Widow B. Gillis from 's -Hertogenbosch in the southern part of Holland. This lady carried on her husband's business when he died and we know that she made complete sewing sets, thimbles and also thread baskets, one of which can be seen in Plate 19. This little basket has a pierced text *Uit Achting*, meaning 'with respect'.

Silver thread baskets and tubs were made between 1780 and 1875. The high-sided tub shown in Plate 22 is exceptional, being of early twentieth century manufacture.

Plate 20
Round silver thread tub in Biedermeier style wirework design with beaded border. Amsterdam, c.1840. Marks: Assay mark 1814–1953. Maker: Jacob Daniel Arnoldi and Johannes Wilhelmus Wielick, Amsterdam (1836–63). 8.4cm (3⅜in) diameter.

KAY SULLIVAN ANTIQUES

Plate 21
Round silver thread basket. Fine 'counted money' pierced design between two ribbed bands. Year letter 1841. Maker: Pieter van Gelderen, Schoonhoven (1819–42). 5.5cm (2¼in) high.

KAY SULLIVAN ANTIQUES

Plate 22
Round, high-sided thread or wool tub. Fluted double row of pierced geometric design. Year letter 1912. Maker: Gerardus Schoorl, Zaandijk/Amsterdam/Haarlem (1875–1914). 8.3cm (3⁵⁄₁₆in) high.

KAY SULLIVAN ANTIQUES

Mini-chatelaine thread holders

Another type of thread holder, in the style of a small chatelaine, consists of a shield with a hook at the back to hang on the belt (Plates 23-28). At the bottom of the shield is an eye on which a large, looped pin is attached, onto which the ball of thread can be fastened. The swivel action of the eye and pin mount allows the thread to flow freely in a continuous supply. There is much variety in the decoration of the shield. Mini-chatelaine thread holders vary in overall length from approximately 8-12cm (3¼in-4¾in).

Plate 23
Silver thread or wool holder with flower basket pattern. Probably Schoonhoven, c.1800. Marks: 'Dolphin' tax mark 1859-93.

PRIVATE COLLECTION

Plate 24
Right: Silver thread or wool holder with sunflower in basket and 'diamond' border. Probably Groningen, c.1820-40. Marks: Assay mark 1814-1905. Maker's mark indistinct.
Left: Silver thread or wool holder engraved with cross and rays. Year letter 1861. Maker: P. Salm, Hoorn (1850-90).

BOTH PRIVATE COLLECTIONS

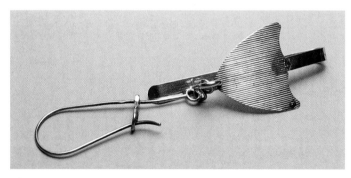

Plate 25
Silver thread holder with ribbed shield. Year letter 1844. Maker: Adriaan Marinus Kalbsfleisch, Vlissingen (1834-67). 11cm (4⅜in) long.

PRIVATE COLLECTION

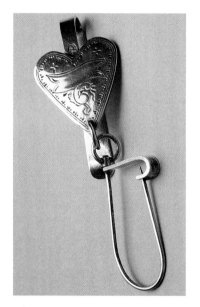

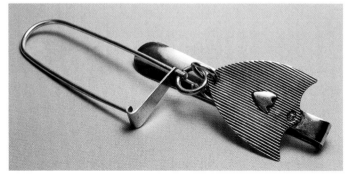

Plate 26
Silver thread holder with ribbed shield and small vacant shield. Year letter 1847. Maker: Jan Johannes Jr. van den Bergh, Schoonhoven (1817-53). 12cm (4¹³⁄₁₆in) long.

PRIVATE COLLECTION

Plate 27
Silver thread holder with heart-shaped shield, c.1890. Marks: Assay mark 1814-1953. Maker: Gebr. v. Straten, Hoorn (1885-91). 10.5cm (4¼in) long.

PRIVATE COLLECTION

Plate 28
Silver thread holder, c.1890. Shield with flower design. Marks: Assay mark 1814-1905. Maker: Wed. Johanna Hendrika Geelen, Schoonhoven (1889-1902). 9.5cm (3¹³⁄₁₆in) long.

PRIVATE COLLECTION

Thread winders

Charming snowflake-shaped winders, ideal for small amounts of silk, were usually included in boxed sets of sewing tools. It is therefore not common to find them as separate items. They are generally made of gold or silver. A decorative winder in the collection of the Fries Museum, Leeuwarden (Plate 29) is intricately worked in bone and mounted on a handle.

Gold thread winders are more often encountered than those of silver. A matching pair of silver winders is illustrated in Plate 30. A silver thread winder belonging to the Museum Boymans van Beuningen bears the initials 'G.v.d.V.' (Plate 31). The information with it tells us that it was from Grietje van der Veen's sewing box and that it was a present from her fiancé, Arjen Taekes Schat, on 19th May 1889. Another silver thread winder is shown in Plate 32. A selection of gold thread winders is illustrated in Plates 33-35.

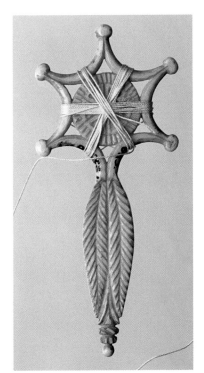

Plate 29
Rare bone winder on a handle, 19th century. 8.2cm (3¼in) high.

FRIES MUSEUM, LEEUWARDEN

Plate 30
Silver thread winders with engraved flower design, c.1840-70. Assay mark 1814-1905. Maker's mark indistinct. 2.75cm (1⅛in) wide.   KAY SULLIVAN ANTIQUES

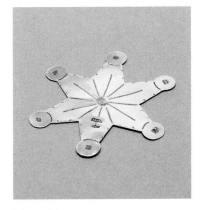

Plate 31
Six-pointed silver thread winder with engraved initials G.v.d.V. (Grietje van der Veen), c.1889.
MUSEUM BOYMANS VAN BEUNINGEN, ROTTERDAM

Plate 32
Six-pointed silver thread winder, c.1850. Marks: Assay mark 1814-1905. Maker: Albertus Antonius Rooswinkel, Leeuwarden (1841-68).
PRIVATE COLLECTION

Plate 33
Eight-pointed gold thread winders. Marks: Assay 18ct. 1814-1905. Probably c.1825-40.

COURTESY OF INEZ EIKELENBOOM/MRS. OAKTREE

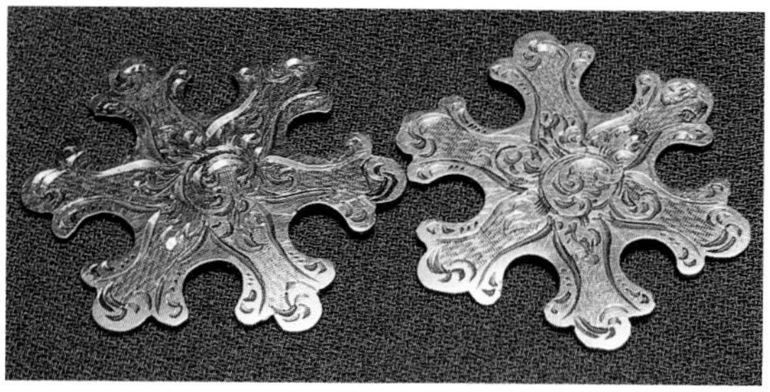

Plate 34
Six-pointed gold thread winders with Biedermeier engraving, c.1850-60. Marks: Assay 18ct. 1814-1905. Maker: Pieter Keizer, Amsterdam (1850-1866).
PRIVATE COLLECTION

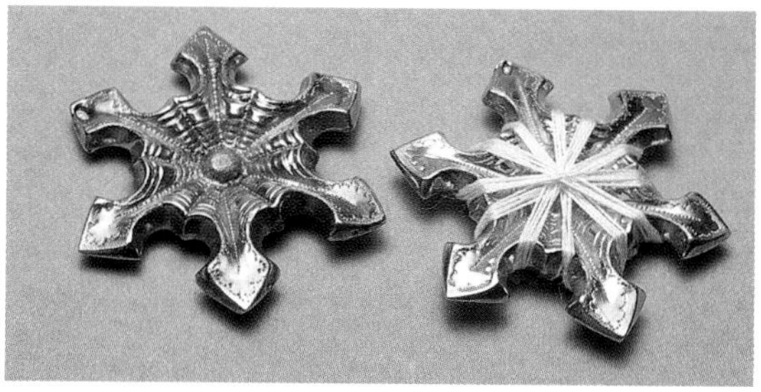

Plate 35
Six-pointed 14ct. gold thread winders, c.1860. Marks: Assay mark 1853-1905.
PRIVATE COLLECTION

Straw and wooden thread containers

Straw baskets have not survived the centuries, but Old Master paintings of domestic interior scenes, a number of which are featured in this book, frequently depict a woman sewing, with a cushion on her lap and a straw basket at her side. A late nineteenth century painting, by Thérèse Schwartze, portrays girls in the Orphanage in Amsterdam, with the girl in the centre sewing (Plate 36). There is also a straw basket containing fabrics standing in the corner of the picture.

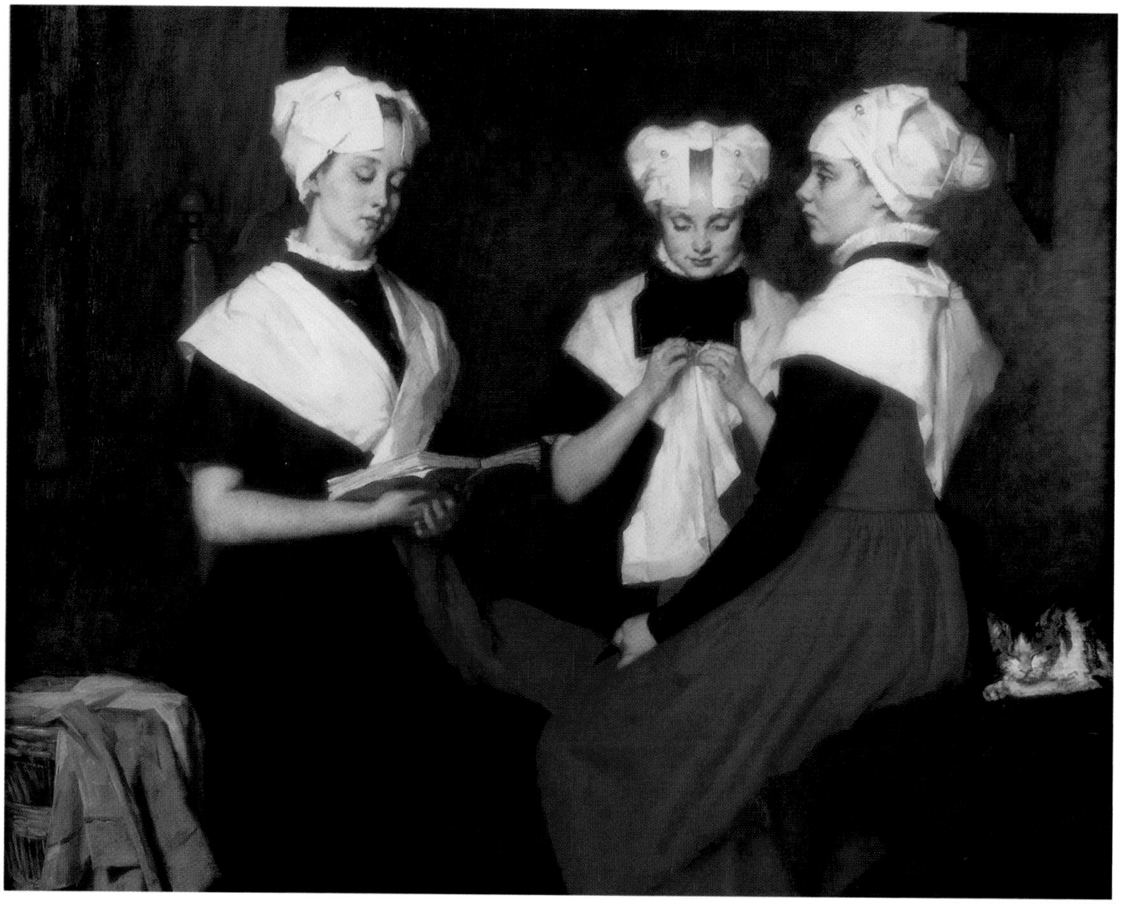

Plate 36
Drie Burgerweesmeisjes van Amsterdam, 1885 (Three Civic Orphan girls in Amsterdam), Thérèse Schwartze (1851-1918). The orphan in the middle is sewing. There is a sewing basket in the corner.
AMSTERDAMS HISTORISCH MUSEUM, ON LOAN: RIJKSMUSEUM, AMSTERDAM

Thread baskets were also made of wood (Plates 38-40). They were mostly plain in design, with practical use in mind. A wooden tub may have been made to resemble the style of the silver versions, as is the case with the one in Plate 37. The maker of this little tub cleverly combined wood, bone, silver and mother-of-pearl to achieve a beautiful and unique result. The base of the tub is lined on the inside with mother-of-pearl.

Many boxes were made in the home to store sewing tools and threads and some of these are illustrated in Chapter 1. The casket with hand painted flower designs in Plate 41, called a *brei en stopkist* (darning wool cabinet) was specifically made to store knitting and darning wool and threads.

Plate 37a
Cylindrical wooden thread basket with bone spokes and mother-of-pearl inlay in bottom, c.1800. Top and bottom rims inlaid with silver. 6.4cm (2½in) high.

KAY SULLIVAN ANTIQUES

Plate 37b
Inside of thread basket showing the unusual mother-of-pearl lining.

Plate 38
Vase/urn-shaped thread tub of tropical wood with dark and light brown veins. First half 19th century. 8.5cm (3⅜in) diameter, 11.5cm (4⅝in) high.

PRIVATE COLLECTION

Plate 39
Engine-turned lignum vitae thread container with cover, shaped as a pot with lid, c.1840-80. 8.6cm (3⁷⁄₁₆in) diameter, 5.4cm (2³⁄₁₆in) high.

PRIVATE COLLECTION

Plate 40
Mahogany thread tub with inlaid brass rings, c.1840–80. 8.8cm
(3½in) diameter, 5.2cm (2¹⁄₁₆in) high.

KAY SULLIVAN ANTIQUES

Plate 41
Wooden knitting and darning wool casket with hand-painted flower design. 19th century.

NEDERLANDS OPENLUCHTMUSEUM, ARNHEM

Thread on wooden reels

One of the easiest and most familiar ways to store thread more recently was on a simple wooden cotton reel. The Carp thread factory in Helmond, Holland, has been responsible for many different versions of thread on reels since opening their doors in 1860. One of their most famous trademarks is the *Zes Vingerhoeden* mark, which was also made in the English 'Six Thimbles' version (Plates 42 and 43). Amongst others, their colourful labels included clowns, cars, buildings and sewing machines.

Plate 42
Wooden thread spool. Carp, Helmond, Holland. Trade mark and illustration: six thimbles mark (in Dutch *Zes Vingerhoeden*). 20th century.

Plate 43
Wooden cotton reels from the Carp factory in Helmond, Holland including 'Six Thimbles' trade mark.

De Druivenplukker (The Grape-picker), 1792. Jacobus Johannes Lauwers (1753–1800)

Tambour Tools

Tambour work and the spool knave

Tambour work involves the making of an embroidered chainstitch on to fine material, such as crêpe, muslin and cambric. Fine, almost transparent fabric is stretched over a frame, named after the French *tambour*, meaning drum. White thread is attached to the underside of the fabric and the tambour needle is then pushed at a right angle through the material with the right hand, catching up the thread under the fabric with the fine hook of the needle, assisted by the needlewoman with her left hand. The loop is then pulled through to the surface of the fabric and fastened again with the next stitch through the material, thereby creating a chainstitch.

For tambour work, a continuous flow of thread was needed, leaving the hands free to manipulate the needle. A spool knave was used for this purpose, comprising a hook and a bow-shaped frame to which a free-turning spindle was attached, sometimes covered by an ivory, bone or wooden spool (Plate 1). The hook of the spool knave was attached to the belt or apron strings and the ball of thread placed on the spindle, thus supplying sufficient thread as required, leaving the hands free. The girl in J.J. Lauwers' painting (opposite) is wearing a spool knave, a detail of which is shown in Plate 2.

This method of tambour work became very popular, as it grew much faster than chainstitch embroidery worked with an ordinary needle. In the eighteenth century, tambour work was carried out in many European countries and the proficient needlewoman could produce a fine piece of embroidery in a minimum of time. Tulle was also used as a basis for tambour work, on which the chainstitch created a lace-like effect. Plates 3a and 3b show details of the tambour work on a stole and apron, part of the traditional costume worn in Friesland.

The earliest known Dutch spool knaves were made in the first half of the eighteenth century, and it would seem that they were made almost exclusively from silver and occasionally from ivory. One rare gold example, made in Middelburg in 1789, is known to have turned up for auction in Amsterdam. The decoration of this spool knave incorporated a pair of ducks, surmounted by a Duke's coronet.

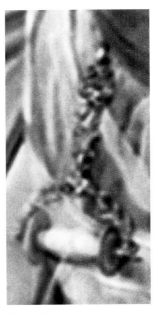

Plate 2
Detail of *De Druivenplukker* (opposite), showing a spool knave attached to the waistband.

Plate 1
Silver spool knave with ivory spool. Mark: Amsterdam 1745. Maker: Jan Borduur, Amsterdam 1731-66. 19.5cm (7¾in) long.

PRIVATE COLLECTION

Plate 3a
Detail of stole embroidery.

Plate 3b
Detail of bottom edge of apron.

Plate 3
A modern lady wearing traditional Dutch costume from Friesland. Her stole and apron are tambour lace on tulle.

Dutch skating event

Who has not seen the familiar Dutch skating scene as portrayed by the Dutch Masters of the seventeenth century? Even in present-day Holland, a cold winter conjures up the wonderland of a skating scene. As in centuries past, sporting events are then organised as a pleasurable pastime.

One such event took place in the exceptionally severe winter of 1762-63 when it was so cold that even the Zuiderzee froze over. Inhabitants of Stavoren skated over the frozen sea, a distance of some twenty miles, to Enkhuizen, the nearest city on the opposite coast. Some even crossed over in horse-drawn sleighs. Late in the seventeenth century, and especially in the eighteenth century, it was customary to commemorate such trips with inscriptions on small silver items such as snuff boxes, spoons, tea caddies or milk jugs. A certain Professor Wigeri skated across the frozen sea to Enkhuizen, bringing an original gift home as a surprise for his wife to commemorate this spectacular achievement. His text is to be found on the spool knave illustrated in Plate 4.

Plate 4

Silver spool knave with ivory spool. City mark Enkhuizen 1762-63. Maker: Possibly Hendrik Jan Tiedeman, Enkhuizen. Souvenir of skating event across the sea to Enkhuizen in January 1763. Text on inside of hook: *Den 22.Jan 1763 met Schaatsen van Enkhuisen gehaalt door Professor Wigeri.* (The 22 Jan 1763 obtained by skating from Enkhuizen by Professor Wigeri.)

ZUIDERZEEMUSEUM, ENKHUIZEN

Plate 5

Silver spool knave with simple shell design and ivory spool. Hoorn, north Holland, first half 18th century. Maker unknown.
15.2cm (6in) long.

PRIVATE COLLECTION

Spool knaves and the silversmith

It is notable how much thought and imagination went into making a spool knave. As will be seen from the following examples, each one produced by the Dutch silversmiths had an individual design and they were all, in their own way, works of art. Designs on silver spool knaves cover a wide range of subjects including flowers, animals, birds, sea shells, figures and religion. The styles of the Louis XV period (1715-74), incorporating C-formed volutes, flowers, leaves, birds and curls in S-form, and the Louis XVI (1774-93) with firm lines, pearl beading, flower garlands, bows and medallions, are royally represented and recognisable on spool knaves from the second half of the eighteenth century. Examples are illustrated in Plates 5-20. The spool knave shown in Plate 7 was probably reconstructed from a bag frame. The Bible scene, in relief, of Jesus kneeling and the Apostle Peter with his feet in a basin of water, is an especially handsome design.

Plate 6
Silver spool knave incorporating female figures, dated 1761. Maker unknown. A similar example is known to have been made in Rotterdam in 1749.

NEDERLANDS OPENLUCHTMUSEUM, ARNHEM

Plate 7
Silver spool knave with wooden spool. Religious scene showing 'The Washing of the Feet'. Schoonhoven, c.1775. Maker unknown. 13.5cm (5⅓in) long.

PRIVATE COLLECTION

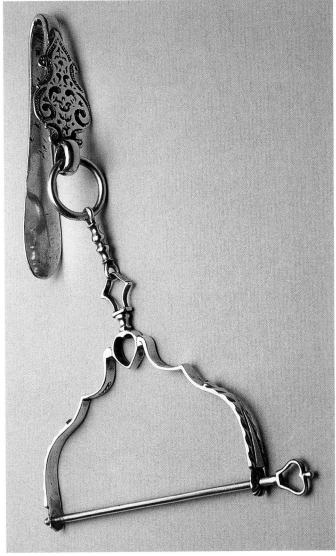

Plate 8
Silver spool knave with ivory spool. Partially openworked design of ribbons, bows and flowers. Amsterdam city mark 1772-95 incorporating year letter 'R': 1776. Maker's mark: Adam Rutgers, Amsterdam (1760-92). 15.6cm (6⅛in) long.   PRIVATE COLLECTION

Plate 9
Silver spool knave with symmetrical 'C' volutes and wavy shaped frame with heart-shaped elements and silver spool. Amsterdam city mark 1772-95 incorporating year letter 'T': 1778. Maker's mark: Rijk Vermoolen, Amsterdam (1756-c.1800). 15.4cm (6⅛in) long.

KAY SULLIVAN ANTIQUES

A frequently recurring name in connection with sewing tools made in the second half of the seventeenth century, is that of Daniel la Feber. This important silversmith was a gifted craftsman who produced articles of beautiful design and very high quality (Plates 11-12).

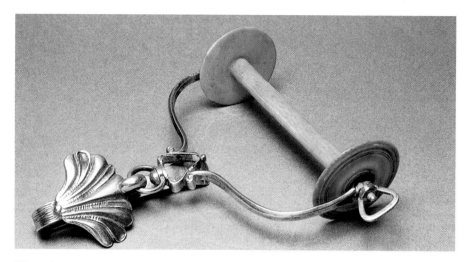

Plate 10b
Detail showing marks on hook of spool knave. From top to bottom: Tax mark crowned 'O': 1807. Leiden city mark and year letter 'Z': 1783. Maker's mark: Probably Evert van Til.

Plate 10a
Silver spool knave with decorative shell-shaped hook and ivory spool. Leiden, 1783. 12.5cm (5in) long.

PRIVATE COLLECTION

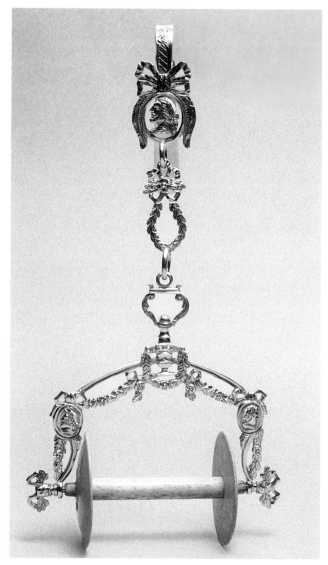

Plate 11
Silver spool knave with bone spool. Beautiful Louis XVI design, including Roman Emperors in a wreath of leaves (see detail). Amsterdam city mark incorporating year letter 'B': 1786. Maker: Daniel la Feber (1780–post-1804). 18cm (7in) long.

PRIVATE COLLECTION

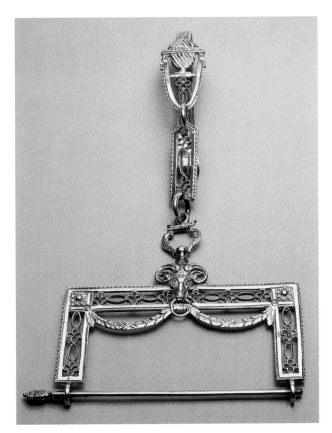

Plate 12a
Silver spool knave decorated with flowers and swags and centre detail of a ram's head (see detail above). Amsterdam, 1790.

Plate 12b
Detail showing marks, from left to right:
Maker: DLF – Daniel la Feber (1780-post-1804). Amsterdam city mark (three crosses) with year letter 'F': 1790.
Axe: mark used 1853-1927 for work stamped with old Guild marks and later returned to the market. 18cm (7in) long.

Plate 13
Silver spool knave, Louis XV/Louis XVI decoration with a vase, bows, garlands of leaves and bust of a Roman Emperor, c.1792 (see detail). Maker: Jan le Minje, Haarlem 1772-1812. 20cm (8in) long.

Plate 14b
Detail showing marks found on hook of spool knave. Amsterdam city mark (three crosses) with year letter 'I': 1793. Maker's mark resembling that of Hendrik Land (1772-1801). Shield crowned 'V': tax stamp 1814-93.

Plate 14a
Silver spool knave in Louis XVI style and with ivory spool. Amsterdam, 1793. 17cm (6¾in) long.

PRIVATE COLLECTION

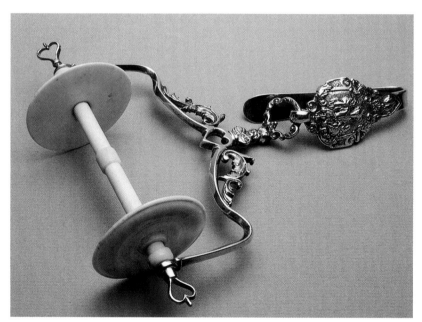

Plate 15
Silver spool knave with heart details, c.1797. Maker: Jacobus Fortman, The Hague (1773-pre-1812). Mark: Stork – The Hague Guild mark. Unusual double section to the ivory spool. 14.5cm (5¾in) long.

KAY SULLIVAN ANTIQUES

Plate 15a
Hook decoration, showing bust of a woman.

Plate 15b.
Centre spindle decoration: bust of a woman wearing a lace ruff.

Hendrik Land was known for casting silver mounts for bags and hooks from which bags, spool knaves or even chatelaines could be suspended from the waistband. His brother, Simon, was known for making spool knaves. The mark on the spool knave in Plate 14 resembles that of Hendrik Land, but it is possible that it was actually made by Simon. An interesting detail of the spool knave made by Jacobus Fortman in The Hague in 1797 (Plate 15) is the double section to the ivory spool. In the middle of the spool is a raised section, presumably to keep two balls of thread separated.

Plate 16
Silver spool knave with ivory spool. Second half 18th century. Maker unknown.
NEDERLANDS OPENLUCHTMUSEUM, ARNHEM

Plate 17
Silver spool knave with ivory spool. Second half 18th century. Maker unknown.
FRIES MUSEUM, LEEUWARDEN

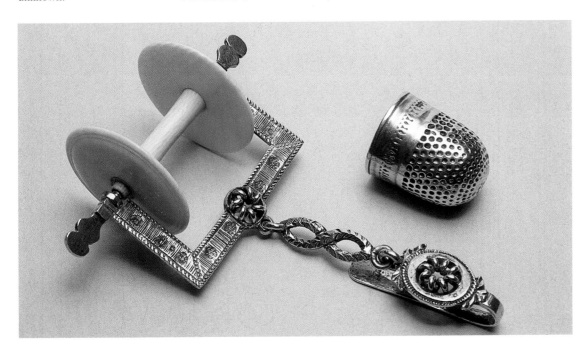

Plate 18
Miniature spool knave made as a toy. Amsterdam city mark 1772-95 incorporating year letter 'Z': 1784. Maker's mark indistinct. 8cm (3¼in) long.
PRIVATE COLLECTION

An extraordinary item is illustrated in Plate 18. This miniature spool knave was made in Amsterdam in 1784. Considering its size, only about three times larger than a thimble, it was undoubtedly made as a miniature for a costume doll. The collecting of silver miniatures, which included all imaginable household items, figures and windmills, was extremely popular in the eighteenth century.

It will have become obvious from the examples illustrated in this chapter that the majority of spool knaves were made of silver. Two exceptions, made completely of ivory, belong to the Fries Museum in Leeuwarden (Plates 19 and 20). These rare spool knaves are estimated to date from the second half of the eighteenth century.

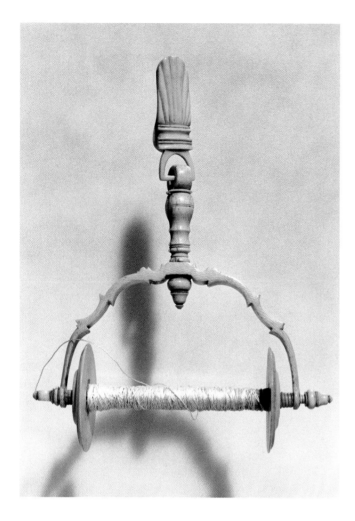

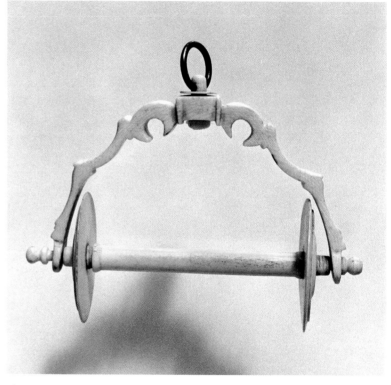

Plates 19 and 20
Ivory spool knaves in Louis XIV style. Second half 18th century.
FRIES MUSEUM, LEEUWARDEN
LOAN: OTTEMA-KINGMA FOUNDATION

Nineteenth century spool knaves

Spool knaves continued to be made until the middle of the nineteenth century. This form of hand embroidery began to decline when it was discovered that the stitches could be produced perfectly and efficiently on a machine. On a smaller scale tambour work continued and is still practised today, when aprons and stoles are needed to complete folk costume. In the second half of the nineteenth century, many existing spool knaves were put to use for other forms of handwork. One use was for knitting wool. Plate 21 portrays a lady knitting, dressed in folk costume. Hanging from her waistband is a spool knave on which a ball of black wool is wound. This model of a lady in the colourful costume of Kampereiland is in the collection of the Stedelijk Museum in Kampen. The spool knave was made by David de Put, an Amsterdam goldsmith who also worked with silver. He is also known to have made scissors, sealing-wax containers and chatelaines. Some early and mid-nineteenth century spool knaves, the most recent of which is dated 1855, are illustrated in Plates 23-26.

Plate 21a
Lady in traditional costume, knitting. A ball of black wool is wound on to a silver spool knave, attached to the waistband.

STEDELIJK MUSEUM KAMPEN

Plate 21b
Spool knave used for knitting, year letter 1753.
Maker: David de Put, Amsterdam (1725-87).

Plate 22
Silver spool knave with leaf and floral decoration and ivory spool. Sneek, Friesland, year letter 1809. Maker: Age Oosterwerf, Sneek (1774-1826). 14cm (5½in) long.

PRIVATE COLLECTION

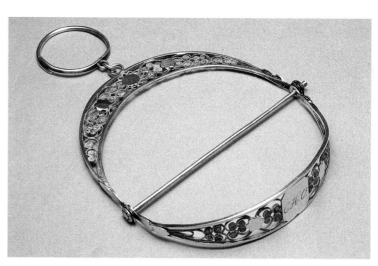

Plate 24

Unusual silver spool knave of circular shape with roundels and cartouche within openwork filigrain scrolls, c.1840. Circular double silver ring for fastening to waistband. Assay mark 1814-1905. Maker: Jean Louis Roch Nez and Charles Julien Nez, Amsterdam. Mark used by brothers between 1831-46. 15cm (6in) long. PRIVATE COLLECTION

Plate 23

Silver spool knave with open diamond-shaped decoration and the letter 'S' incorporated in the bow. Narrow bone spool. Amsterdam 1796-1807. Amsterdam city mark. Maker's mark indistinct. 14.5cm (5⅝in) long. KAY SULLIVAN ANTIQUES

Plate 25

Silver spool knave with ivory spool decorated with lions and sun-like clasp. Bolsward, Friesland, year letter 1844. Maker: Jan Piers Fennema (1827-48). 14cm (5⅜in) long. PRIVATE COLLECTION

Plate 26

Silver spool knave in romantic style, the hook showing a milkmaid with pails, and the bow two turtle doves in scrolled surrounds. Spindle and spool of silver. Sneek, Friesland, 1855. Maker: Laurens van Manen (1844-71).

FRIES MUSEUM, LEEUWARDEN

Tambour hooks and needles

Needles for tambour embroidery were available in varying sizes according to the thickness of the thread used (Plate 29). The handle into which the needle fits flares out towards the top and has a winged nut which secures the needle. Fancy holders for tambour hooks in ivory and mother-of-pearl were made mostly in England or France. Those made by the Dutch silversmiths were usually of silver or gold and occasionally contained in a luxury box with a hook and needles of different sizes, such as that displayed in Plate 27.

Sometimes, a tambour hook was made in two pieces, with a separate section at the top, which can be screwed on to the handle when working, and over the bottom part of the hook when work is laid aside. Other tambour hooks are made in one piece, such as those of beautifully coloured agate with a silver tambour hook shown in Plates 28 and 29. The handle of the tambour hook in Plate 30 has an additional section in which to store needles of different sizes.

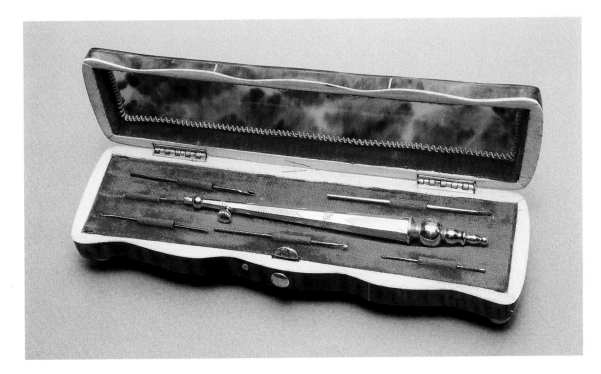

Plate 27
Tortoiseshell box lined with purple velvet on ivory feet, containing a 14ct. gold tambour hook and needles of various sizes. Amsterdam c.1860–70. Assay mark 1853-1905. Box 13cm x 4cm (5⅛in x 1⅝in). Needle holder 9.5cm (3¾in) long.

PRIVATE COLLECTION

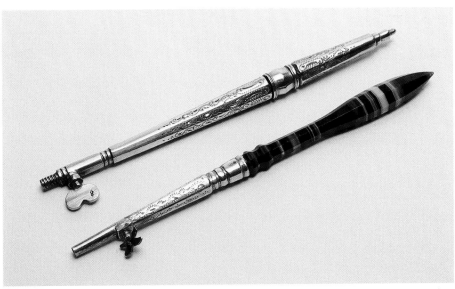

Plate 28
Top: Silver tambour hook, c.1880. Cornelis Rietveld, Schoonhoven (1865-1912). 11.7cm (4⅝in) long.
Bottom: Silver tambour hook with black and white striped agate handle, c.1880-1900. Assay mark: 1814-1905. 11.6cm (4⅝in) long.

PRIVATE COLLECTIONS

Plate 29
Silver tambour hooks with faceted agate handles c.1900. Maker: S. Rins, Purmerend (1896–1926). Assay mark 1814–1905.
Top: 11.6cm (4⅝in). Bottom: 11.4cm (4¹¹⁄₁₆in).
PRIVATE COLLECTIONS

Plate 30
Silver tambour hook with section for storing needles. Probably Friesland, c.1850–70. Assay mark: 1814–1905. Maker's mark indistinct. 14.5cm (5¾in) long.
PRIVATE COLLECTION

Crochet hooks

From several sources it is known that crocheting has existed for many centuries, although it seems that the purpose and methods differed from modern crochet, as we know it today. Crocheting, unlike tambour work, is not surface embroidery. A series of chainstitches is looped together independently to make complete articles or to be used for trimmings or edging pieces. For this work a slightly flared needle is used, but a crochet hook does not have the winged nut of the tambour needle. The crochet hook featured in Plate 31 provides evidence that the art of crochet is considerably older than tambour work. Although the marks are now indecipherable, judging from the style and decoration, it is believed that this crochet hook is of seventeenth century manufacture. A two-part crochet hook is featured in Plate 32. The silver sheath slides over an exceptionally long needle, leaving the fine needle protruding through the bottom of the sheath.

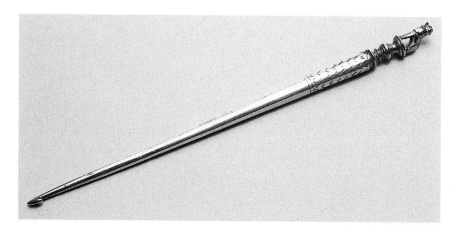

Plate 31
Silver crochet hook, c.1650. Probably region Alkmaar, Haarlem or Amsterdam. Lion figure on top(see detail). Remnants of maker's mark. 11.7cm (4⅝in) long.
PRIVATE COLLECTION

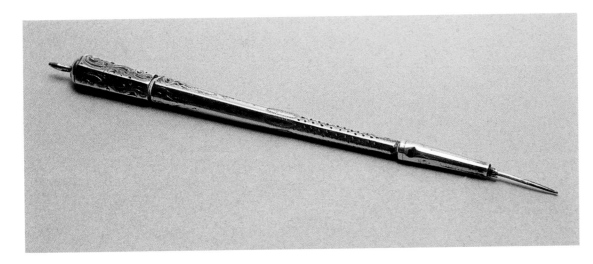

Plate 32
Silver crochet hook, c.1820-40 decorated with 'C' scrolls and dots. Unusual two-part construction. The sheath slides over the long needle leaving the fine hook protruding through the bottom (see below). Assay mark: 1814–1905. 17.5cm (7in) long.

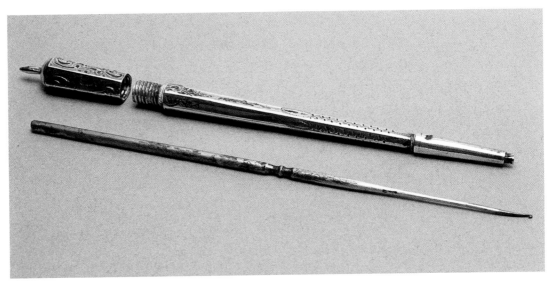

Plate 33
Bronze crochet hook, 18th century. 18.1cm (7¼in) long.

De jonge breister van Hindelopen (Young knitter from Hindelopen), Pieter Willem Sebes (1827–1906).

ZUIDERZEEMUSEUM, ENKHUIZEN

CHAPTER 10
Knitting Accessories

Knitting has been a means to an end for many centuries. It is thought to have originated in the Middle East, where knitted carpets and wall hangings are known from the fourth and fifth centuries. The art of knitting probably travelled to Europe via Spain and Italy. There are many references to knitting in Scotland, going back beyond medieval times.

The knitting needle sheath

From documented research we know that the sheath was used extensively in the British Isles as an extension of the knitting needle and as a support for the knitting as early as the seventeenth century. A few examples have been preserved with engraved texts dating from the 1680s.

Having looked into extensive collections of this item, it appears that the majority of existing Dutch sheaths are eighteenth and nineteenth century. It was therefore very exciting to discover a wooden sheath in the Fries Museum, Leeuwarden (Plate 1) bearing the date 1588 and a profound message. Early knitting sheaths are generally straight and often have very fine carving. From the eighteenth century onwards, the designs took on a different character, incorporating all sorts of animals and imaginative subjects.

Plate 1
A wooden sheath bearing the text: *Samson was een sterck man noch is hi stercker die siin tonghe bedwinghen kan 1588.* (Samson was a strong man, but not as strong as he who could hold his tongue, 1588).
FRIES MUSEUM, LEEUWARDEN

A knitting sheath is a type of tube that was thrust into the waistband of apron or trousers and used to support the working needle. In the top of the sheath is a hole large enough to take one knitting needle. This support made it unnecessary to hold the needle, and with practice, the speed of knitting could be increased, as the sheath bore the weight of the knitting. The needle was 'lengthened' and the clothing was protected from the point of the needles. Use of a knitting sheath had many advantages and therefore it seems strange that this handy little gadget has been cast aside, never to be used again. There is perhaps a logical explanation for this as although a knitting sheath was secured by hooking it on to the waistband, it was held in position by the thick skirts and trousers of the folk costume. It is therefore possible that when slimline modern clothing came into fashion in the first half of the twentieth century the use of a sheath was no longer practical.

Sheaths for knitting were made in all kinds of materials including wood, leather, straw, ivory, bone, brass, pewter, silver and perhaps even in gold. Combinations of these materials were also used, as will be seen later in this chapter.

The Wiegersma Collection

An important collection of wooden knitting sheaths is housed in the Nederlandse Openluchtmuseum in Arnhem. Before the Second World War the General Practitioner, artist and collector Hendrik Wiegersma (1891-1969) of Deurne collected a large number of small wooden objects, of which knitting sheaths, knife handles and walking sticks made up the core of the collection. He called these objects 'folk art', in accordance with the prevailing romantic concept of folk culture.

Plate 2
De Breischei (The Knitting Sheath) by Dr Hendrik Wiegersma.
Book cover decorated with symbols found on wooden sheaths.

KAY SULLIVAN ANTIQUES

The vast majority of the knitting sheaths in Wiegersma's collection were made by shepherds and peasants for personal use or as gifts. The items in the collection come from all parts of the country and date from the eighteenth to the twentieth century. Many of the wooden sheaths shown here come from this extensive and prestigious collection.

A remarkable collection of eighty-four knitting needle sheaths is housed in the Museum Boymans van Beuningen in Rotterdam, donated in 1988 by Mr M. van Hoogstraten. The majority of the collection consists of silver sheaths, or silver combined with other materials, but there are also a number of unusual wooden examples.

With the help of the Nederlands Openlucht Museum, Museum Boymans van Beuningen and the Fries Museum, who provided dates, descriptions and photos, it has been possible to include in this chapter a large number of sheaths from various collections.

The first book to be published with information about knitting sheaths was, to the author's knowledge, *De Breischei* (The Knitting Sheath) by Dr Hendrik Wiegersma. Many of the symbols seen on the cover of his book, published in 1926 (Plate 2), can be found in the decorations on wooden knitting sheaths made in Holland.

The knitting sheath in daily use

The knitting sheath carries with it a remarkable history. The vast variety of surviving sheaths, with a large assortment of texts, designs and symbols, gives us a truly wonderful insight into the lives and minds of the people living and working at that time. Perhaps this information, not published in any great detail until now, will stimulate the interest of the collector and give new food for thought.

Many early sheaths were made by shepherds, farmers and fishermen, often from the simplest and least expensive materials. Examples made from simple branches and twigs can be seen in Plate 3.

Women and girls, as well as shepherds, farmers and fishermen, knitted with the help of a sheath. Generally speaking, men used a curved or rounded sheath made of wood, which was placed centrally in the waistband of their trousers in a vertical position (Plates 4, 5 and 6). Often there was a slit in the sheath through which to thread a belt. Women and girls put the sheath behind the waistband of their apron, slanted on the right-hand side, almost in a horizontal position. Woman mainly used the round and tapered types of sheath (Plates 7, 8 and 9).

A sheath could also be pushed under the arm to be used as a support whilst knitting. A silver sheath sometimes had a pin to attach it to the bodice of the dress, and some had rings to hang on a chatelaine, or a cord around the waist.

Plate 4
Palm wood sheath. 'Christening in Jordan'. Text: 'HENRICEUS GALEN 1789'. 18.2cm (7¼in) long.
NEDERLANDS OPENLUCHT MUSEUM

Plate 3
Simple knitting sheaths made from twigs and branches. Probably 18th century or earlier.
MUSEUM BOYMANS VAN BEUNINGEN, ROTTERDAM

Plate 5
Palm wood sheath. Bald man in checked waistcoat. Front and back *Kerfsneewerk*. Probably 19th century. 22.6cm (9in) long.

Plate 6
Shepherd's sheath with cage and slit to take belt. Brabant, early 19th century. 18.5cm (7⅜in) long, 2cm (¾in) wide.

KAY SULLIVAN ANTIQUES

Plate 7
Palm wood sheath. Woman and musician in relief, early 18th century. 23cm (9⅛in) long, 2cm (¾in) wide.

Plate 8
Symbols for Faith, Hope, Charity and life tree. Probably Zeeland. Dated 1863. 17cm (6⅞in) long

KAY SULLIVAN ANTIQUES

Plate 9
Black lacquered palm wood sheath with cage. Men in high hats, a hunter, deer and horses, mid-19th century, 18.3cm (7¼in) long.

PLATES 5, 7 AND 9: NEDERLANDS OPENLUCHTMUSEUM, ARNHEM

Time was money

Knitting provided a welcome supplement to the meagre family income. In the eighteenth century shepherds, farmers and fishermen knitted while they worked. The most important items, necessary in every household, were warm stockings. Under the long skirt of the folk costume, long black stockings were worn to keep out the fierce Dutch winter. To keep a family with many children in warm stockings throughout the bitterly cold weather, took many hours of knitting. Knitted goods could also be exchanged for other basic necessities. Therefore, if the knitting of stockings was an important source of income, or there were many little legs in the family needing warm stockings, then no time could be lost. People knitted when visiting friends, or when out walking. Shepherds

Plate 10
Girl and boy in traditional
costume. The girl is knitting.
NEDERLANDS
OPENLUCHTMUSEUM, ARNHEM

knitted whilst tending their sheep and fishermen when out on the water netting fish. The use of a sheath increased the speed of knitting – some reports state a remarkable speed of two hundred stitches per minute. One old lady in Zeeland is known to have said that she knitted stockings in exchange for flannel for her mother. After two years of doing nothing else, and being unable to face another stocking… she went to work for the baker.

A Dutch newspaper reported Catharina Angenieta van Dam as being the oldest resident in Holland, having reached an age of 111 years and 242 days. The article goes on to say that 'Katje', after just three years' schooling, started her working life in the nineteenth century, knitting socks!

Wooden sheaths

The use of wooden knitting sheaths extended over a period of more than four centuries. Woodcarving was an important folk-art into which the people could, and often did, put their hearts and souls. The making of a little sheath for a loved one, or for one's own use, was often a masterpiece involving many hours of patient work. Lonely hours spent out on the heath tending sheep could be whiled away by adding decorations to a wooden sheath. Much is to be learned from the decorations and messages carved into a sheath by people from past centuries, at a time when this tool was most definitely a way of life. We see names and dates, messages of joy and sorrow, words of love, religious themes, pictures of animals and flowers, and the most intricate and beautiful designs. The wooden sheaths found whilst researching this book make an impressive display. A selection has been made, to give the reader a good idea of the types and shapes of sheaths used when this little tool was a necessity, rather than a luxury.

Plate 11
Palm wood sheath with pewter bands and lead point. Masks and text: Anno 1714. 22.5cm (9in) long.

Plate 12
Black painted pear wood sheath, in the shape of a young girl in folk costume, around 1900. 19.2cm (7¹¹⁄₁₆in) long.

Plate 13
Elm wood sheath in the shape of a skeleton. Man's head with beard. Hole in skull for knitting needle. 19th century. 18.2cm (7¼in) long.

Plate 14
Palm wood sheath with cage and two wooden beads. Twisted design ending in a clog. 19th century. 18.5cm (7⅜in) long.

Plate 15
Palm wood sheath with primitive decoration. Text: 1825 *MVD Borg* and *Eene. Goede. Herder. Moet. Veel. Zoerig. Dragen (A good shepherd has many worries).* 19cm (7½in) long.

Plate 16
Ash wood sheath with cage and wooden ball. Text: *Geloof, Hoop, Liefde* (Faith, Hope, Love). 30.5cm (12in) long.

PLATES 11–16: NEDERLANDS OPENLUCHTMUSEUM, ARNHEM

Although all the knitting sheaths shown here are equally admirable examples of a long-lost folk art, some deserve special reference. Dated sheaths are of ultimate importance as they enable us to accurately pin-point the period in which this handy tool was used. Apart from the sheath dated 1588 mentioned at the beginning of this chapter, the oldest sheath with a carved date is that of 1714 (Plate 11).

Elaborately decorated sheaths were still in use around 1900, as demonstrated by the example in Plate 12, of a young girl standing on a pedestal. The skeleton in Plate 13 certainly makes an impressive knitting sheath.

An intricate 'cage', made with finely carved rungs, is worked into a number of sheaths, sometimes also containing little wooden beads. This is similar to the technique used with lace bobbins in the nineteenth century, the so-called church window bobbin. Knife handles are also found with a cage and wooden beads. What could be more Dutch than the slender sheath shown in Plate 14, with wooden beads contained in a cage, and ending in a clog.

Texts sometimes help us to appreciate the hard lives led by our knitting ancestors. Plate 15 carries the message *Eene. Goede. Herder. Moet. Veel. Zoerig. Dragen* (A Good Shepherd Has Many Worries). Another popular theme was Faith, Hope and Love (Plate 16). The sheath belonging to Klaas Eising, shown in Plate 17, tells an interesting story. Apart from being a shepherd, Klaas Eising was also a calligraphic artist. He was well known in his home town near Emmen in Drenthe for his talents in this field. When a document at the Town Hall was in need of a fancy text, someone was sent to look for Klaas. His 'fee' was always a glass of brandy. He registered this fact on his sheath by carving a glass with a crown above it as well as his name and the date, 1873.

Plate 17
Sheath made of lime wood, with a pewter cap and dated 1873. Klaas Eising was shepherd and calligraphic artist. 19.5cm (7¹³⁄₁₆in) long, 6.2cm (2½in) wide, 1.5cm (⅝in) high.

NEDERLANDS OPENLUCHTMUSEUM, ARNHEM

Religious themes were often used and the carving of a holy figure can show true craftsmanship, as can the sheaths carved as a man's head or those in the shapes of animals. There are numerous animal themes, including horses, goats, snakes, dogs and lions, to mention a few (Plates 21-26). Plate 20 shows an unusual nineteenth century sheath shaped as a monk with a carved measuring stick at the bottom, probably to measure the length of the knitting.

Plate 18
Palm wood sheath, man's head with hat, cage with four rungs and slit for belt. Engraved 'AVDH' and 'IE'. 19th century. 21cm (8⅜in) long.

Plate 19
Palm wood sheath, man's head with flat beret with hole for needle. Design in primitive relief, dated 1885. 19.7cm (7⅞in) long.

Plate 20
Elm wood sheath, top half carved as a standing Capuchin monk. Bottom half carved for use as a measure. 19th century. 19.1cm (7⅜in) long.

PLATES 18-20: NEDERLANDS OPENLUCHTMUSEUM, ARNHEM

Plate 21
Top: Mahogany knitting sheath with long silver tip. Dutch lion with a crowned shield engraved 'LWS Anno 1820' (see detail).
Bottom: Wooden knitting sheath with silver mountings and belt hook, c.1860–80. Engraved 'Anna Crol'. 18.5cm (7⅜in) long.
PRIVATE COLLECTION

Plate 22
Palm wood sheath; horse's head and human mask. Tools and flowers tell us something about the user. Probably 19th century. 21cm (8⅜in) long.
NEDERLANDS OPENLUCHTMUSEUM, ARNHEM

Plate 23
Wooden goat's head knitting sheath with hole for needle between the horns. 19th century. 20.5cm (8¼in) long.
NEDERLANDS OPENLUCHTMUSEUM, ARNHEM

Plate 24
Palm wood sheath, shaped as a snake with an apple in its mouth. Probably 19th century. 22.5cm (9in) long.
NEDERLANDS OPENLUCHTMUSEUM, ARNHEM

Plate 25
Palm wood sheath crowned with a dog's head. Probably 19th century. 20.5cm (8⅛in) long.
NEDERLANDS OPENLUCHTMUSEUM, ARNHEM

Plate 26
Palm wood sheath, lion sitting on a pedestal supported by four columns. Elaborate pattern with text 'LUN' and 'Helmond 1840'. 22.7cm (9in) long.
NEDERLANDS OPENLUCHTMUSEUM, ARNHEM

Plate 27
Lime wood sheath, spatula-shaped with two holes in top for knitting needles. Image of Christ carved on front. On back text: *Uit Vriendschap* (Friendship). Underneath, a cage with small ball. 21.1cm (8⅜in) long.
NEDERLANDS OPENLUCHTMUSEUM, ARNHEM

Plate 28
Walnut knitting sheath shaped as a hip-bone with face. 18th century. 15.6cm (6⅛in) long.
NEDERLANDS OPENLUCHTMUSEUM, ARNHEM

Plate 29
Front of sheath, 'M.Redeker' Back, 'Cadeau 1889' (A present 1889).
MUSEUM BOYMANS VAN BEUNINGEN, ROTTERDAM

Plate 30
Palm wood sheath in the shape of a totem pole. Letters 'FHI'; dated 1869. 20.1cm (8in) long.
NEDERLANDS OPENLUCHTMUSEUM, ARNHEM

A humourist must have carved the sheath shaped as a hip-bone with a face in Plate 28. From the text on the sheath in Plate 29 it would seem that the owner received it as a present. On one side is his name, and on the reverse the text *Cadeau 1889*, meaning Present 1889. Symbols of a pair of scissors, a knife, fork, spoon, and a hammer and chisel are carved into the narrow end with a monogram 'AS'. A little cage with tiny wooden balls had been painstakingly worked into the shaft of the sheath. The 'totem pole' shown in Plate 30 is ornately carved and dated 1869.

Dogs and dates

As the use of knitting sheaths extended over a number of centuries, it is exceedingly difficult, if not impossible, to date all wooden sheaths accurately. We are therefore very grateful to the craftsmen who did indeed date their sheaths. Six beautiful dated examples, all showing pictures of dogs, can be seen in Plates 31-35. These six sheaths, of similar shape, are typical of the type used by shepherds. Most were actually made by the shepherd who used them and those featured here span more than a century. Sometimes, sewing items are encountered with decoration related to historical events. This is the case with the oldest of these four sheaths, dated 1793 (Plate 31). The design depicts a *keeshond*. In the period 1780-95 the patriotic movement was very strongly anti-Orange, the ruling aristocracy. Their sympathies were with the French Revolution, who believed in liberty, equality and brotherhood. This dog was their symbol, making this little sheath, at the time that it was made, politically dangerous. The sheath shown in Plate 32 is carved in the shape of a dog's head drinking from a square bottle. The hole for the needle is in the bottle and the carved date is 1870. It is to be expected that many of these typical shepherds' sheaths will have pictures of their sheepdogs. The knitting sheaths in Plates 33 and 35 were made by Geert Stevens, a shepherd from North Sleen in the north-eastern part of Holland. The shepherd's sheath in Plate 34 comes from Gees, also in this area.

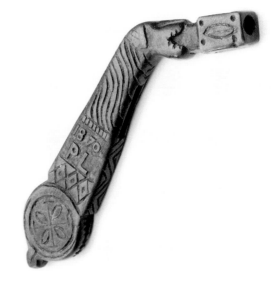

Plate 31
Shepherd's sheath, *Keeshond* (ship's dog). Dated 1793 and initials 'LJ'.
MUSEUM BOYMANS VAN BEUNINGEN, ROTTERDAM

Plate 32
Shepherd's sheath shaped as a dog's head. Dated 1870 and initials 'PL'.
MUSEUM BOYMANS VAN BEUNINGEN, ROTTERDAM

Plate 33
Palm wood sheath, made by Geert Stevens, shepherd, dated 1883. Running dog and hare design. 19.8cm (7⅞in) long.
NEDERLANDS OPENLUCHTMUSEUM, ARNHEM

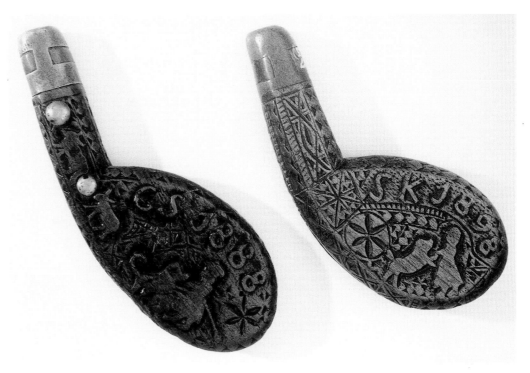

Plate 35

Left: Maple wood shepherd's sheath, dated 1888. 16.6cm (6⅝in) long. Right: Maple wood shepherd's sheath, Geert Stevens, dated 1898. 15.5cm (6¼in) long.

Plate 34

Palm wood sheath, made by shepherd, Jan Strijks. Dated on back, 1891. 16.2cm (6½in) long.

Kerfsneewerk

The art of *kerfsneewerk* (chip-carving) was widely used in the making of sheaths in the late eighteenth and all of the nineteenth century. The decoration of these sheaths is of the highest quality, their surfaces often being entirely covered with intricate designs composed of incised triangles formed in circles and/or straight lines. The variations in design of *kerfsneewerk* are limitless. A few wonderful examples can be seen here (Plates 36-39), giving an idea of the variety of shapes and patterns used, depicting a type of folk art rarely, if ever, used today.

Plate 36

Palm wood, *kerfsnee* (chip-carving) shepherd's sheath showing primitive carving of horses with rider and dated 1788. 18cm (7⅛in) long.

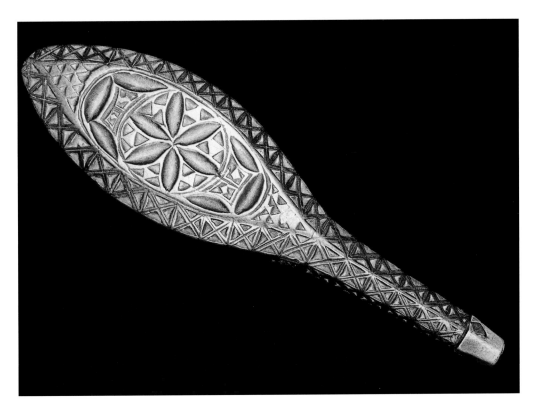

Plate 37
Kerfsnee (chip-carving) decoration with lead cap. Initials 'A.H.' and dated 1866.
NEDERLANDS OPENLUCHTMUSEUM, ARNHEM

Plate 38 (below left)
Walnut knitting sheath with *kerfsnee* (chip-carving) decoration. On the inside, 'FB en 1836'. 19.2cm (7¹⁰⁄₁₆in) long.
NEDERLANDS OPENLUCHTMUSEUM, ARNHEM

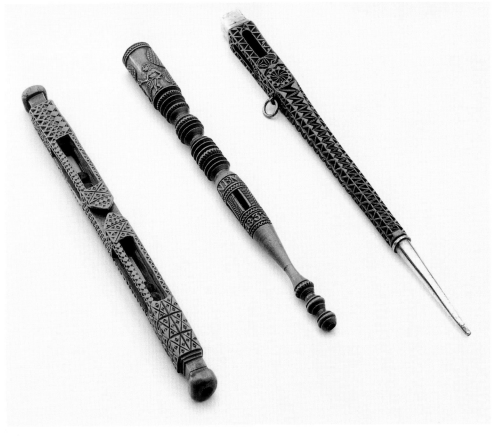

Plate 39
Left and right: Fine women's knitting sheaths with *kerfsnee* decoration, one with silver mountings. 19th century. Centre sheath finely carved (not *kerfsnee*). Dated 1833.
MUSEUM BOYMANS VAN BEUNINGEN, ROTTERDAM

Spindle sheaths

Spindle sheaths, illustrated in Plate 40, were turned on a lathe in small workshops. Six of these seven sheaths were most likely made in the first half of the nineteenth century. The middle sheath is hand carved. Plate 41 features lathe-turned spindle sheaths of varying designs, luxuriously mounted with silver tops and tails.

Plate 40
Middle sheath: hand carved. All the others are lathe-turned. First half 19th century.

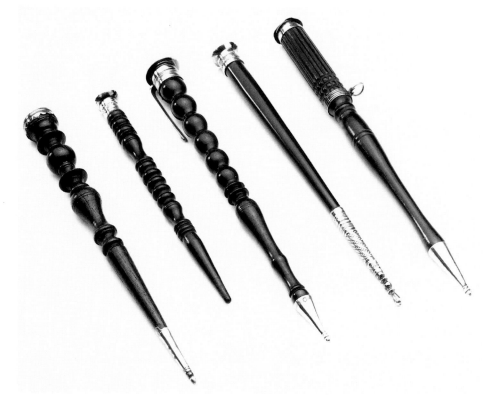

Plate 41
Lathe-turned women's knitting sheaths with silver decoration. Second from left: Maker's mark: H. Reitsma, Sneek/Leeuwarden 1862-85. Middle sheath has hook to hang on belt and monogram 'JSH'. Others unmarked, all 19th century.

Decoration

Much imagination went into decorating a simple wooden knitting sheath. Often other materials were used, including brass, pewter, nails, beads and ivory or bone. Two examples decorated with nails can be seen in Plate 42. Other wooden examples, completely covered with brass wire in intricate designs, are shown in Plates 43 and 44. The latter is shaped as a fish, the wire forming the pattern of the scales. In the middle is a small decoration with beads. From late in the eighteenth century, silver was used extensively as decoration for a wooden sheath.

Plate 42
Right: Palm wood sheath with 19 headed nails and *kerfsnee* decoration. Dated 1761.
Left: Chestnut sheath with eight brass-headed nails. Letters 'AR'. 23cm (9¼in) long.
NEDERLANDS OPENLUCHTMUSEUM, ARNHEM

Plate 43
Wooden sheath covered with brass wire. 19th century.
MUSEUM BOYMANS VAN BEUNINGEN, ROTTERDAM

Plate 44
Sheath shaped as a fish decorated with wire and beads. 17.5cm (7in) long.
NEDERLANDS OPENLUCHTMUSEUM, ARNHEM

169

Knitting sheaths of other materials

The simplest and least expensive materials used for knitting sheaths would have been a bunch of straw or feathers, bound together with string. Unfortunately most of these have not survived. A tube made of leather, filled with thin pieces of wood or feathers also made a usable sheath. Ivory, bone and brass were used as decoration, but these materials were also used for the actual sheath (Plates 45, 46 and 47). The sheath on the left in Plate 45 is made of bone with a silver hook engraved with the initials 'F.d.J.' and the one second from right is trimmed with silver.

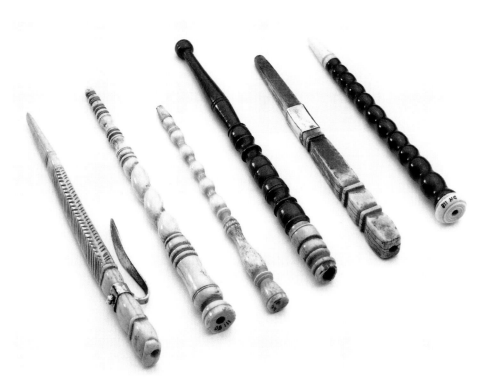

Plate 45
Knitting sheaths made of ivory, bone or wood, some with silver trimmings. 18th and 19th century.
MUSEUM BOYMANS VAN BEUNINGEN, ROTTERDAM

Plate 46 (right)
Knitting sheaths made of solid brass. Two far right, probably made from brass pipe. The other three of turned brass. 19th century.
MUSEUM BOYMANS VAN BEUNINGEN, ROTTERDAM

Plate 47 (left)
Horn knitting sheath in chain design, with last ring free to fasten to belt. Probably 18th century. 16.9cm (6¾in) long.
NEDERLANDS OPENLUCHTMUSEUM, ARNHEM

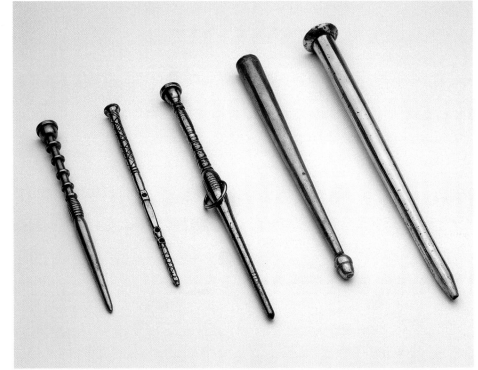

Feather quills and fishskin

Knitting sheaths made of woven feather quills were popular at the end of the eighteenth century. These sometimes colourful creations were always topped and tailed with silver, the silver cap containing a hole for the needle. The design and stained colour combinations made each sheath individual. A number of these attractive knitting sheaths are displayed in Plates 48-52. An example in Plate 49 is engraved 'ADM' and dated 1795. Another, made by Jacob Ages Oosterwerf from Sneek, bears the text 'JPB 1829'.

Fishskin was also used to cover small items such as boxes and knife and knitting sheaths. The sheath shown in Plate 53 is covered in skin from a ray.

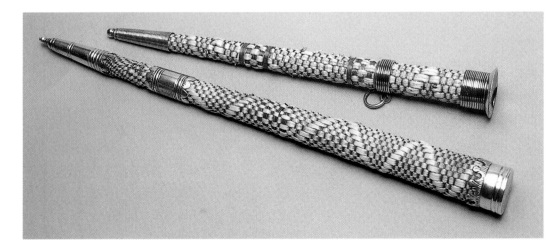

Plate 48
Top: Woven feather quill sheath also has a brass wire coil to which a brass ring is attached.
Friesland c.1820-40. Silver marked 1814-1905. Maker's mark indistinct. 17.3cm (6⅞in) long.
Bottom: Knitting sheath of woven feather quills and decoration of brass wire and silver mountings. 21.6cm (8½in) long.

PRIVATE COLLECTION

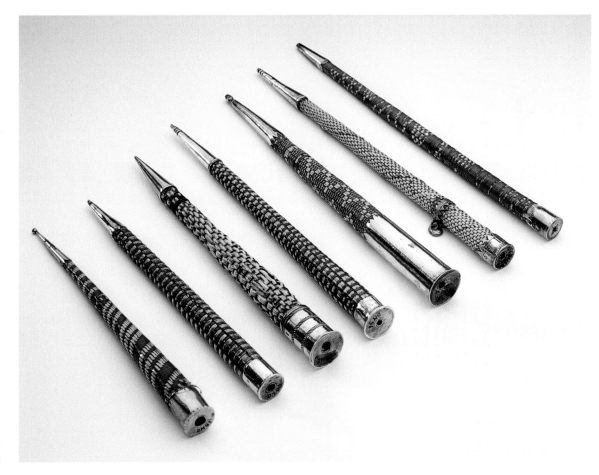

Plate 49
Knitting sheaths decorated with feather quills and silver mountings. Friesland, late 18th/early 19th century. Sheath second from right bears engraved text 'ADM 1795'. Third from right: engraved 'JPB 1829'. Maker: Jacob Ages Oosterwerf, Sneek (1827-42).

MUSEUM BOYMANS VAN BEUNINGEN, ROTTERDAM

Plate 50
Knitting sheaths decorated with feather quills and silver mountings. Some knitting sheaths have more than one hole. Friesland, late 18th/early 19th century.

MUSEUM BOYMANS VAN BEUNINGEN, ROTTERDAM

Plate 51
Knitting sheath with unusual coloured feather quills. Silver mountings: Assay mark 1814-1905. Maker's mark indistinct. Probably Friesland, c.1820.

KAY SULLIVAN ANTIQUES

Plate 52
Knitting sheath decorated with feather quills, c.1825. Silver mountings: Assay 1814-1905. Maker's mark: Rudulphus J. Feenstra, Sneek (1810-45). Engraved 'AK'.

PRIVATE COLLECTION

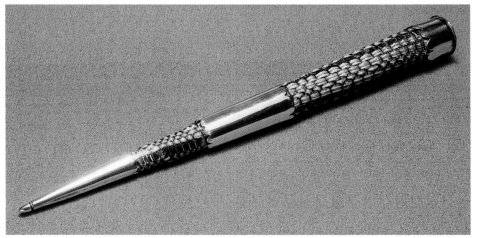

Plate 53
Knitting sheath covered in ray skin, with silver mountings. Friesland, late 18th/early 19th century.
MUSEUM BOYMANS VAN BEUNINGEN, ROTTERDAM

Silver sheaths

It would not be Holland if there were not silver sheaths. We have seen that many of the early sheaths were made of wood, but in the eighteenth century silver sheaths began to appear. Whilst the poorer folk still made much of their wooden sheaths, daughters of rich farmers and tradesmen could afford to have a sheath made of precious metal. Silver sheaths therefore came into fashion. Mr Wttewaall tells us in his book *Nederlands Klein Zilver* (Dutch Small Silver) that the oldest known silver sheath dates from 1736. Ladies' silver knitting sheaths are generally round and tapered. Sometimes a silver sheath will be fitted with a hook to hang it on the waistband, or a ring to attach it to a chatelaine or to suspend it from a simple cord around the waist.

Plate 54 shows two silver knitting sheaths, one from Amsterdam and one from Friesland. The maker of the Amsterdam sheath is Isaak Lingenaar, who made the sheath between 1796 and 1802.

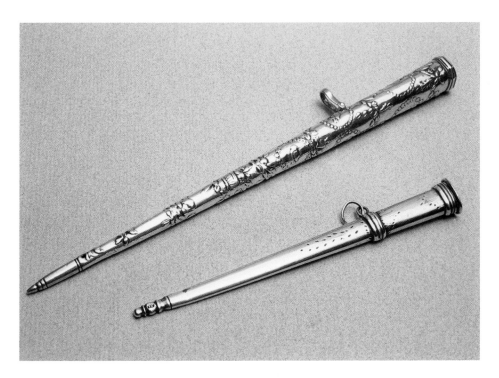

Plate 54
Top: Silver knitting sheath with allegorical figures with *guirlande* design and ring for chain. Amsterdam city mark 1796-1807. Maker's Mark: Isaak Lingenaar, Amsterdam (1751-1802). 17.9cm (7⅛in) long.　PRIVATE COLLECTION

Bottom: Oval shaped knitting sheath with ring for chain. Simple decoration, typical for the period 1830-40. Maker's mark 1826-44. Maker: Jurjen Harmanus Yskamp, Harlingen (1807-44). 13.6cm (5⅜in) long.

KAY SULLIVAN ANTIQUES

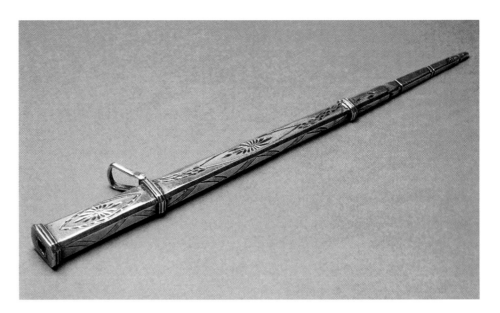

Plate 55
Silver sheath engraved with sunflower design, ring for chain, c.1770-90. Marks: Crowned 'O' for work present in 1807. 16.5cm (6⅝in) long.
KAY SULLIVAN ANTIQUES

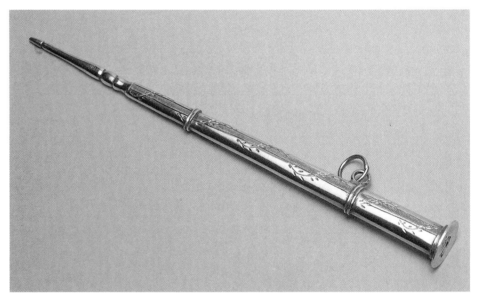

Plate 56
Finely engraved silver sheath with ring for chain, c.1790. Marks: Crowned 'O' for work present in 1807. Indistinct marks: Possibly three fishes of Enkhuizen; discharge mark of 1795. 19cm (7½in) long.
PRIVATE COLLECTION

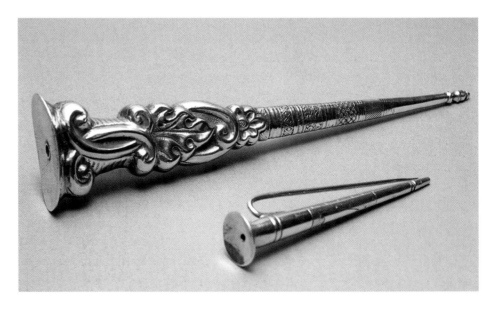

Plate 57
Top: Silver knitting sheath with hook to attach to waistband, c.1840. Assay mark: 1814-1905. Maker's mark indistinct. 14.3cm (5⅝in) long.
Bottom: Small silver knitting sheath with pin to attach to bodice. Assay mark: 1815-1905. Maker's mark indistinct. Early 19th century. 6.5cm (2⅝in) long.

KAY SULLIVAN ANTIQUES

The system of marking silver in Holland enables us to find much information about the silver and goldsmiths. We know that Isaak Lingenaar was born in 1722, the son of Cornelis (a carpenter by profession) and Catherina van Beeren. He became a silversmith in 1751 and died in 1806 in the Old Men's House in Amsterdam. He was of the Dutch Reformed Religion and lived on the Rozengracht in Amsterdam. He was known as the maker of knife handles, needle cases, babies' rattles and tobacco boxes. Apparently, he also made other sewing items.

The two knitting sheaths shown in Plates 55 and 56 are both marked with a crowned 'O'. This mark was deposited on old goods, already present in 1807. If we compare these sheaths with others from the period 1770-90, then we see that the shape and decoration conforms to this period.

Silver knitting sheaths of varying styles and ages are shown in Plates 57-63. Both sheaths shown in Plate 57 have the addition of a hook. The large sheath has a hook on the back to fasten on to the waistband. The small sheath has a hooked pin, to attach it to the bodice. A selection of similar sheaths with a pin is shown in Plate 58. Two silver sheaths of an unusual shape (Plate 59), have hinged pins to secure them in the style of a brooch. An unusual combination is the sheath made of amber and mounted in silver with a pin fastener (Plate 60).

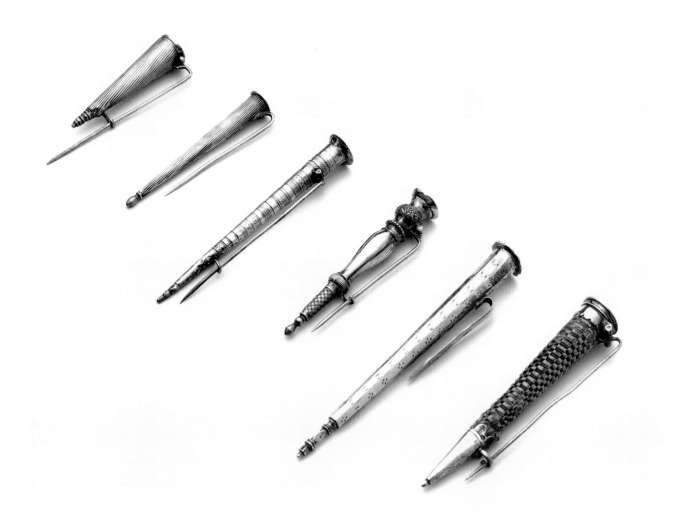

Plate 58
Small 19th century silver knitting sheaths with pin. Second from right c.1880. Maker: Cornelis Rietveld, Schoonhoven (1865-1912).
MUSEUM BOYMANS VAN BEUNINGEN, ROTTERDAM

Plate 59
Silver knitting sheaths of unusual shape with hinged pin. Right: c.1850-70. Maker: Cornelis Monteban, Schoonhoven
(1843-80). Left: mid-19th century, maker's mark indistinct.

MUSEUM BOYMANS VAN BEUNINGEN, ROTTERDAM

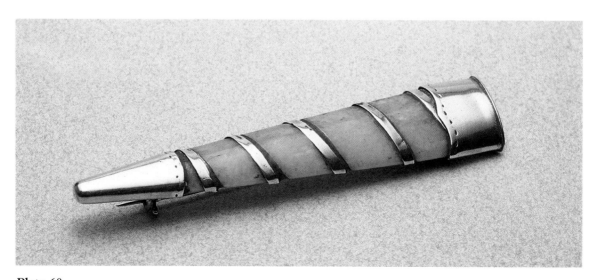

Plate 60
Silver knitting sheath c.1800. Amber mounted in silver, with pin fastener. 8.3cm (3⅜in) long.

PRIVATE COLLECTION

The two small knitting sheaths in Plate 63 are decorated with a beautiful design regularly encountered on needlework tools in the nineteenth century, and typical for Friesland. A maker's mark frequently found on sewing and knitting tools from this area is that of the silversmith Reitsma. It would appear that this too was a family business as, although these two sheaths are similar in design, the marks tell us that one was made by Reitsma Senior, and the other considerably later by Reitsma Junior.

Plate 61
Silver knitting sheath with hook. c.1845. Assay mark: 1814–1905. Maker: Andries Jzn. Graves Kooiman, Schoonhoven (1838–79). 14.5cm (5¾in) long.
KAY SULLIVAN ANTIQUES

Plate 62
Silver knitting sheath with hook on back, c.1860–70. Biedermeier style, engraved with flowers and letters 'LMV'. Maker: Jan Schijfsma, Woudsend/Sneek (1844–98). 13.8cm (5½in) long.
PRIVATE COLLECTION

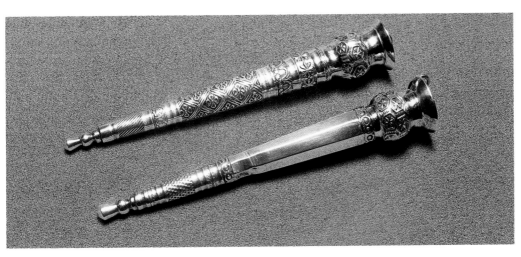

Plate 63
Top: Small silver sheath with intricate decoration, c.1840. Assay mark: 1814–1905. Maker: S.T. Reitsma Sr. Lemmer/Sneek (1814–57). 8.5cm (3⅜in) long.
Bottom: Small silver sheath with decorated top and bottom and octagonal middle section, c.1860. Assay mark: 1814–1905. Maker: S.T. Reitsma Jr. Heerenveen/Sneek (1859–92). 8.7cm (3½in) long.
KAY SULLIVAN ANTIQUES

Knitting needle guards

Up to this point, this chapter has been dedicated entirely to the knitting sheath, but how were knitting needles stored? This has been an age-old problem, as Gertrude Whiting so colourfully describes in her book *Tools and Toys of Stitchery*, published in 1928:

> *Knitting-needles are 'pesky critters' to carry around – they bore through pockets and push through bags, they fall through cracks and catch and bend. They are dangerous too. Our cook, for off moments, kept knitting in her pocket. One morning, Mother was out marketing and the maid thrust her hand into her long pocket to pull out the ever-present knitting. A steel needle ran right through the palm of her hand.*

She goes on to warn knitters that they should invest in 'needle ends' or at least use corks as protectors. At the beginning of the nineteenth century the problem was solved as the ungainly corks were replaced by handsome knitting needle guards. These were especially useful when the knitting was laid aside, as the needles and the knitting could be placed within the guards, holding the stitches securely in place.

Although knitting needle guards were made in different materials, the vast majority of those made in Holland were of gold or silver. A simple and effective method of storing needles is illustrated in Plate 64, showing guards of gold. The guards in this picture are joined together in the middle by ribbon, gathered up to cover a brass spiral. This can then be stretched to allow the distance between the guards to be extended to the desired length, to fit the needles. Plate 65 conveniently illustrates this technique, as the ribbon has come loose from its brass spiral. Other gold and silver guards from the

Plate 64
14ct. gold knitting needle guards. Amsterdam, c.1855.
Maker: Pieter Cuypers, Amsterdam (1849-52).

KAY SULLIVAN ANTIQUES

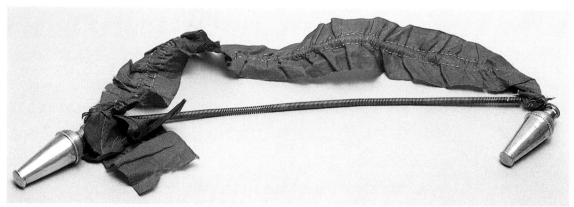

Plate 65
Silver knitting needle guards, c.1820-40 Maker: Pieter Loopuyt, Hoorn (1820-53). 3.2cm (1¼in) long.

PRIVATE COLLECTION

second half of the nineteenth century constructed in this way are shown in Plates 66-69.

It was the tradition in many areas of Holland to recognise a period of mourning by wearing black clothing for a certain length of time following a death. The tradition was strictly adhered to, as the rare mother-of-pearl knitting needle guards on a black ribbon in Plate 69 illustrate. Knitting needle guards were also joined together by a cord, chain or later in the nineteenth century with elastic.

Plate 66
14ct. gold octagonal/conical-shaped knitting guards, c.1860-70. Maker: Nicolaas Hermanus van Veen, Amsterdam (1844–82). 3.7cm (1½in) long.
PRIVATE COLLECTION

Plate 67
Vase-shaped silver knitting guards, c.1870. Maker: Pieter Oostrom, Schoonhoven (1861–82). 4.2cm (1¹¹⁄₁₆in) long.
PRIVATE COLLECTION

Plate 68
Baluster-shaped 14ct. gold knitting guards, c.1860-70. Maker: Nicolaas Hermanus van Veen, Amsterdam (1844–82). 4.5cm (1¾in) long.
KAY SULLIVAN ANTIQUES

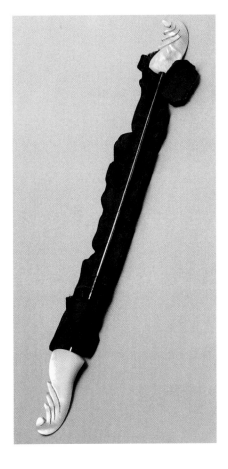

Plate 69
Rare mother-of-pearl knitting guards with black mourning ribbon, c.1850-80. 4.2cm (1¹¹⁄₁₆in) long.
PRIVATE COLLECTION

179

Plate 70
Left: Silver-plated knitting needle guards shaped as slippers, c.1920. Right: Silver guards shaped as boots, c.1840. Maker: A. Meurs, Rotterdam (1831-?).

KAY SULLIVAN ANTIQUES

Plate 71
Silver knitting needle guards shaped as shoes, c.1890. Assay mark: 1814-1905.

KAY SULLIVAN ANTIQUES

Plate 72
Silver knitting needle guards shaped as clogs, c.1870-90. Assay mark: 1814-1905. Tax mark: 1864-1905.

KAY SULIVAN ANTIQUES

Plate 73
Silver knitting needle guards shaped as keys, c.1840-60. Assay mark: 1814-1905.

KAY SULLIVAN ANTIQUES

Distinctive and figural knitting needle guards

With the introduction of knitting needle guards, gold and silversmiths allowed their fantasies to roam. Gold and silver were used in many themes to make their products attractive. Mostly joined by a silver or gold chain, shoes, boots and slippers were amongst the most popular novelties (Plates 70-72). Plate 73 shows a pair of silver guards shaped as keys, but considerably more rare are the guards in the shape of dogs' heads in Plate 74.

An exceptional pair of gold guards, shaped as gargoyles of a mythological water snake or dragon, is illustrated in Plate 75. These guards, made in Groningen, hang on their original gold chain, indicating that they were to be worn as a necklace. This beautiful piece of craftsmanship was obviously owned by someone from the affluent elite who did not need to knit.

Plate 74
Silver knitting needle guards shaped as dogs' heads (see detail).
Maker: Johannes Wendels, Schoonhoven (1879-1908), c.1880-90.
4.9cm (2in) long.

Plate 75
18ct. gold knitting needle guards on 18ct. gold chain. Shaped as gargoyles of a mythological water
snake or dragon (see detail). Willem Schutter, Groningen, c.1841-49. 3.4cm (1⅜in) long.

Plate 76
Baluster-shaped knitting needle guards with stippled pattern,
c.1860-80. Assay mark: 1814-1905.

Plate 77
Baluster-shaped knitting needle guards with stippled pattern, c.1880. Assay
mark 1814-1905.

Plate 78
Silver knitting needle guards with panelled, stippled pattern,
c.1840-60. Assay mark: 1814-1905.

KAY SULLIVAN ANTIQUES

Plate 79
Silver knitting needle guards with stars and French lilies, c.1840. Maker: S.T.
Reitsma, Lemmer/Sneek (1814-57).

KAY SULLIVAN ANTIQUES

Plate 81
Vase-shaped silver knitting needle guards, c.1880. Maker's mark
indistinct. Assay mark: 1814-1905 plus weight mark 1865-1906

KAY SULLIVAN ANTIQUES

Plate 80
Vase-shaped silver knitting needle guards, c.1850-70. Maker's
mark indistinct. Assay mark: 1814-1905.

KAY SULLIVAN ANTIQUES

Plate 82
Baluster-shaped silver knitting needle guards, c.1840-50.
Maker's mark indistinct. Assay mark: 1814-1905.

KAY SULLIVAN ANTIQUES

Plate 83
Six-sided baluster-shaped silver knitting needle guards with Biedermeier decoration,
c.1870-80. Maker: Jan Petrus Sperna Weiland, Schoonhoven (1831-83).

KAY SULLIVAN ANTIQUES

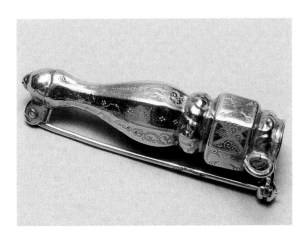

Plate 84
14ct. gold knitting needle guard with pin to attach to
bodice, c.1860. Maker: P.A. Zonne, Gouda (c.1855-?).

KAY SULLIVAN ANTIQUES

Plate 85
Silver acorn-shaped knitting needle guards, c.1850.
Assay mark: 1814-1905.

KAY SULLIVAN ANTIQUES

Guards were made in many different distinctive shapes and with beautifully engraved designs (Plates 76-85). Maker's marks on small objects such as sewing tools are rarely clear, if present at all. Easy to identify is the assay mark demanded by law. It will be noticed that almost all items bear this mark. A stippled pattern, made up of tiny dots engraved into patterns, is a very recognisable design on silver sewing items made in Holland.

A more sophisticated storage case looks rather like an elongated needle case. A commonly used style with ribbed design is typical for needle cases and other sewing tools made in the first half of the nineteenth century (Plate 86). Such a knitting needle case has a slit down the middle through which to hang the knitting in progress. One end of the case can be removed, to slide in the needles with the knitting, as Plate 87 demonstrates.

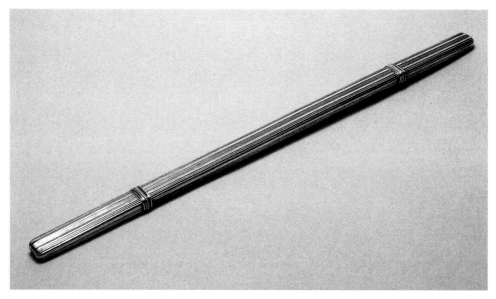

Plate 86a
Silver knitting needle case with ribbed design, c.1820-30. Maker: Christiaan Straater, Amsterdam (1816-46).
KAY SULLIVAN ANTIQUES

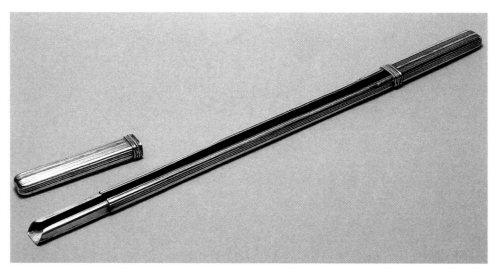

Plate 86b
Needle case shown with end removed.

Plate 87a
Knitting needle case with removable end for sliding in needles and knitting.

Plate 87b
Knitting needle case in use as storage case.

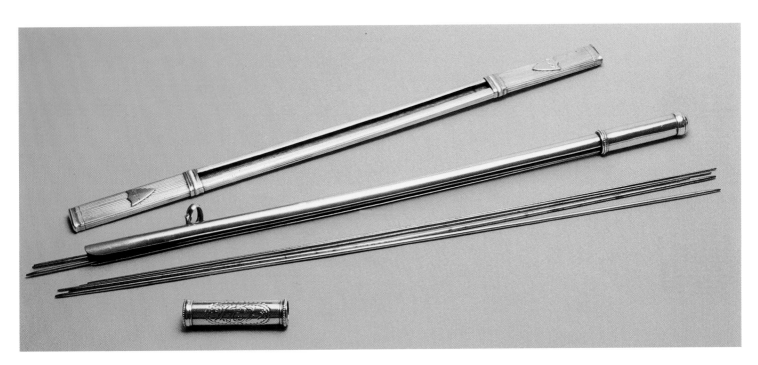

Plate 88a
Top: Silver knitting needle case with two shields, one engraved 'GdV' and dated 1868. Maker's mark indistinct. 24.6cm (9⅝in) long.
Bottom: Silver knitting needle storage case-cum-sheath, engraved monogram 'AM' (see detail below), c.1790. Unmarked. 27.3cm (10⅞in) long.

Plate 88b
Top of case, with engraved monogram. It can be used as a knitting sheath when in place.

185

Plate 88 shows two storage cases for knitting. The ribbed case at the top is similar to that shown in Plates 86 and 87, with the addition of a shield on both ends as decoration. One of the shields bears the monogram 'GdV' and is engraved 1868. A rare late eighteenth century knitting needle case is seen at the bottom of this picture. The case can be used to store needles and knitting as previously illustrated, but this one has an additional function, and can also be used as a knitting sheath. The removable end has a hole for the knitting needle. Another combined silver knitting needle case and sheath is pictured in Plate 89.

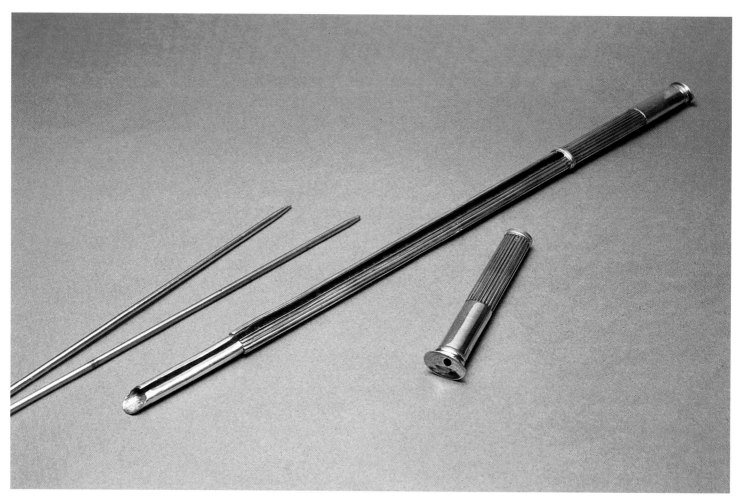

Plate 89
Silver knitting needle case and knitting sheath c.1820. Ribbed design with plain ends. Removable end with hole for needle. Assay mark: 1814-1905.

KAY SULLIVAN ANTIQUES

Knitters' chatelaines

The knitter's chatelaine was a handy accessory and often combined a number of functions. Although our German neighbours made chatelaines for knitters with many imaginative decorations, those made in Holland seem to have been limited to the shape of a key (Plate 90). This chatelaine, made in Amsterdam, has a hole in the key end to enable it to be used as a sheath whilst knitting, at the same time hanging the ball of wool on the hook suspended from the chain. The work-in-progress can be stored when not knitting by extending the chain to fit the length of the needles. Another example (Plate 91) can also be pinned to the clothing and has a hole in the bottom to use as a sheath and a chain for extension when storing the knitting.

Plate 90b
Detail, seen hanging from the waistband.

Plate 90a
Knitter's chatelaine with chain and hook on which to hang wool. Can also be used as knitting sheath. Amsterdam, c.1840. Maker: Pierre Louis Uriot (1812-62).

KAY SULLIVAN ANTIQUES

Plate 91
Knitter's silver chatelaine shaped as a key. First half 19th century. Maker unknown.

MUSEUM BOYMANS VAN BEUNINGEN, ROTTERDAM

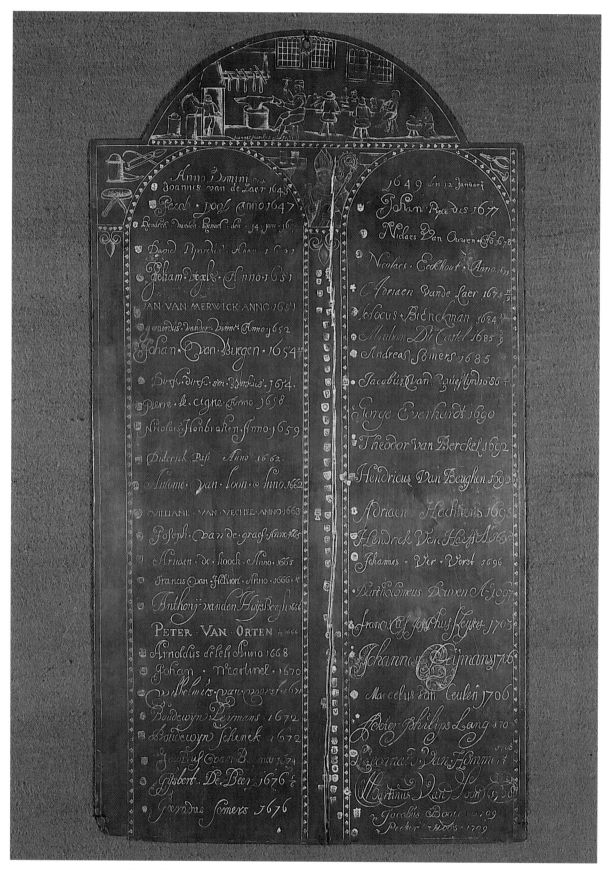

Copper marking plate of the Guild of Gold and Silversmiths, 's-Hertogenbosch, Joannes Matthiae, 1649.

CHAPTER 11

Marks on Gold and Silver Needlework Tools

Holland

The marking of gold and silver in Holland, as laid down in ordinances and laws, spans a long period of time. It seems to have started in 1382 and is still in legal practice today. In that period, the territory now referred to as 'The Kingdom of The Netherlands' was subjected to influences of mighty neighbouring rulers, such as Burgundy, Hapsburg and the Holy Roman Empire, and around 1800 became supervised by France. In 1814, Holland became an independent Kingdom, reuniting the seventeen provinces of the Northern and Southern Netherlands. This was not to last long. In 1830 the Southern Netherlands proclaimed itself an independent state called 'The Kingdom of Belgium'.

In the context of this book, 'made in Holland' refers to the present borders of The Kingdom of The Netherlands (see below).

1. Friesland
2. Groningen
3. Drente
4. Overijssel
5. Gelderland
6. Utrecht
7. Noord-Holland
8. Zuid-Holland
9. Zeeland
10. Noord-Brabant
11. Limburg

Through the ages, many thousands of different state marks, city marks, year letters, makers' marks and assay marks are deposited on objects of precious metal. This chapter deals only with the most common marks which might be found on gold and silver sewing tools made in Holland.

The Guilds

The marking of gold and silver, as it has been carried out in Holland to the present day, started in Burgundy where, in 1275, it was ordered that products would be stamped with the symbol of the town or city in which they were made. In the same decree, makers' marks were also mentioned.

The guilds played an important role in the marking of gold and silver. They were local interest organizations which, amongst other duties, kept control of the alloy standard and the quality of the articles produced by their members.

In 1355, the authorities of Montpellier in France dictated that articles of gold and silver must be stamped with a maker's mark, prior to presentation to the Assay Masters of the Guild for providing the city symbol. This practice seeped into Holland and in 1382 was also dictated in an ordinance in Utrecht. In the decree of Philip the Fair from 1502 it became mandatory to mark with both the maker's mark and the city mark within the territory of what was then Holland.

Date letters started to appear around 1450 and became normal practice for most of the towns and cities around 1600. These date letters often coincided with the annual appointment of a new assay master. This system of city marks, date letter and maker's mark remained in force until the French occupation in 1795. The Guilds were abandoned around this time and, with a few exceptions, their valuable records were destroyed.

In the eighteenth century there were approximately fifty-six cities and towns with guilds, each with their own city mark. A very useful book, *Goud-en Zilvermerken van Voet* by L.B. Gans, shows the marks and date letters of these guilds. An example is shown below.

City, state and date letter for the city of Amsterdam.
The three columns left were used for large work.
The right-hand column was used for small work.

Reproduced from
Goud-en Zilvermerken van Voet

Transition period from 1795

In 1795 French troops invaded Holland to support the Dutch revolutionary movement. The Batavian Republic was proclaimed, modelled on the French system. Although the guilds were officially abolished, they remained in existence as so called 'destroyed' guilds only, for the purpose of assaying and hallmarking precious metals. These were bewildering times, and this shows in the inconsistencies in marking during that period. The old city marks, date letters and makers' marks remained more or less valid during this period.

Kingdom of Holland 1806-1810

In 1806, Napoleon proclaimed the Batavian Republic a part of the French Empire and moreover, a Kingdom, with his youngest brother, Louis Napoleon, as its King. New hallmarking rules and marks were introduced in 1807.

Re-examination marks 1807

found on old assayed work which was on hand in Holland before the new rules of 1st July 1807. Used only for a few months.

Duty mark for gold and silver objects not stamped with crowned O on time.

Assay marks period 1807-1812

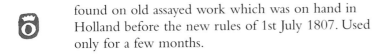

Gold of 22ct. (916/1000) or higher

Gold of 20ct. (750/1000) or higher

Gold of 18ct. (750/1000) or higher

Silver of 1st fineness (934/1000)

Silver of 2nd fineness (833/1000)

Small gold work 22ct.

Small gold work 20ct.

Small gold work 18ct.

Date letters 1807-1812

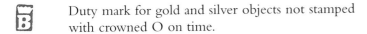

7th October 1807 – 18th March 1809

18th March 1809 – 21st December 1809

21st December 1809 – 17th December 1810

17th December 1810 – 1st March 1812

Assay Offices 1807-1812

There were thirty-seven Assay Offices operative in Holland. Needlework tools, being generally small objects, are hardly ever marked with the Assay Office mark. A few examples are shown here.

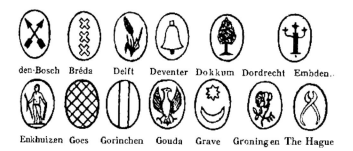

Makers' Marks 1807-1812

All old makers' marks became extinct and new makers' marks were introduced. W. Koonings lists 1051 makers' marks in his book, *De Keuring van Goud en Zilver tijdens het Koninkrijk Holland.*

The French period 1810-1813

To prevent a repeat of the unsuccessful English invasion of Zeeland and the annoyance of his brother Louis' independent actions, Emperor Napoleon decided to annex the Kingdom as a department of France. In phases the French marking system for provinces was enforced between the middle of 1811 and March 1812 and makers' marks also had to be placed in a 'lozenge'. The French marking system is detailed in the books by Tardy.

1809-1814
large work

1809-1814
small work

These two French marks are sometimes found on objects bearing the older marks of the guilds, duty marks or hallmarks of the 1807-12 period. In France they were meant for objects of foreign origin, but in Holland they were used as a tax-free census mark.

Kingdom of the Netherlands 1814 – present

The defeat of Napoleon by a European Coalition at Leipzig in 1813 signalled the retreat of French troops from Dutch soil. On 2nd December 1813, Willem I was inaugurated as King of the Netherlands. New hallmark punches came into use.

Assay marks

There are different assay marks for large and small sized work. Knitting baskets, spool knaves and chatelaines are generally classed as large or medium sized work. Other sewing tools come under the category of small sized work.

Assay marks for large-sized work

22ct.gold	20ct.gold	18ct.gold	Silver	Silver
916/1000	833/1000	750/1000	1st fineness	2nd fineness
1814-1953	1814-1953	1814-1953	1814-1953	1814-1953

In 1853, the gold standard of fineness for 14 carat was introduced.

Gold 14ct.   Gold 14ct.
583/1000   583/1000
1853-1905   1906-1953

Gold 20ct.	Gold 18ct.	Gold 14ct.	Silver 1st fineness	Silver 2nd fineness
833/1000	750/1000	585/1000	925/1000	834/1000
1953-present	1953-present	1953-present	1953-present	1953-present

Typical Assay Office marks

Gold	Silver	Gold	Silver
1814-1905	1814-1905	1906-present	1906-present

C=office The Hague   K=office Bois-Le-Duc

Large-sized work should always be punched with four marks:
– assay mark as above
– assay office mark as above
– date letter
– maker's mark

Assay marks for small-sized work

Small-sized work is not punched with office mark and date letter, but with assay mark and maker's mark only.

Gold	Silver	Gold
18ct.	minimum	18ct.
750/1000	833/1000	750/1000
1814-1905	1814-1905	1814-1865

The mark, above far right, was punched on articles with appendices which made it impossible to punch each individual part, such as chains.

Gold	Gold	Silver
18ct.	14ct.	minimum
750/1000	583/1000	833/1000
1906-1953	1906-1953	1906-1953

Gold 18ct.	Gold 14ct.	Silver	Silver	Gold 20ct.	Silver
750/1000	585/1000	835/1000	800/1000	833/1000	925/1000
1953–present	1953–present	1953–present	1953–present	1955–present	1955–present

Special marks, Duty marks, Import marks

Duty marks for gold and silver objects of Dutch origin of which the fineness is not guaranteed.

1853–1859   1859–1893   1893–1905   1906–1953

Duty marks for imported, unmarked or invalid marked objects of foreign and national origin. Marks do not give any guarantee of standard of fineness. Except for the flowered V (1814–31), objects with these marks are generally not considered to be of Dutch origin.

1814–1893   1814–1831   1831–1893
large work   small work   small work

1893–1905   1893–1905   1906–1953
large work   small work   large and small work

Duty marks for old gold and silver objects of national origin, returned to the trade.

 1853–1927

 1865–1905

Weight indication stamps can contain a number in the cartouche from 1 to 20. Multiply the number by five to obtain gross weight in grams. Mark must always occur with hallmarks or duty marks.

 1906–present

Date letters

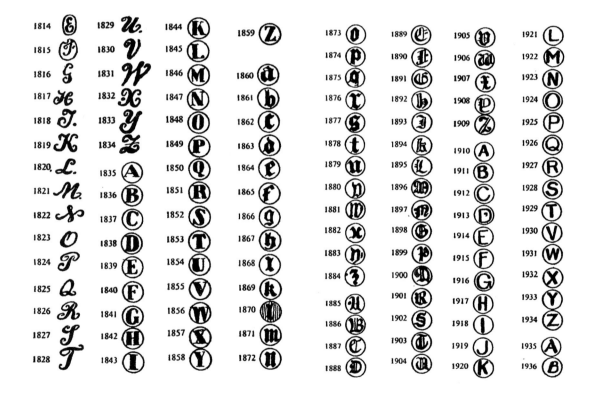

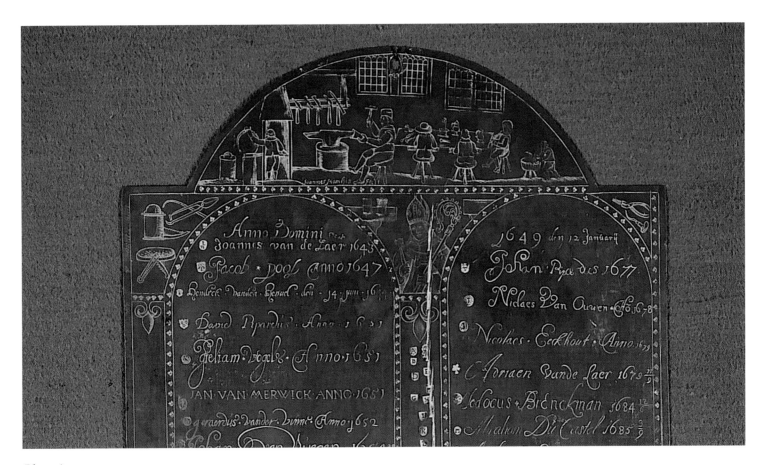

Plate 1

Top section of marking plate used in 's-Hertogenbosch between 1643 and 1709, showing the interior of a master silversmith's workshop with five men or apprentices. In the middle St. Eloy (Eligius) is portrayed in full Bishop's robes, with a chasing hammer in his right hand. Silversmiths' tools are pictured in the corners. In the right and left columns are the marks and names of the silversmiths, together with the year of deposit. In the small middle column are the year letters and city marks, the first one at the top being an A for 1652/53 and the crowned forest tree.

Makers and their marks

Karel Citroen brought together in his book, *Dutch Goldsmiths' and Silversmiths' Marks and Names prior to 1812*, a total of 10,500 names of craftsmen with and without attributed marks. Casper van Dongen's book, *Netherlands Responsibility Marks since 1797* lists more than 20,000 marks of other makers, assayers and importers.

In the listing of makers' marks on needlework tools in this section, reference was gratefully made to the works of Voet, Citroen, Koonings and van Dongen. Since a number of books are unobtainable for the non-specialist collector, it was not possible to merely refer to the identification numbers in the reference books. Gold and silver needlework tools have tiny marks and have generally had to contend with a good deal of handling. Therefore, the marks are often rubbed and unsuitable for photographic reproduction. The makers' marks listed in this chapter are limited to those on items pictured in this book, together with a number of marks on objects from the author's private collection.

Makers' marks

Anderlee, Josephus Servatius
Amsterdam.

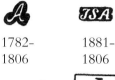

| 1782–1806 | 1881–1806 | 1882–1806 |

| 1807–1812 | 1818–1818 | 1812–1818 |

Born 1755, died 1818, active 1782-1818.
Known to have made: bag hooks, scissors.
Illustration: Plate 6-25.

Arnoldi, Jacob Daniel and Wielick, Johannes Wilhelmus
(Arnoldi & Wielick), Amsterdam.

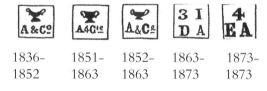

| 1836–1852 | 1851–1863 | 1852–1863 | 1863–1873 | 1873–1873 |

Arnoldi born 1806, died 1873, active 1836-73.
Between 1836 and 1863 he was in partnership
with Wielick, who then left the company.
Arnoldi continued alone until 1873.
Known to have made: thread tub.
Illustration: Plate 8-20.

Bergh, Jan Johannes Jr. van den
Schoonhoven.

| 1807–1810 | 1817–1834 | 1830–1836 | 1834–1837 | 1836–1837 |

| 1837–1853 | 1837–1853 | 1837–1853 |

Born 1771, died ?, active 1807-10 and 1817-53.
Between 1810 and 1817 stopped temporarily
as workmaster.
Known to have made: thread holder.
Illustration: Plate 8-26.

Beuningen, Jan van
Amsterdam.

    1701– after 1754

Born 1679, died after 1754, active 1701 –
after 1754.
Known to have made: chatelaine hook.
Illustration: Plate 2-11.

Boltjes, Jacob
Leeuwarden.

    1760-1783

Baptized 1731, died 1783, active 1760-83.
Known to have made: bag hook, vinaigrette
on chatelaine.
Illustration: Plate 2-21a.

Borduur, Jan
Amsterdam.

    1731-1766

Born 1698, died 1766, active 1731-66.
Known to have made: toys, scissors, spool knave.
Illustration: Plate 6-12, 9-1.

Bormeester, Cornelis
Amsterdam.

1730-1785   1730-1785   1730-1785

Born 1708, died 1785, active 1730-85.
Known to have made: toys, scissors.
Illustration: Plate 6-8.

Breda, Jan
Amsterdam.

  1688-1725

Born 1665, died 1725, active 1688-1725.
Known to have made: cast silver thimble,
miniature pin tray.
Illustration: Plate 3-13/2.

Brouwer, Volkert

Kampen, Zwolle, Deventer.

1827- 1865	1828- 1865	1828- 1865	1838- 1865	1848- 1865

Born 1801, died 1865, active between 1827-65.
Known to have made: knitting basket.

Cabboes, Widow Johan Coenraad Gottfried

Leeuwarden.

 1839-1841

Active 1839-41.
Widow of Johan Coenraad Gottfried
Cabboes (1812-1839).
Known to have made: sewing barrel, thread
winder.

Canté, Cornelis Balthus Hermanus

Amsterdam.

1837- 1852	1837- 1852	1852- 1870

Born 1810, died 1877, active alone 1852-70.
Between 1837-52 in partnership with his
brother-in-law Louis Frederik Schmidt
(Schmidt & Canté).
Known to have made: thimbles, small gold
sewing tools.
Illustration: Plate 1-25a, 3-61.

Croix, Pieter du

Leiden.

1835- 1864	1835- 1864

Active 1835-64.
Known to have made: bodkin case, bodkin.
Illustration: Plate 4-51.

Cuypers, Pieter

Amsterdam.

 1849-1852

Active 1849-52.
Known to have made: knitting needle guards.
Illustration: Plate 10-64.

Dam Kooyman, Cornelis van

Schoonhoven.

1812- 1816	1816- 1834	1816?- 1837?	1830 1834

1834- 1837	1834- 1837	1837- 1862

Active 1812-62.
Known to have made: thimbles, scissors.

Dauw, Hendrik

Leeuwarden.

1764-1807

Born 1734, died before 1818, active
1764-1807.
Known to have made: knitting sheath, bag
hook.
Illustration: Plate 4-38.

Denderen, Jan Hendrik van

Wildervank.

 1878-1891

Active 1878-91.
Known to have made: thimble.
Illustration: Plate 3-73.

Duncan, J.A.
's-Hertogenbosch.

| 1815-1821 | 1815-1821 | 1817-1821 |

| 1817-1821 | 1821-1853 | 1821-1853 |

Active 1815-53.
Known to have made: thread basket.
Illustration: Plate 8-13.

Dussen, Gerrit van der
Schoonhoven.

| 1867-1912 | 1867-1912 | 1879-1912 |

Active 1866-1912.
In the period October 1866-August 1867
he worked with maker's mark of
G. Kuylenburg.
Known to have made: needle case, bodkin.
Illustration: Plate 4-49, 5-31.

Eersten, Hendrik Theodorus van den and
Hofmeijer, Dirk Carl
(van den Eersten Hofmeijer)
Amsterdam.

| 1867-1893 | 1893-1906 | 1906-1920 |

van den Eersten: born 1836, died 1926.
Hofmeijer: born 1831, died 1894.
Association active 1867-1920.
Company remained in existence under the
same name until 1955.
Known to have made: sewing sets.
Illustration: Plate 1-29, 1-30.

Egmond, Christiaan van
Amsterdam.

 1862-1869

Active 1862-69.
Known to have made: thimble.
Illustration: Plate 3-64.

Feber, Daniel la
Amsterdam.

 1780-1804

Born 1741, died after 1804.
Active 1780-after 1804.
Known to have made: sewing barrel,
miniature spool knave.
Illustration: Plate 9-11, 9-12.

Feenstra, Rudulphus
Sneek.

| 1807-1811 | 1812-1815 | 1815-1834 |

| 1822-1845 | 1829-1835 | 1835-1845 |

Born 1783, active 1810-45.
Known to have made: knitting sheath,
pincushion.
Illustration: Plate 10-52.

Fennema, Jan Piers
Bolsward.

| 1827-1837 | 1837-1848 |

Active 1827-48.
Known to have made: spool knave.
Illustration: Plate 9-25.

Fortman, Jacobus
The Hague.

1773-   1807-
1806   c.1810

Active 1773 - after 1807/before 1812.
He was assay master between 1792 and 1798.
Known to have made: spool knave.
Illustration: Plate 9-15.

Gaillard, Johannes
Schoonhoven.

1852-   1863-   1883-
1863   1883   1910

Active 1852-1910.
Worked with W. Littel (1848-49) and E. van
Ewyck (1849-52) before starting his own
business.
Known to have made: needle case.
Illustration: 4-48.

Gastmans, Johannes
Amsterdam.

                1717-1774

Born 1696, died 1774, active 1717-74.
Known to have made: vinaigrettes, thimble
house, needle case.
Illustration: Plate 3-20.

Geelen Cz., widow Jacobus van
(Kuijlenburg, Johanna Hendrika)

                1889-1902

Active 1889-1902.
Widow of Jacobus Cornelis (1868-89).
Known to have made: thread holder.
Illustration: Plate 8-28.

Gelderen, Laurens van
Schoonhoven.

1837-   1861-
1873   1873

Active 1837-73.
Known to have made: thimble, scissors.
Illustration: Plates 6-15, 6-29.

Gelderen, Pieter van
Ameide/Schoonhoven.

1819-   1821-   1821-   1834-
1821   1834   1834   1837

1834-   1837-   1837-
1836   1842   1842

Active 1819-42.
Started in 1781 as apprentice to his father,
Jan (1738-1794).
Known to have made: scissors, thread basket.
Illustration: Plates 2-20a, 6-33, 8-21.

Geyskes, Pieter
Schoonhoven.

1788-   1807-   1812-   1816-   1816-
1806   1812   1816   1832   1832

Active 1788-1832.
Known to have made: needle case.
Illustration: Plate 4-44.

Gillis, Bernardus

's-Hertogenbosch.

| 1820-1821 | 1821-1833 | 1822-1830 | 1830-1833 |

Active 1820-33.
Known to have made: thimble.
Illustration: Plate 3-39.

Gillis, Widow Bernardus

's-Hertogenbosch.

| 1833-1834 | 1833-1859 | 1834-1859 | 1840-1859 |

Active 1833-59.
Carried on the business after her husband's death. The company continued after 1859 under Antonius van Grinsven until 1872.
Known to have made: thimbles, sewing sets, needle case, thread basket.
Illustration: Plates 1-22, 3-57, 4-56, 8-19.

Goedhart, Dirk

Amsterdam.

| 1782-1806 | 1807-1812 | 1812-1816 |

Born 1755, died after 1816, active 1782-1816.
Known to have made: needle case, thimble holder.
Illustration: Plates 2-21a, 4-34.

Gonzal, Salomon

Amsterdam.

| 1776-1806 | 1807-1812 |

Born 1751, died 1844, active 1776-1812.
Known to have made: spool knave.

Grauhart, Hendrik

Amsterdam.

   1683-1732

Born 1661, died 1732, active 1683-1732.
Known to have made: thimble house, viniagrettes.
Illustration: 3-19.

Graves Kooiman, Andries Jzn.

Schoonhoven.

   1838-1879

Born 1811, died 1879, active 1838-79.
Took over his father-in-law's business (Arie Mopman, active 1819-38). His widow continued in 1879 and her son, Adrianus Graves Kooiman, took over until 1911.
Known to have made: knitting sheath, stiletto, finger guard, needle case.
Illustration: Plates 4-45, 4-18, 4-44, 10-61.

Greup, Dirk Hendrik

Schoonhoven.

| 1815-1866 | 1834-1837 | 1837-1837 | 1837-1864 | 1837-1864 |

Active 1828-64.
Father of Gerrit Greup who took over the business in 1864 and continued until 1915.
Known to have made: thimble, needle case, sewing set.
Illustration: Plate 3-45, 4-46.

Greup, Gerrit

Schoonhoven.

| 1864-1888 | 1864-1888 | 1888-1915 |

Active 1864-1915.
Son of Dirk Hendrik Greup (1828-1864).
Known to have made: thread winder, thimble.

Groen, Eva
Amsterdam.

 c.1892–1895

Active c.1892–95.
Known to have made: thimble.
Illustration: Plate 3-71.

Halteren, Wed.Hermanus Jacobus van
Schoonhoven.

  1863–1895

Active 1863–95.
Widow of Hermanus Jacobus van Halteren (1832–1863).
Her son, Johannes, took over the business in 1895 and continued until 1908.
Known to have made: boxes, needlecase, thimble.
Illustration: Plate 1-23, 4-53.

Ham, Carolus Wilhelmus ten
Amsterdam.

  1743–1793

Born 1717, died 1793, active 1743–93.
Known to have made: needle case, toys.
Illustration: Plate 4-30, 4-33.

Hasselbeek, Pieter
The Hague/Middelburg.

  1712–1717

Active: 1712–17.
Known to have made: needlecase.
Illustration: Plate 4-27.

Heijema, Rinse
Sneek.

 1820–1833

Active 1820–33.
Known to have made: scissors.

Hicht, Thomas Sibrand
Dokkum.

 1675–1719

Born 1650, died 1719, active 1675–1719.
He was also the Mayor of Dokkum.
Known to have made: pin trays, chatelaine girdle.
Illustration: Plate 2-3a.

Hoek, Cornelis van
Amsterdam.

1786–   1807–   1812–   1812–
1806   1812   1813   1813

Born 1753, died 1813, active 1786–1813.
His son, Johannes van Hoek (1813–47), continued with the business in 1813.
Known to have made: knitting sheath, needle cases.
Illustration: Plate 4-32.

Hoep, Dirk
Hoorn.

Rose

1768–   1807–   1812–
1806   1812   1813

Born 1734, died 1813, active 1768–1813.
Known to have made: needle case, knitting sheath.
Illustration: Plate 4-31.

Hoop, Anthony de
Amsterdam.

 1767–1785

Born 1742, died 1785, active 1767–85.
Son of Jan de Hoop (1731–69).
Known to have made: needle case.
Illustration: Plate 2-13.

Hoop, Jan de
Amsterdam.

 1731-1769

Born 1704, died 1769, active 1731-69.
Father of Anthony de Hoop (1767-85).
Known to have made: thimble holder,
chatelaine, toys.
Illustration: Plate 2-30.

Jansen, Wessel
Amsterdam.

 1642-1696

Active 1642-96.
Known to have made: toys.
Illustration: Plate 1-7a,b.

Joekes, Hendrik
Leeuwarden.

1790- 1807-
1806 1812

Active 1790-1811.
Known to have made: scissors.
Illustration: Plate 2-25.

Jong, Arie de
Schoonhoven.

1865- 1865-
1873 1873

Active 1865-73.
Later employed by D.H. Greup and in 1877
went to Rotterdam to become a pub keeper.
Known to have made: pin box.
Illustration: Plate 5-29.

Kalbfleisch, Adriaan Marinus
Vlissingen.

1834- 1834- 1840- 1862-
1867 1862 1867 1867

Active 1834-67.
Upon his death in 1867 the company
continued as Wed. Adriaan Marinus
Kalbfleisch & Zoon.
Known to have made: thread holder.
Illustration: Plate 8-25.

Kaldenbach, Herman
Hoorn.

1853-1862 1853-1862

Active 1853-62.
Known to have made: needle case.

Kassen, Jan van
Schoonhoven.

 1883-1885

Active 1883-85.
Known to have made: needle case.
Illustration: Plate 4-48.

Keijzer Leeflang, Cornelis de
Leiden.

1820- 1822- 1824- 1824- 1825-
1824 1824 1825 1825 1843

Active 1820-43.
Known to have made: thread basket.
Illustration: Plate 8-16.

Keizer, Pieter
Amsterdam.

 1850–1866

Active 1850-66.
Known to have made: scissors, thread winders.
Illustration: Plate 1-20, 8,34.

Kleinhout, Gerrit Hendriksz and Koene, Jan Jacob Eduard
Amsterdam.

 1842–1846

Active 1842-46.
Known to have made: knitting needle guards.
Illustration: Plate 8-13.

Kooiman, Adrianus G.
Schoonhoven.

1807– 1812– 1814– 1834–
1811 1814 1834 1837

Born 1780, died 1840, active 1807-37.
In 1808, Adrianus took over the tools of his father, Andries Graves Kooiman (1755-1809), and probably also the business. After his death his widow continued the business until 1860, whereafter son Jacob continued until 1893. He was followed by grandson Andries Cornelis until 1920 (he imported thimbles from Germany).
Known to have made: finger guard, pin box.
Illustration: Plate 3-51.

Kooiman, Andries Graves
Schoonhoven.

1777-1806 1777– 1777– 1777–
1808 1808 1808

Born 1755, died 1809, active 1777-1808.
In 1808 he turned his tools over to his son, Adrianus.
Known to have made: scissors.

Kooiman, Jacob A.G. Zn.
Schoonhoven.

1812– 1814– 1830– 1834– 1834–
1834 1834 1834 1837 1837

1837– 1837– 1837–
1853 1853 1853

Active 1812-53.
Son of Andries Graves (1755-1809).
Father of Andries Graves (1813-1896) and Willem Verhey (1819-1886).
Known to have made: bodkins.
Illustration: Plate 1-17.

Koster, Laurens
Rotterdam.

1807– 1807– 1807– 1812– 1815–
1811 1811 1811 1815 1828

Active 1796-1828.
Known to have made: thread basket.
Illustration: Plate 8-12.

Kouwenberg, C.
Breda.

1858– 1858–
1901 1901

Born 1829, died 1901, active 1858-1901.
Known to have made: scissors.
Illustration: Plate 6-17.

Kuilenburg, Pieter
Schoonhoven.

1818– 1830– 1831–
1831 1837 1834

1834– 1837– 1837–
1837 1857 1857

Active 1818–57.
Known to have made: finger guard, pin box/cushion.
Illustration: Plate 3-50, 5-17.

Kuipers, Albert H.
Workum.

1807– 1812– 1823–
1811 1823 1831

Born 1767, died 1831, active 1807–31.
Known to have made: chatelaine, thread winder.
Illustration: Plate 2-27.

Kuylenburg, Adrianus
Schoonhoven.

1784– 1812– 1816–
1812 1816 c.1831

Born 1760, died after 1835, active 1784–1831.
Known to have made: knitting sheath, thimble, needle case.

Kuylenburg, Gerrit
Schoonhoven.

1854– 1854– 1865– 1865–
1865 1865 1867 1871

Active 1854–75.
Known to have made: needle case.
Illustration: Plate 4-47.

Kuylenburg, Jan
Schoonhoven.

1816– 1834– 1837–
1834 1837 1844

Active 1816–44.
Known to have made: sewing ring.

Lameer, Gysbert
Schoonhoven.   1779–1811

Born 1755, died after 1811, active 1779–1809. In 1809 he possessed, together with Jacob Kooiman, a thimble machine for making the indentations.
Known to have made: needle case, thimbles.
Illustration: Plate 4-42.

Lameer, Jacobus Ferdinandus
Zwolle, Rotterdam, Groningen, Schoonhoven, Amsterdam.

1854– 1854– 1854– 1854–
1880 1880 1880 1880
22ct. 20ct. 18ct. 14ct.

1880– 1880– 1880– 1880–
1885 1885 1885 1885
22ct. 20ct. 18ct. 14ct.

Active as Assay Master 1849–85.
Mark found on: thimble.
Illustration: Plate 3-60.

Land, Hendrik
Amsterdam.

 1772-1801

Born 1746, died 1801, active 1772-1801.
Known to have made: spool knave.
Illustration: Plate 9-14.

Lazonder, Adrianus Haalbos
Schoonhoven.

| 1822-
1837 | 1830-
1837 | 1837-
1857 | 1837-
1857 |

Active 1822-57.
In 1857 his son, Jacobus Johannes Lazonder, took over the business because his father went to prison for speculation in assurance companies.

Lazonder Sr., Gerrit
Schoonhoven.

| 1796-
1811 | 1812-
1816 | 1816-
1824 |

Born 1770, died after 1837, active 1796-1824.
Assay master between 1807-12.
Known to have made: scissors.
Illustration: Plate 6-28.

Leersum, David van
Utrecht.

| 1814-
1826 | 1826-
1866 |

Active 1814-66.
Known to have made: thimble.

Leeuwen, Martinus van
Amsterdam.

| 1830-
1866 | 1830-
1866 |

Active 1830-66.
Between 1823 and 1830 in partnership with Kornelis van Zante.
Known to have made: needle case.
Illustration: Plate 4-52.

Lely, Gabynus van der
Leeuwarden.

 1731-1754

Active 1731-54.
Known to have made: bag mount.
Illustration: Plate 1-4.

Leuven Sr., Johannes van
Alkmaar.

| 1802-
1811 | 1812-
1816 | 1816-
1858 | 1820-
1858 | 1822-
1853 |

Active 1802-58.
In 1796 he was apprentice to his father, Jacob.
Known to have made: thread basket.
Illustration: Plate 8-17.

Lingenaar, Isaac
Amsterdam.

 1751-1802

Born 1722, died 1805, active 1751-1802.
Known to have made: knitting sheath, needle case, thimble house, vinaigrettes.
Illustration: Plate 3-21, 10-54.

Lintvelt, Hermanus
Amsterdam.

1797–   1797–   1812–
1811   1811   1816

1816–   1821–   1824–
1833   1833   1833

Born 1770, died 1848, active 1797-1833.
In 1833 he transferred the business to his son, Jan.
Known to have made: sewing clamp, thread baskets.
Illustration: Plate 5-21, 5-22.

Littel, Willem
Schoonhoven/Amsterdam.

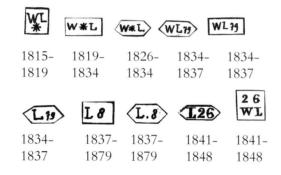

1815–   1819–   1826–   1834–   1834–
1819   1834   1834   1837   1837

1834–   1837–   1837–   1841–   1841–
1837   1879   1879   1848   1848

Active 1814-41 in Schoonhoven and 1841-48 in Amsterdam.
In 1861 he associated with Gilles Grevink to continue fabrication as W. Littel & Cie. until 1863. In 1864 he started up business again on his own, probably as salesman.
Known to have made: thimbles.
Illustration: Plate 3-41, 3-56.

Loopuijt, Pieter
Hoorn.

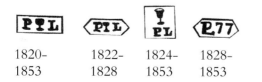

1820–   1822–   1824–   1828–
1853   1828   1853   1853

Active 1820-53.
Known to have made: knitting needle guards, tape measure.
Illustration: Plate 7-11.

Maarseveen Sr., Dirk van
Amsterdam.

   1816–1840

Active 1816-40.
Son of Joost van Maarseveen (1752-1825).
Known to have made: sewing clamp.
Illustration: 5-23.

Maarseveen, Petrus Franciscus van
Amsterdam.

1868–   1868–
1880   1880

Active 1868-80.
Known to have made: needle case.

Manen, Laurens van
Sneek.

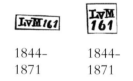

1844–   1844–
1871   1871

Active 1844-71.
Known to have made: scissors, spool knave.
Illustration: Plate 6-19, 9-26.

Massee, Jean Pierre
Nieuwer Amstel/Amsterdam.

1809–   1812–   1816–
1811   1816   1822

1816–   1822–   1844–
1822   1832   1846

Active 1809-46.
From 1832 to 1844 he served in the Army.
Known to have made: thread basket.
Illustration: Plate 8-7.

Meurs, A.

Rotterdam.

 1831-?

Active 1831-?
Known to have made: knitting needle guards.
Illustration: Plate 10-70.

Minje, Jan le

Haarlem.

 1772-1812

Active 1772-1812.
Known to have made: spool knave.

Mirani, J.

Rotterdam

c.1834-? c.1834-?
Active c. 1834-?
Known to have made: thimble.
Illustration: Plate 3-69.

Monteban, Cornelis

Schoonhoven.

1843- c.1843- 1846- 1874?-
1880 c.1880 1874? 1880

Active 1843-80.
Known to have made: thimble, finger guard, knitting sheath.
Illustration: Plate 3-49, 10-59.

Morellon La Cave, Frans

Amsterdam.

All marks used 1753-86.
Born 1726, died 1786, active 1753-86.
Known to have made: scissors, thimble, parts for child's chatelaine.
Illustration: Plate 2-14, 3-15.

Nez, Jean Louis Roch and Nez, Charles Julien

Amsterdam

1831- 1831- 1831-
1846 1846 1846

Active 1831-46.
Known to have made: thimble, thread basket, spool knave. Illustration: Plate 3-59, 8-10, 9-24.

Nieuwmeijer, J. and Schwab, J.W.

Amsterdam.

 1834-1875

Active 1834-75.
Known to have made: needle case.
Illustration: Plate 1-20.

Noorman, Wed. Hindrik

(Klaasje Teunisse Noorderwijk)
Nieuwe Pekela.

1831- 1831- 1831-
1832 1832 1832

Active 1831-32.
Her husband, Hendrik, was active 1815-31.
Known to have made: bodkin.
Illustration: Plate 4-7.

Oepkes Sr., Christoffel

Amsterdam.

1795- 1807- 1812- 1816-
1806 1812 1816 1837

1816- 1818- 1822-
1837 1822 1837

Born 1772, died 1837, active 1795-1837.
Known to have made: stiletto, sewing clamp with pincushion.

Oling, Lucas
Leeuwarden.

1779–1806

Born 1748, died 1806, active 1779–1806.
He was apprenticed to Hendrik Dauw.
Known to have made: gold bag mount and
hook, knitting basket.
Illustration: Plate 1-6.

Oosterwerf, Age
Sneek.

| 1774–1811 | 1812–1815 | 1815–1827 | 1815–1827 |

Born 1749, died 1826, active 1774–1827.
His son, Jacob Ages, continued with his father's
mark until 1827 when he obtained his own mark.
Known to have made: needle case, spool knave.
Illustration: Plate 9-22.

Oosterwerf, Jacob Ages
Sneek.

| 1827–1842 | 1827–1842 |

Active 1827-42.
Known to have made: knitting sheath.
Illustration: 10-49.

Oosterwout, Willem Lucas van
Amsterdam.

1805–1812

Born 1783, died 1849, active 1805-12.
Associated with his father, Jan van
Oosterwout (1753-1835).
Known to have made: thimble.

Oostrom Sr. Pieter
Schoonhoven.

1861–1882

Active 1861-82.
Due to insufficient work, he worked for
Jacob van Geelen between 1871 and 1874.
Later, he worked with his son-in-law, P. van Os.
Known to have made: knitting needle guards.
Illustration: Plate 10-67.

Oyen, Johannes van
Gouda.

Mark: Three onion bulbs in contour.

Active 1675-1725.
Known to have made: pin tray.
Illustration: Plate 5-6.

Pluut, Arie
Schoonhoven.

| 1865–1880 | 1865–1880 | 1865–1895 |
| 1865–1895 | 1865–1895 | 1880–1895 |

Active 1865-95.
After his death his widow (she was from the
Kooiman family) continued until 1896, after
which her sons, Jan and Frank, continued as
Fa. Wed.A. Pluut until 1926.
Known to have made: scissors.

Preyers, C.
Amsterdam.

| 1822–1834 | 1824–1834 |

Active 1822-34.
Known to have made: wax holder-pincushion.
Illustration: Plate 5-15.

Put, David de
Amsterdam.

                1725-1787

Born 1700, died 1787, active 1725-87.
Known to have made: scissors, spool knave.
Illustration: Plate 9-21.

Reitsma, H.
Sneek/Leeuwarden.

| 1862-
1879 | 1862-
1885 | 1879-
1885 |

Active 1862-85.
Known to have made: knitting sheath.
Illustration: Plate 10-41.

Reitsma Jr., S.T.
Heerenveen/Sneek.

| 1859-
1892 | 1859-
1892 |

Active 1859-92.
Known to have made: knitting needle guards, knitting sheath.
Illustration: 10-63.

Reitsma Sr., S.T.
Lemmer/Sneek.

| 1814-
1857 | 1823-
1847 |

Active 1814-57.
Known to have made: knitting sheath.
Illustration: Plate 10-63, 10-79.

Rembrants, Magdalena
Amsterdam.

                1753-1787

Born 1718, died 1787, active 1753-87.
She was the daughter of Johannes Rembrants who was a goldsmith.
Known to have made: toys and cast bag hooks.
Illustration: Plate 2-31.

Remmers, Hendrik
Amsterdam.

| 1806-
1811 | 1812-
1820 | 1820-
1830 | 1821-
1828 |

| 1822-
1826 | 1828-
1830 | 1830?-
1835? | 1830-
1847 |

Active 1806-47.
Son of Hermanus Remmers (1757-1826).
Known to have made: thread basket, tape measure.
Illustration: Plate 8-15.

Renkhoff, Johannes
Amsterdam.

                1824-1828

Active 1824-28.
Known to have made: wax holder.
Illustration: Plate 5-16.

Rethmeijer, Diederik Willem
Amsterdam.

| 1785-
1806 | 1807-
1812 | 1812-
1821 |

Born 1756, died 1821, active 1785-1821.
Known to have made: thread tub.

Riel, Hendrik Willem van
Arnhem/Schoonhoven/Amsterdam.

| 1837-
1854 | 1837-
1854 | 1854-
1880 22ct. |

| 1854-
1880
20ct. | 1854-
1880
18ct. | 1854-
1880
14ct. |

Active 1837-80.
He was not a silversmith.
His mark appears as assayer.
Illustration: Plate 1-20, 3-61, 3-62, 3-63.

Rietveld, Cornelis
Schoonhoven.

1865– 1865–
1912 1912

Active 1865–1912.
In 1912 he passed the business to his sons
who continued until 1920.
Known to have made: tambour hook.
Illustration: Plate 9-28, 10-58.

Rins, S.
Purmerend.

1896– 1896– c.1920–
1926 1914 1926

Active 1896–1926.
Known to have made: tambour hook.
Illustration: Plate 9-29.

Roelofse, Coenraad Roelof
Middelburg/Goes.

Mark:
cock to right
between two 'Rs'

1801– 1811– 1811– 1816–
1811 1816 1816 1840

1811– 1827– 1834–
1816 1840 1855

Active 1801–55.
Known to have made: bodkin.
Illustration: Plate 4-8.

Rond, Wed. Mensje
(born van Baaren)
Schoonhoven.

1860– 1860–
1863 1863

Active 1860–63.
Continued with the business of her husband,
Christiaan Albertus, who was active 1849–60.
She passed it on to her son, Christiaan Louis,
active until 1904.
Known to have made: bodkin.
Illustration: Plate 4-5.

Roos, Willem Johannes de
Dokkum.

 1763–1790

Active 1763–90.
Known to have made: scissors.

Rooseboom, Jan
Amsterdam.

1730– 1730–
1773 1773

Born 1698, died 1773, active 1730–73.
Known to have made: needle case, toys.

Rooswinkel, Albertus Antonius
Leeuwarden.

1837– 1841– 1841–
1868 1868 1868

Active 1837–68.
Known to have made: thread winder.
Illustration: Plate 8-32.

Rozendaal, Johan
Hoorn.

| 1833–1863 | 1833–1863 | 1853–1874 |

| 1853–1863 | 1863–1874 | 1868–1874 |

Active 1833–74.
Known to have made: finger guard.
Illustration: Plate 3-52.

Rutgers, Adam
Amsterdam.

                    1760–1792

Born 1744, died 1792, active 1760–92.
Known to have made: spool knave.
Illustration: Plate 9-8.

Salm, Pieter
Hoorn.

| 1850–1876 | 1869–1890 | 1869–1890 | 1876–1890 |

Active 1850–90.
Known to have made: thread holder.
Illustration: Plate 8-24.

Sandt, David van 't
Haarlem.

| 1779–c.1790 | c.1790–1811 | c.1790–1811 | 1812–1816 |

| 1816–1822 | 1822–1826 |

Active before 1779–1826.
Known to have made: thimble.
Illustration: Plate 3-37.

Schalkwijk, Jacobus
Rotterdam.

| 1818–1847 | 1818–1847 |

Active 1818–47.
Known to have made: thread basket.
Illustration: Plate 8-18.

Schijfsma, Jan
Woudsend/Sneek.

| 1843–1847 | 1844–1898 | 1844–1898 |

Active 1843–98.
Known to have made: knitting sheath.
Illustration: Plate 10-62.

Schijfsma Jz., Johannes
Woudsend.

| 1848–1902 | 1848–1902 |

Active 1848–1902.
Known to have made: scissors.
Illustration: Plate 6-20.

Schoorl, Gerardus
Zaandijk, Amsterdam/Haarlem.

| 1875–1914 | 1875–1914 |

Active 1875–1914.
Known to have made: thread tub.
Illustration: Plate 8-22.

Schrader, Jacobus
Gorkum.

                    1773–1812

Active 1773–1812.
Known to have made: spool knave.

Schutter, Willem
Groningen.

| 1815-1817 | 1817-1820 | 1817-1829 | 1820-1849 |

| 1822-1849 | 1829-1841 | 1841-1849 |

Active 1814-49.
The business was continued by his widow, Frouwke Brands, until 1854.
Known to have made: knitting needle guards.
Illustration: Plate 10-75.

Siedenburg I, Nicolaas
Amsterdam.

  1757-1802

Born 1739, died 1802, active 1757-1802.
Father of silversmiths Nicolaas (1768-1838) and Christoffel (1762-1807).
Known to have made: gold chatelaine.
Illustration: Plate 2-10.

Simonis, Jacobus
The Hague.

  1839-1844
Active 1839-44.
Known to have made: scissors.
Illustration: Plate 6-8.

Smets, Johannes Ferdinandus
Amsterdam.

| 1813-1816 | 1816-1820 | 1817-1828 |

| 1820-1846 | 1828-1846 |

Active 1813-46.
Known to have made: scissors.

Smits, Hendrik
Amsterdam.

| 1798-1811 | 1812-1817 | 1817-1836 | 1817-1836 |

Born 1772, died 1841, active 1798-1836.
He was between 1800 and 1825 one of the most important suppliers of Diemont retailers.
Known to have made: thread tub.
Illustration: Plate 8-11.

Somerwil, Pieter van
Amsterdam.

| 1833-1850 | 1833-1850 |

Active 1833-50.
Son of Johannes van Somerwil II.
Grandson of Pieter van Somerwil II.
Great-grandson of Johannes van Somerwil I.
Great-great-grandson of Pieter van Somerwil I.
Known to have made: bodkin.
Illustration: Plate 4-3.

Somerwil I, Johannes van
Amsterdam.

  1737-1764

Born 1715, died 1764, active 1737-64.
Father of Pieter van Somerwil II.
Son of Pieter van Somerwil I.
Known to have made: chatelaines, needle cases, hook, scent box and thimble holder for chatelaine.
Illustration: Plate 2-14.

Somerwil II, Johannes van
Amsterdam.

| 1786-1806 | 1807-1811 | 1812-1820 | 1820-1833 |

Born 1761, died 1833, active 1786-1833.
Great-grandson of Pieter van Somerwil I.
Father of Pieter van Somerwil.
Known to have made: stiletto.
Illustration: Plate 4-12/2.

Somerwil I, Pieter van
Amsterdam.

                1706-1753

Born 1686, died 1753, active 1706-53.
Father of Johannes van Somerwil I.
Grandfather of Pieter van Somerwil II.
Known to have made: doll's chatelaine, waist
plaque; specialist in toys.
Illustration : Plate 2-29, 2-30.

Sperna Weiland, Jan Petrus
Schoonhoven.

| 1831– | 1831– | 1837– |
| 1837 | 1837 | 1864 |

| 1837– | 1864– |
| 1883 | 1883 |

Active 1831-83.
Known to have made: knitting needle sheath.
Illustration: Plate 10-83.

Stavoren, Jan van
Amsterdam.

                1727-1750

Born 1689, died 1750, active 1727-50.
Known to have made: chatelaine scissors,
needle cases, thimble holder.
Illustration: Plate 2-11.

Straater, Christiaan
Amsterdam.

| 1816– | 1816– | 1827– |
| 1846 | 1846 | 1846 |

Active 1816-46.
Known to have made: needle cases, knitting
needle sheath.
Illustration: Plate 1-16a, 4-50, 10-86.

Straten, Gebr. van
Hoorn.

| 1885– | 1885– |
| 1891 | 1891 |

Active 1885-91.
Known to have made: thread holder.
Illustration: Plate 8-27.

Stuurman, Pieter
Alkmaar.

Mark: P S

Active 1786-1807.
Known to have made: chatelaine hook.
Illustration: Plate 2-32.

Swalue, Nicolaas
Leeuwarden.

| 1775– | c.1790– | 1807– |
| c.1790 | 1806 | 1811 |

Active 1775-1811.
He was Assay Master in 1795 and 1796.
Known to have made: gold bag mount and
hook, filigree needle case.
Illustration: Plate 1-5, 4-41.

Sylstra van der Lely, Frederik
Leeuwarden.

                1748-1788

Born 1723, died 1788, active 1748-88.
Known to have made: bag mount, hook.
Illustration: Plate 1-4.

Teunissen Sr., Andries
Schoonhoven.

| 1859– | 1862– |
| 1900 | 1900 |

Active 1859-99.
He was employed by C. van Gelderen.
After his death his son, Andries Jr., continued
with the business (active 1900-23).
Known to have made: tape measures.
Illustration: Plate 7-18, 7-19.

Tiedeman, Hendrik Jan,
Enkhuizen.

Mark: swan.

Active before 1745-73.
Known to have made: spool knave.
Illustration: Plate 9-4.

Uriot, Pierre Louis
Amsterdam.

1812-   1816-   1820-   1822-
1816   1862   1822   1862

Born 1785, died 1864, active 1812-62.
Father of Theodorus Lambertus (1817-91).
Known to have made: tape measure, needle case,
stiletto, finger shield, knitting chatelaine.
Illustration: Plate 1-17, 7-12, 10-90.

V(F)aust, Christiaan
Kollum/Rotterdam.

1792-   1807-
1811   1811

Born 1765, Active 1792-1811.
Registered his mark in 1807 in Dokkum.
No further information available after 1812.
Known to have made: chatelaine hook.
Illustration: Plate 2-20a.

Veen, Nicolaas Hermanus van
Amsterdam.

    1844-1882

Active 1844-82.
Known to have made: thread winders,
knitting needle guards.
Illustration: Plate 1-19, 10-66, 10-68.

Vermoolen, Rijk
Amsterdam.

    1756-before 1807

Born 1732, died after 1798,
active 1756-before 1807.
Known to have made: spool knave.
Illustration: Plate 9-9.

Visscher, Saco
Dokkum.

    1764-1786

Born 1743, died 1797, active 1764-86.
Known to have made: knife of chatelaine.
Illustration: Plate 2-21a.

Visser, N.S. & Huijvenaar, C.
(Visser & Co. N.S.)
's-Hertogenbosch.

1837-   1837-   1852-
1852   1852   1868

Active 1837-68.
In 1852 the business became N.S.Visser & Zonen
until 1868. In 1868 the business became Nicolaas
Bernardus Antonius Visser (Visser & Co., N.S.).
Known to have made: needle case.

Voet, Elias
Haarlem.

    1800-1812

Born 1774, died 1812, active 1800-12.
Known to have made: stiletto with sheath.

Voorschoten, N.V. Zilverfabriek
Voorschoten.

    1925-1961

Known to have made: sewing set.
Illustration: 1-33.

Weenink, Willem Harmanus
Zwolle.

1809-   1809-   1812-   1812-
1811   1811   1818   1818

  (more marks)

1818-   1818-   1818-
1836   1836   ?

1830-   1836-
c.1847 1847

Born 1785, died 1848, active 1809-47. Son of
Hermen Weenink (active 1775-1808). In 1847 his
son, Jacob Hermen, became partner and carried
on until 1883. Known to have made: scissors.
Illustration: Plate 6-30.

Weessich, D.H.
Middelburg.

1801–	1811–	1811–	1815–
1811	1815	1815	1828

1815–	1817–	1822–
1828	1828	1828

Active 1801-28.
In 1774 apprenticed to Martinus van de Pol.
Known to have made: bodkin.
Illustration: Plate 4-51.

Wendels, Cornelis
Middelburg.

1828–	1828–	1828–
1849	1849	1849

Active 1828-49.
Known to have made: thimble.
Illustration: Plate 3-43.

Wendels, Johannes
Schoonhoven.

1879–	1888–
1908	1898

Active 1879-1908.
Between 1888 and 1898 he was associated
with Frederik Verkerk (Wendels & Verkerk).
Known to have made: knitting needle guards.
Illustration: Plate 10-74.

Wientjes, Egidius J.
Oldenzaal/Ootmarsum.

1807–	1812–	1826–
1811	1826	1856

1826–	1826–	1843–
1856	1856	1856

Active 1807-56. Known to have made:
scissors. Illustration: Plate 6-32.

Wolf, Samuel Machoel
(Fa. Wolf-Hellendall)
Breda.

     1901-1926

Known to have made: sewing set.
Illustration: 1-31.

Wouters, Martinus
's-Hertogenbosch.

1840–	1835–	1841–
1852	1841	1852

Active 1835-52.
Known to have made: sewing sets.
Illustration: Plate 1-28a and b.

Yskamp, Jurjen Harmanus
Almenum/Midlum/Harlingen.

1807–	1812–	c.1815–
1811	c.1815	1826

1826–	1829–
1844	1844

Born 1772, died 1844, active 1807-44.
Known to have made: knitting sheath.
Illustration: Plate 10-54.

Zijlstra, Rein Sipkes
Drachten.

1818–	1826–	1835–
1835	1835	1861

      1835-1861

Active 1818-61.
Known to have made: scissors.
Illustration: Plate 6-27.

Zonne, P.A.
Gouda.

c.1855-? c.1855-?

Active c. 1855-?
Known to have made: knitting needle guards.
Illustration: Plate 10-84.

Other silver and goldsmiths, known to have made needlework tools and not featured in this book, are listed below:

Bennema, Berend Jans, Winschoten.
Active 1804-32.
Known to have made: filigree tape measure.

Boldijn, Michiel, Amsterdam.
Born 1697, died 1770, active 1721-70.
Known to have made: needle case.

Bos, Hendrikus, Utrecht.
Active 1798-1819.
Known to have made: scissors.

Buyn, Andries, Amsterdam.
Born 1751, died after 1807, active 1773-c.1807.
Known to have made: stiletto.

Coutrier, Cornelis, Amsterdam.
Active 1730-49.
Known to have made: toys, scissors.

Cuperus, Hendrik, Leeuwarden.
Born 1755, died 1831, active 1783-1815.
Known to have made: sewing etui of chatelaine.

Dam, Jacobus van, Schoonhoven.
Active 1849-88.
Known to have made: thimble.

Das, Jacobus, Amsterdam.
Born 1686, died 1744, active 1727-44.
Known to have made: needle case for chatelaine.

Douma, Fonger, Leeuwarden.
Born 1721, died 1776, active 1740-76.
Known to have made: necessaire etui, thread winder.

Faber, Jan Luitjen, Kollum.
Born 1779, died 1822, active 1807-22.
His widow continued until 1830.
Known to have made: knitting needle case.

Froger, Dirk, Amsterdam.
Born 1708, died 1780, active 1731-80.
Known to have made: spool knaves, bodkin.

Gaastra, Sjoerd Hendriks, Gorredijk.
Active 1830-1901.
Known to have made: scissors.

Geleen, Hendrik van, Schoonhoven.
Born 1759, died 1812, active 1779-1812.
Known to have made: needle case.

Geleen, N.C. Jz., Hendrik van, Schoonhoven.
Active 1872-75.
Known to have made: needle case.

Giffen, Jan van, Groningen.
Active 1766-81.
Known to have made: scissors.

Graaff, Meijer Hartog de, Den Haag.
Active 1844-55.
Known to have made: thimble.

Groeneveld, Arnoldus van, Utrecht.
Active 1807-32.
Known to have made: scissors.

Haas, Jacob, Amsterdam.
Born 1776, died 1831, active 1806-27.
Known to have made; needle case.

Hallegraaf, Johannes, Deventer.
Born 1698, died 1775, active c.1722-75.
Known to have made: stiletto.

Jongh, David de, Amsterdam.
Born 1749, died after 1811, active 1777-1811.
Known to have made: thimble.

Kooiman, Willem Jan, Schoonhoven.
Active 1856-86.
Known to have made: thimble.

Koop, Hendrik, Amsterdam.
Born 1743, died 1802, active 1764-1802.
Known to have made: knitting sheath.

Kuypers, Huybert Jr., Schoonhoven.
Born 1748, died after 1791, active 1775-91.
Known to have made: knitting sheath.

Meijer Jr., Johan Georg, Amsterdam.
Active 1860-82.
Known to have made: knitting needle case.

Pereboom, Jan, Leeuwarden.
Born 1724, died 1805, active 1751-1805.
Known to have made: chatelaine hook.

Reek, Gerrit, Hoorn.
Active 1772-1823.
Known to have made: wax box, scissors.

Ridder, Hermanus, Groningen.
Active 1812-33.
His widow continued from 1833 to 1859.
Known to have made: scissors.

Roozenburg, Jan, Schoonhoven.
Active 1765-after 1806?
Known to have made: scissors.

Schut, Arnoldus, Amsterdam.
Born 1772, died 1811, active 1794-1811.
Known to have made: scissors.

Smedema, Jippe Klases, Dokkum.
Born 1750, died 1832, active 1781-1832.
Known to have made: scissors.

Smits, Johannes, Gouda.
Active 1761-1811.
He was assay master from 1768 to 1795.
Known to have made: scissors.

Snoek, Roelof, Leeuwarden.
Born 1749, died 1817, active 1772-1817.
Known to have made: scissors.

Vergeer, Pieter, Schoonhoven.
Active 1762-1806.
He was deacon (1788-93) and assay master in 1787.
He administered the joint coal storage for guild.
Known to have made: chatelaine hook.

Vergeer, Willem, Schoonhoven.
Born 1740, died after 1812, active 1779-1806.
Known to have made: needle case.

Verkerk, Barend Cornelis, Amsterdam.
Active 1842-64.
Known to have made: needle case.

Vlijmen, Evert van, Schoonhoven.
Born 1713, died 1749, active 1735-49.

Warren, Jan, Groningen.
Active 1782-1820.
Known to have made: scissors.

Warren, Meinardus Wilhelmus, Sneek.
Active 1811-64.
Known to have made: needle case.

Wingerden, Pieter van, Schoonhoven.
Active 1806-23.
Known to have made: needle case.

Bibliography

Aangekleed Gaat Uit Streekklleding en cultuur in Noord-Holland 1750-1900
M. Havermans-Dikstaal, Waanders Uitgevers, Zwolle, 1998.

Amsterdam in 1585
Het kohier der capitale impositie van 1585
Dr. J.G. van Dillen, Genootschap Amstelodanum, 1941.

Amsterdam Silversmiths and Their Marks
K.A. Citroen, North-Holland Publishing Company, Amsterdam, 1975.

Antiek van het Nederlandse Platteland
Noortje de Roy van Zuydewijn, J.H. Gottmer, Haarlem, 1982.

Antique Needlework Tools and Embroideries
Nerylla Taunton, Antique Collectors' Club Ltd., Woodbridge, Suffolk, 1997.

(De) Bloemen Velden
J.W. de Groot, N.V. Haarlemsche Stoomzeepfabriek 'Het Klaverblad', 1918.

(The) Book of Trades
Jost Amman, Dover Publications Inc., 1973.

(De) Breischee als Voorwerp van Volkskunst
H. Wiegersma, Van Munster's Uitgevers Maatschappij, Amsterdam.

Catalogus met Handleiding voor Friesch Houtsnijwerk en Figuurzaagwerk
W.H. Steelink & Zonen, Amsterdam

"Dat is 'et haakie, daar de kluw an hangt"
J.R. ter Molen, Antiek, 13ᵉ jaargang no.6 1979.

Dictionnaire des Poinçons de Fabricants d'Ouvrages d'Or Et d'Argent, Paris 1798-1838
Cahiers de L'Inventaire No.25 – Paris, Imprimerie Nationale, 1991

Dutch Goldsmiths' and Silversmiths' Marks and Names prior to 1812
Karel Citroen, Primavera Press, Leiden, 1993.

Dutch Silver 1580-1830
A.L. Den Blaauwen, Staats Uitgeverij, Den Haag, 1979.

Economisch-Historisch Jaarboek
G. van Klaveren, Martinus Nijhoff, 's-Gravenhage, Derde deel, 1917.

Fashion in Friesland 1750-1950
Gieneke Arnolli, Friese Pers Boekerij, Leeuwarden, 2000.

(Het) Fries Kostuum
S.J. van der Molen, Lykele Jansma, Augustinusga, 1987.

Fries Zilver
Catalogue Fries Museum, Leeuwarden, 1968.

Gebruiksvingerhoeden in Amsterdam tussen 1550 en 1700
Henny Holthuizen, De Vingerhoed, Amstelveen, nummer 6, juni 1984.

Gelders Zilver
Gemeentemuseum Arnhem catalogus 12 juni – 4 september, 1955.

Glans Langs De Ijssel
Zilver uit Zutphen, Deventer, Zwolle en Kampen. Waanders Uitgevers, Zwolle, 1999.

(De) Gilden in Gouda
P. Lourens a.o., Museum Het Catharina Gasthuis, Gouda, 1996.

Gorcums Zilver
R.F. van Dijk, Museum Dit is in Bethlehem, Gorinchem, 1992.

Goud-en Zilvermerken van Voet
L.B. Gans, Martinus Nijhoff, Leiden, 1992.

Graves Kooiman of Kooiman, Een Dynastie Van Goud-en Zilversmeden in Schoonhoven 1776-1977
R. Kappers, Zilvercahier nr. 4.0 Stichting Vriendenkring, Schoonhoven, 1998.

Groninger Keur
Zilver uit de Stad en Ommelanden.
Jean-Pierre van Rijen, Goud, Zilver – Klokkenmuseum – Schoonhoven/Groninger Museum, 1997.

Haarlemsche Goud-en Zilversmeden en Hunne Merken
Elias Voet Jr., De Erven F. Bohn, Haarlem, 1928.

Handwerken zonder grenzen
'De Breischede', Sietske van der Ley, 1991.

(The) History of Needlework Tools and Accessories
Sylvia Groves, Davis & Charles (Holdings) Ltd., 1973.

Hollands Arcadia – Den Amstel
Leonardus Schenk, Amsterdam, 1730.

Huisraad van een molenaarsweduwe
Drs. A.P.E. Ruempol a.o., Museum Boymans-van Beuningen, Rotterdam/De Bataafsche Leeuw, Amsterdam, 1986.

(An) Illustrated History of Needlework Tools
Gay Ann Rogers, John Murray (Publishers) Ltd., 1983.

International Hallmarks on Silver
collected by Tardy, Paris, 1985.

Kantbrief:
'Ierse Kant, uit hongersnood geboren', I.M.E. Sonderman.
17e jaargang, nr.2, juni, 2000.
'De Tamboereernaald', Anneke den Herder.
17e jaargang nr. 4, december, 2000.

(De) Keuring van Goud en Zilver Tijdens Het Koninkrijk Holland
W. Koonings, De Tijdstroom, Lochem, 1968.

Kinderen van Amsterdam
J.Th. Engels, De Walburg Pers, 1989.

(The) Knitting Sheath
Peter C.D. Brears, reprinted from FOLK LIFE A Journal of Ethnological Studies, Volume Twenty, 1981-82.

Kohier van de Personele Quotisatie te Amsterdam over Het Jaar 1742
Mr. W.F.M. Oldewelt, Genootschap Amstelodanum, 1945.

Kostuum – Relaties: Mode en Streekdracht 2000
Zichtbaar of verborgen, Sigrid Ivo, Nederlandse Kostuum Vereniging voor Mode en Streekdracht, Amsterdam, 2000.

Lace and Bobbins
T.L. Huetson, David & Charles (Holdings) Ltd., Newton Abbot, Devon, 1973.

Meestertekens van Nederlandse Goud-en Zilversmeden
Deel 1, 3e editie. W. Koonings, Government Publishing

Office, The Hague, 1981.
(Of) Meissen Thimbles
Ann Blakeslee Black, Thimble Collectors International, USA, 2000.

Merken van Amsterdamsche Goud-en Zilversmeden
Elias Voet Jr., Martinus Nijhoff, Den Haag, 1912. Reprint 1981.

Merken van Haagsche Goud-en Zilversmeden
H.E. van Gelder/Elias Voet Jr., Martinus Nijhoff, 's-Gravenhage, 1941.

Merken van Friese Goud-en Zilversmeden
Elias Voet Jr., Martinus Nijhoff, Den Haag, 1932. 2nd print 1974.

More Beautiful Purses
Evelyn Haertig, Gallery Graphics Press, Carmel, California, USA, 1990.

Museum Stukken 'Ellen, Duimstokken en Meters'
Ferdi van de Vijver, Heemkundig Handboekje voor de Antwerpse Randgemeenten, jaargang 22, nr.4.

(Het) Nederlands Interieur in beeld 1600-1900
C. Willemijn Fock, Waanders Uitgeverij, Zwolle, 2001.

Nederlands Klein Zilver 1650-1880
B.W.G. Wttewaall, Uniepers B.V. Amsterdam/Allert de Lange B.V. Amsterdam, 1987.

Netherlands Responsibility Marks Since 1797
Casper van Dongen, Waarborg, Holland, Gouda, 1999.

(De) Nijverheidsvereniging van Goud- en Zilversmeden in Schoonhoven
R. Kappers, 1999, Zilvercahier nr. 3.1. Stichting Vriendenkring, Schoonhoven, 1997.

Nederlandse Zilveren Vingerhoeden van af de 16e tot het einde van de 18e eeuw
Catherine A. Langedijk, Antiek januari 1995, Waanders Uitgevers, Zwolle.

Notes and Queries, numbers 2 and 3
E.F. Holmes, London, 1989.

Old-Time Tools & Toys of Needlework
Gertrude Whiting, Dover Publications, New York, 1971.
Originally published in 1928 under the title *Tools and Toys of Stitchery.*

Ons Amsterdam
Maandblad van de Commissie Heemkennis, 11e jaargang nr. 3, maart, 1959.

Opgravingen in Amsterdam
Dr. J. Baart, W. Krook e.a., Dienst der Publieke Werken/Amsterdams Historisch Museum Afdeling Archeologie. Unieboek B.V. Bussum, 1977.

(Le) Petit Journal – Supplément Illustré
Dimanche 29 Novembre, 1896.

Phaidon Guide to Silver
Margaret Holland, Elsevier International Projects Ltd., Oxford, 1978.

Recht en Slecht in het Land van Vianen
Piet Horden, 1952.

Rembrandt: alle etsen op ware grootte
Gary Schwartz, SDU Uitgeverij, Maarssen, 1988.

Sewing Accessories – An Illustrated History
Victor Houart, Souvenir Press Ltd., London, 1984.

(The) Story of Bilston Painted Enameled Thimbles
John von Hoelle, Dine American, Delaware, 1988.

(A) Short History of The Netherlands
Prof. Dr. P.J.A.N. Rietbergen, Bekking Publishers, Amersfoort. 4th edition, 2000.

Thread Winders for Collectors
Diane Pelham Burn, Thimble Collectors International, USA, 1989.

(Een) Twentse Ellemaat
B. Dubbe, Antiek, april, 1985.

Uit Grootmoeders Kastje
De Verzameling Antiek Handwerkgerei van mevrouw C.M.

Kuttschrutter
Exhibition catalogue: Centraal Museum, Utrecht, 1973.

(De) Verzameling van de Stichting Willem Van der Vorm
Museum Boymans van Beuningen, Rotterdam, 1994.

Vingerhoeden en Naairingen uit de Amsterdamse Bodem
Catherine A. Langedijk, Herman F. Boon, Archeologische Werkgemeenschap voor Nederland, Amsterdam, 1999.

Vingerhoeden van Mariken Pieters en Antonis van Gesteren
Herman F. Boon and Catherine A. Langedijk, Oud Utrecht maart/april, 1997.

Zeeuws Zilver
J. de Bree, Interbook International B.V., Schiedam, 1978.

Zilver
Dr. J.R. ter Molen. Catalogue van de voorwerpen van edelmetaal in de collectie van het Museum Boymans van Beuningen, Rotterdam, 1994.

Zilver en Zilversmeden uit de Baronie van Breda
Jean-Pierre van Rijen, Stichting Stedelijk Museum, Breda, 2000.

Zilversmeden van de Stad Schoonhoven
Exhibition catalogue Goud – Zilver – en Klokkenmuseum, Schoonhoven, 1981.

Zilver uit 's-Hertogenbosch
Noordbrabants Museum, 's-Hertogenbosch, 1985.

Zilver van het Noorder Kwartier
Exhibition catalogue: Westfries Museum, Hoorn, 1957.

Photographic Credits
(Chapter and Plate number)

Amsterdams Historisch Museum, Amsterdam: page 52, 8-14.

Museum Boymans van Beuningen, Rotterdam: page 122, 8-31.

Bureau Monumenten & Archeologie, Amsterdam: 1-2, 2-1, 4-1, 5-2, 5-3, 6-1, 6-2, 6-7.

Christie's, London: page 72.

Fries Museum, Leeuwarden: 1-4, 1-5, 1-6, page 34, 2-3a/b, 2-5, 2-27, 2-28, 2-33, 3-2, 3-4, 4-60, 5-20, 6-11, 7-7, 7-8, 7-9, 8-29, 9-17, 9-19, 9-20, 9-26, 10-1a/b.

Tom Haartsen, Ouderkerk aan de Amstel: 1-3, 3-75, 4-25, 5-6, 6-4, 8-18, 10-3, 10-29a/b, 10-31, 10-32, 10-39, 10-40, 10-41, 10-43, 10-45, 10-46, 10-49, 10-50, 10-53, 10-58, 10-59, 10-91.

National Gallery of Ireland, Dublin: page 90.

Nederlands Openluchtmuseum, Arnhem: 1-35, 1-37, 1-38, 1-42, 2-4a/b, 2-6, 2-7, 2-8, 2-9a/b, 2-22, 2-23, 2-24, 2-25, 2-26, 4-61a/b, 4-62, 4-63, 4-64, 4-65, 4-66, 5-11, 5-12, 5-25, 5-26, 5-27, 5-28, 5-29, 6-5, 6-35, 6-36, 8-5, 8-9, 8-41, 9-6, 9-16, 10-4, 10-5, 10-7, 10-9, 10-10, 10-11, 10-12, 10-13, 10-14, 10-15, 10-16, 10-17, 10-18, 10-19, 10-20, 10-22, 10-23, 10-24, 10-25, 10-26, 10-27, 10-28, 10-30, 10-33, 10-34, 10-35a/b, 10-36, 10-37, 10-38, 10-42, 10-44, 10-47.

Noordbrabants Museum, 's-Hertogenbosch: page 188, 11-1.

Rijksbureau voor Kunsthistorische Documentatie, Den Haag: page 138, 9-2.

Rijksmuseum, Amsterdam: page 10, 1-8a/b, 5-24a/b, page 116, 8-36.

Royal Cabinet of Paintings, Mauritshuis, Den Haag: page 102.

Zuiderzeemuseum, Enkhuizen: 2-13, 9-4, page 154.

From private collections: 1-12a/b, 1-22, 1-23a/b, 2-10a/b, 3-62a/b, 3-73, 4-15, 4-28.

All other photographs by Kay Sullivan.

INDEX